School Rampage Shootings and Other Youth Disturbances

EARLY PREVENTATIVE INTERVENTIONS

**Edited by
Kathleen Nader**

Routledge
Taylor & Francis Group
New York   London

ROUTLEDGE PSYCHOSOCIAL STRESS SERIES
Charles R. Figley, PhD, Series Editor

This book is part of the Psychosocial Stress Series, edited by Charles R. Figley.

Routledge
Taylor & Francis Group
711 Third Avenue
New York, NY 10017

Routledge
Taylor & Francis Group
27 Church Road
Hove, East Sussex BN3 2FA

© 2012 by Kathleen Nader
Routledge is an imprint of Taylor & Francis Group, an Informa business

Printed in the United States of America on acid-free paper
Version Date: 20111107

International Standard Book Number: 978-0-415-87747-3 (Hardback) 978-0-415-87748-0 (Paperback)

Library of Congress Cataloging-in-Publication Data

Nader, Kathleen.
    School rampage shootings and other youth disturbances : early preventative interventions / Kathleen Nader. -- 1st ed.
        p. cm. -- (Psychosocial stress series)
    Includes bibliographical references and index.
    ISBN 978-0-415-87747-3 (hardcover : alk. paper) -- ISBN 978-0-415-87748-0 (pbk. : alk. paper)
    1. Child psychology. 2. School shootings--Prevention. 3. School violence--Prevention. I. Title.

BF721.N26 2012
372.17'82--dc23   2011029456

**Visit the Taylor & Francis Web site at
http://www.taylorandfrancis.com**

**and the Routledge Web site at
http://www.routledgementalhealth.com**

Contents

Series Editor's Foreword

How could a child suddenly take the life of another? Rampage shootings such as those at Virginia Tech, Northern Illinois, Columbine, and schools outside the United States force civilized society to face this question and a host of others. How can school shootings be prevented? What motivates violence? Fundamentally, all of these questions are focused on finding explanations—whether neurobiological, demographic, psychological, psychoneuroimmunological, sociological, traumatological, or psychosocial.

This book is about those explanations.

As editor of the Psychosocial Stress Book Series, the oldest of its kind in the world, the series editorial board welcomes Kathleen Nader's *School Rampage Shootings and Other Youth Disturbances: Early Preventative Interventions* as the latest addition to the series. Nader, a long-time colleague, is a frequent contributor to the series as an editor, author, chapter author, and reviewer. She is a pioneer in the field of child trauma, violence-related psychological mitigation, grief and loss, and child-related assessments.

School Rampage Shootings and Other Youth Disturbances joins a long and illustrious line of books, the first of which, *Stress Disorders Among Vietnam Veterans*, was released in 1978. That book focused on another kind of shooting—war combat—and examined ways to best understand and help combat veterans of the Vietnam War. In contrast, Nader's book focuses on children who were undiagnosed and unsuspected by parents and teachers but were ticking time bombs. Both books were conceived to cover new and relatively unexplored areas of research and practice, and as such, constitute milestones. As Nader points out in her introduction, "Aggression in schools has long been a problem," but rampage shootings are a rarity. More often, they are stopped by school authority—thanks, in a large part, to parents and friends of those who appeared to be ready to explode emotionally and in violent directions. Yet, as Nader notes in this book, during the 2008–2009 school year, an estimated 55.6 million students were enrolled in schools (prekindergarten through high school), and in 2008, there were approximately 1.2 million victims of nonfatal crimes at school among students ages 12–18 (e.g., 619,000 thefts, 629,800 violent crimes). Clearly, violence in schools is a significant problem.

Nader notes that preparing schools for rampage shootings also prevents them. She discusses what is known about youth-targeted school shootings and shooters and what kinds of factors—related to family, school, culture, and community—put them at risk for violence. The chapters explore the various options we have for the reduction of aggression, other delinquency, and psychopathology in youth, and the final section of the book provides lessons and methods for helping to offset the risk of school violence. These include methods for improving social skills, coping skills, self-control, and empathy, as well as methods for customizing these skills to work within specific cultural and environmental conditions

It is encouraging to learn from Nader and others that there is considerable resilience among those who have witnessed school violence. Recent reports indicate that, overall, students exposed to violence in schools utilized their own support systems to recover fully. These students employed a variety of coping methods, styles, and their own timetable; gender-based coping styles (e.g., competitive versus cooperative) were common.

School Rampage Shootings and Other Youth Disturbances will be a turning point in efforts to offset, control, eliminate, and prevent school violence. Our children deserve to go to school without fear and, rather, experience the joyful parts of learning that can only happen without fear.

Charles R. Figley, PhD
Series Editor
New Orleans

Acknowledgments

This book was inspired by the many children who were exposed to violence and disasters at their schools, and their families. Although their trauma and other distressing reactions were of great concern and engendered considerable efforts toward repair, their courage and recovery were uplifting. After many years of work with children exposed to traumatic events and traumatic losses, prevention of such events and their long-term consequences are of great import.

I am very grateful for the excellent contributions of a well-respected group of chapter authors. My sincere appreciation also is extended to a number of esteemed colleagues who reviewed chapters and materials of the book and CD and provided very helpful feedback. Among them are some who chose to remain anonymous as well as the following: Randy Borum, John Briere, Jonathan Cohen, Nancy Richards Colocino, Dewey Cornell, May Britt Drugli, Joseph Durlak, Charles Figley, Pat Goreman, Karen Lee, Butch Losey, Page Smith, and Carolyn Zahn-Waxler. I am also very thankful for the assistance of Routledge's Anna Moore, Tara Nieuwesteeg, and the staff of Taylor & Francis. I am grateful for Sherry Moore's help with the index.

To my beloved family and friends: Thank you for all of your support and help through this process. You are a great part of my joy and a treasured part of my own sense of connection.

NOTE TO READERS

With one exception, the methods presented in the book chapters to follow have been well tested. Chapter 9 presents a means to teach children skills to deal with bullies directly. A pilot study of the method's effectiveness has been submitted for publication, and it has received the endorsement of numerous school professionals who have used it. It is offered along with other methods (i.e., those used to reduce bullying in schools and to teach important skills and methods) that are associated with a reduction in problem behaviors and an increase in positive and prosocial outcomes.

Contributors

Edmund Bruyere, MS, a First Nation Indian of Ojibwa decent, currently holds the Maude C. Clarke graduate research assistantship under Professor James Garbarino of Loyola University, Chicago. His doctoral work is focused on identifying the developmental pathways that lead to thriving among Native American youth. He is currently a member of the National Congress of American Indians and the International Society for the Prevention of Child Abuse and Neglect.

John Eller, PhD, is director of the Doctoral Program in Educational Administration at St. Cloud State University. He served as an assistant professor in educational leadership and coordinator of the Principal Preparation Program in the National Capital Region for Virginia Tech. Dr. Eller has authored articles and books through Solution Tree and Corwin Press. He is former assistant superintendent and a National Distinguished Principal through the U.S. Department of Education.

Dorothy L. Espelage, PhD, is a professor of child development in the Department of Educational Psychology at the University of Illinois, Urbana–Champaign. She is a university scholar and has fellow status in Division 17 (Counseling Psychology) of the American Psychological Association. She earned her PhD in counseling psychology from Indiana University in 1997. She has conducted research on bullying and homophobic bullying for the last 17 years and is author of over 80 professional publications and 4 edited books.

Lisa Ferentz, LCSW-C, DAPA, has been in private practice for 27 years. She received the 2009 Social Worker of the Year Award from the Maryland Society for Clinical Social Work. She provides clinical consultation, workshops, and lectures across the United States, as well as two certificate programs in advanced trauma treatment through the Institute for Advanced Psychotherapy and Education, Inc. She has published articles on self-harm and is the author of *Treating Self-Destructive Behaviors in Traumatized Clients: A Clinician's Guide.*

James Garbarino, PhD, holds the Maude C. Clarke Chair in Humanistic Psychology and was founding director of the Center for the Human Rights of Children at Loyola University, Chicago. He is a fellow of the American Psychological Association and a scientific expert witness in criminal and civil cases involving issues of violence and children. His authored or edited books include *Children and the Dark Side of Human Experience* (2008), *See Jane Hit* (2006), and *Lost Boys* (1999).

Israel C. Kalman, MS, NCSP, has been working as a school psychologist and psychotherapist for over 30 years. He has developed quick, effective role-playing techniques that teach the practical application of psychological and moral principles to solve interpersonal problems. Over 40,000 professionals have attended his full-day seminars on anger control and bullying. He is director of Bullies to Buddies, Inc., and has produced numerous products and publications for solving the problem of bullying.

Karen W. Lee, MEd, received her bachelor's degree in physical education from Texas Tech University and a master's degree in administration from Texas State University. She taught physical education to kindergarten and first grade for 10 years in central Texas, and kindergarten through fifth grade for 13 years. She is involved with her disabled son in Special Olympics. She studied movement as an enhancement to brain development, intelligence, and classroom performance before positron emission topography proved their association.

Sabina Low, PhD, is an assistant professor of clinical psychology at Wichita State University. She earned her PhD in child clinical psychology from the University of Denver, followed by an internship and post-doctoral studies at the University of Washington School of Medicine. She has conducted research for the last 10 years on peer and familial determinants of health-risk behaviors and bullying using social–developmental and ecological frameworks.

Christine Mello, PsyD, has been a school psychologist for 25 years in upstate New York. She has worked with elementary through high school students, addressing social skills and coping skills with individual students, small groups, and classrooms. Dr. Mello has worked in a school-based clinic following a school disaster, providing long-term treatment for children and families. She has contributed to other publications related to school-based treatment of traumatized children.

Ellen Moss, PhD, is a professor of developmental psychology at the University of Quebec at Montreal and director of the Centre for the Study of Attachment and the Family. She has published extensively about the effects of attachment relationships on cognitive, social, and emotional development, and is currently involved in clinical intervention projects for at-risk children. Dr. Moss is active in training professionals who work with troubled youth and their families.

Kathleen Nader, DSW, has provided national and international consultations, training, and specialized interventions that include school training and intervention programs following shootings, bombings, disasters, and war or terrorism. Dr. Nader has written and co-authored publications, assessment scales, and videotapes regarding youth trauma, treatment, and school interventions. Her books include *Honoring Differences: Cultural Issues in the Treatment of Trauma and Loss* (1999) and *Understanding and Assessing Trauma in Children and Adolescents: Measures, Methods, and Youth in Context* (2008).

Wallis Nader, BA, graduated from the University of Texas at Austin where she received her BA in history and Russian, East European, and Eurasian studies. She has provided research and other assistance in a number of locations during her matriculation. Her recent internships include the Kennan Institute in Washington, DC, and an international business in Moscow. She is currently attending law school.

Katherine Pascuzzo, MA, is currently completing her PhD in developmental psychology at the Center for the Study of Attachment and the Family at the University of Quebec at Montreal, under the supervision of Dr. Ellen Moss. She is conducting research on the longitudinal impact of insecure parent–child attachment relationships on adult adaptation, particularly in romantic relationships. She is pursuing her post-doctoral degree at McGill University.

William S. Pollack, PhD, ABPP, is an associate clinical professor in the Department of Psychiatry at Harvard Medical School. He is a senior consultant for the Mental Health of Men, Young Men, and Boys at the Cambridge Health Alliance. Dr. Pollack founded the Centers for Men and Young Men at McLean Hospital, both teaching affiliates of the Harvard Medical School. He is also president of the independent Centers for Men/Young Men and the Real Boys® Anti-Violence/Anti-Bullying & Positive School Climate Programs. The author of numerous books, book chapters, and articles on boys, bullying, violence, and safe schools, he served as an investigator for the Federal Safe Schools Initiative, and coauthored the U.S. government publication *Threat Assessment in Schools: A Guide to Managing Threatening Situations and to Creating Safe School Climates.*

Kimberly Schonert-Reichl, PhD, is an applied developmental psychologist and associate professor in the Faculty of Education, University of British Columbia. For over 20 years, her child social, emotional, and moral development research has emphasized identifying psychological and contextual mechanisms that foster children's positive traits, including empathy, altruism, and optimism. Her current research includes school-based social and emotional learning programs, including the Roots of Empathy and MindUP™. Dr. Schonert-Reichl is a member of the Research Advisory Group for the Collaborative for Academic, Social, and Emotional Learning.

Eitan D. Schwarz, MD, FAACAP, DLFAPA, is a clinical assistant professor of psychiatry at the Feinberg School of Medicine, Northwestern University, Chicago. He received his MD from Johns Hopkins University and is certified by the American Board of Psychiatry and Neurology in psychiatry and in child and adolescent psychiatry. Dr. Schwarz is the author of publications related to the reactions and needs of youth, including *Kids, Parents, & Technology: A Guide for Young Families and Alternatives to Violence.*

Valerie Simard, PhD, is a clinical child psychologist and a professor in the Department of Psychology at the University of Sherbrooke. Her research interests include child development, sleep, parent–child relationships, and attachment. The aim of her current research program is to further our understanding of the association between parenting and the development of emotional and physiological regulation in children.

Factors That Contribute to School Rampage/Targeted Shootings, Other Aggression, and Other Youth Problems

CHAPTER 1

School Shootings and Other Youth Problems
The Need for Early Preventive Interventions

Kathleen Nader

School safety is important to learning and to well being (Allen, Cornell, Lorek, & Sheras, 2008; American Psychological Association [APA] Zero Tolerance Task Force, 2008; Robers, Zhang, Truman, Snyder, 2010). Aggression in schools has long been a problem. Although barricaded captive events and rampage or targeted shootings are infrequent occurrences (Borum, Cornell, Modzeleski, & Jimerson, 2010; Daniels, Royster, Vecchi, & Pshenishy, 2010a), their long-term impact on schools, individuals, and families can be significant. In addition to school preparedness for the possibility of such events is the need for early preventive interventions that reduce the likelihood of their occurrence. Because some of the traits, circumstances, and conditions associated with the individuals who commit such events are also associated with other youth difficulties, engaging in early interventions such as those presented in the second half of this book may prevent a number of youth and later adult problems including aggression.

Section I of this book examines school shooters, especially youth-targeted school shooters, as well as the family, school, and community environmental conditions associated with school shootings. A number of interventions may assist the reduction of aggression, other delinquency, and psychopathology in general as well as reduce the likelihood of targeted (sometimes called rampage) shootings by those with the potential to carry them out. In Section II of this book, methods to improve social skills, coping skills, self-control, empathy, and environmental conditions for elementary school children are described. Addressing insecure and disorganized attachments and creating supportive environments with increased connection among individuals are also important to the prevention of school violence and other youth-related problems.

SCHOOL SHOOTINGS

Incidence of Violence in Schools

In 2006, homicide was the second leading cause of death for youth ages 10 to 24 (5,958 murdered; CDC 2009a) (Suicide was the third leading cause for adolescents in 2002; Gould et al., 2006). The incidence of violence, including violence resulting in deaths, is greater outside of schools than within schools (National School Safety Center [NSSC], 2006). Arrest rates for murder increased from 1980 to 1993 and declined through 1997 (Snyder, & Sickmund, 1999). The number of youth arrested for committing homicides decreased from 3,092 (1993) to 1,354 (1998) (Brooks, Schiraldi & Ziedenberg, 2000).

The 1994 Gun-Free Schools Act requires expulsion of students carrying firearms to schools. During the 1996–1997 school year, 5,724 students were expelled, and in 1997–1998, 3,927 students were expelled for carrying weapons to school (NSSC, 2006). Nevertheless, in 2007, youth in grades 9–12 reported carrying a gun or other weapon on school grounds—28.5% males versus 7.5% of females; 5.2% carried a gun on school grounds (CDC, 2008b).

On school property, 7%–8% of students sampled were threatened or injured with a weapon in 1993, 1995, 1997, and 1998 (Kaufman et al., 1999, 2000). Although response rates suggest that statistics are incomplete, a 2007 nationally representative sample of youth grades 9–12 reported threat rates similar to the 90s (CDC, 2008b). That is, nearly 8% of youth (7.8%) reported being threatened or injured with a weapon on school property one or more times in the past 12 months. In addition, 12.5% of reporting students were in physical fights in the past 12 months (16.8% of male students; 8.5% of female students fought on school property). During the 2008–2009 school year, an estimated 55.6 million students were enrolled in schools (prekindergarten through high school; Snyder & Dillow, 2010). In 2008, there were approximately 1.2 million victims of nonfatal crimes at school among students ages 12–18 (e.g., 619,000 thefts, 629,800 violent crimes) (Robers et al., 2010). Again in 2009, 8% of students reported being threatened or injured with a weapon, such as a gun, knife, or club, on school property.

School-associated student homicide rates decreased between 1992 and 2006 and have remained relatively stable in recent years (CDC, 2008). In 2008–2009, there were approximately 38 school-associated violent deaths among youth ages 5–18 (24 homicides; 14 suicides). Like other youth homicides, most school-associated homicides are generally gang or drug related or otherwise associated with criminal activity or interpersonal disputes (Borum et al., 2010). Targeted school shootings are rare. Between 1996 and 2005, 17 school shootings perpetrated by students, with multiple victims, resulted in deaths of 39 youth and 13 adults as well as 111 physical injuries (Kaiser, 2005; see Table 1.1). The numbers of deaths and injuries reported do not include other victims, such as the many students and families who suffered psychological traumas and traumatic grief, as well as loss of a sense of safety at school for students, teachers, other school personnel, and parents. In recent years, school shootings and stabbings have occurred all over the world (Allen et al., 2008).

Manifestation of Aggression

Multiple pathways may lead to aggression (Cornell, 1990; Cornell, Benedek, & Benedek, 1987; Nader, 2008). Among factors associated with aggression are environments (e.g., home, community), attachment issues, age, humiliation, moral socialization, personality, neurobiology, past traumas, and information processing. For example, from an information processing perspective, Sutton et al. (1999) suggest that maladaptive behaviors (e.g., persistent aggression) are the result of deficits in any one or more of the steps identified by Crick and Dodge (1994) in a child's behavioral responses to social stimuli: (1) encoding of cues, (2) interpretation of encoded cues, (3) clarification of goals, (4) response access or construction, (5) response decision, and (6) behavioral enactment (Peeters, Cillessen, & Scholte, 2010). No single factor or trait explains violence, and the traits identified in shooters can be found in those who do not commit aggression. Additionally, youth's skills, traits, and styles combine in a complex way to influence behavioral and social outcomes (Angold & Heim, 2007; Nader, 2008). For example, genetic vulnerabilities combine with home, community, and/or traumatic adversities to result in specific types of psychopathology. Cumulative or extreme stresses may contribute to emotional reactivity (Nader, 2008; Sapolsky, 1998; van der Kolk & Sapporta, 1991). One skill may influence multiple interrelated skills or outcomes. For example, the ability to take the perspective of another is important to social skills including the ability to influence others, express and understand humor, and display empathy (Semrud-Clikeman & Glass, 2010). Empathy and moral development are

TABLE 1.1 Completed U.S. School Shootings With Multiple Victims (1966 Onward)

School and University Mass Shootings (from 1966)	Shooter	Event and Number of Deaths/Injuries
August 1, 1966 University of Texas–Austin	Charles Whitman (CJW)	Whitman strangled his mother and stabbed his wife the night before the shooting. The next morning he arrived at school and began to ascend the UT clock tower. His first victim was a receptionist, whom he knocked unconscious. She later died. He then shot two more people before he reached the upper deck of the tower. There, he unpacked his weapons and proceeded to shoot people at random. Whitman killed a total of 15 people, including his wife and mother, and injured 31.
January 20, 1983 Parkway South Junior High School St. Louis, Missouri	David F. Lawler (DFL)	Lawler entered a classroom and shot two classmates, killing one and injuring the other. He then shot and killed himself.
November 1, 1991 University of Iowa–Iowa City	Gang Lu (GL)	Lu, a graduate student, was angry that his dissertation did not receive an award. He went to school carrying a revolver and handgun with the intent of shooting specifically targeted people, including his academic advisor and the student who won the award. He killed five people in total, and severely injured another. He committed suicide.
May 1, 1992 Lindhurst High School Olivehurst, California	Eric Houston (EH) Age 20	Houston was being laid off because he had no high school diploma. He killed a teacher who flunked him and went on a shooting spree in the hallways, holding 70–85 students hostage for over 8 hours. He killed three students and injured nine.

Date/Location	Name	Description
December 14, 1992 Simon's Rock College of Bard Great Barrington, Massachusetts	Wayne Lo (WL)	Wayne took an SKS rifle to school and shot six people, killing two and injuring four.
November 15, 1995 Richland High School Lynnville, Tennessee	Jamie Rouse (JR) Age 17	Rouse walked into the school and started shooting with a semiautomatic weapon at the first teacher he saw. He killed one teacher and one student and seriously injured another teacher. He was wrestled to the ground before he could hurt anyone else.
February 2, 1996 Frontier Junior High School Moses Lake, Washington	Barry Loukaitis (BL)	Loukaitis, dressed up like a western gunslinger, walked into his algebra classroom with two pistols and a rifle, and proceeded to shoot three students and his teacher. Three were killed and one injured.
October 1, 1997 Pearl High School Pearl, Mississippi	Luke Woodham (LW) Age 16	Woodham killed his mother and then went to school. With a rifle he killed two girls and wounded seven other students. He was stopped by the assistant principal when trying to go to the middle school to continue his rampage.
December 1, 1997 Heath High School West Paducah, Kentucky	Michael Carneal (MC) Age 14	Carneal used a pistol to kill three students and wound five, after they participated in a school prayer circle in the lobby of the school and were starting to go to class.
December 15, 1997 Stamps, Arkansas	Joseph "Colt" Todd (JT) Age 14	Todd used sniper fire to shoot two students outside of their high school.
February 19, 1997 Bethel Regional High School Bethel, Alaska	Evan Ramsey (ER)	Ramsey went to school with a shotgun. He shot three students, killing one and injuring two. He then shot and killed his principal.

Continued

TABLE 1.1 (*Continued*) Completed U.S. School Shootings With Multiple Victims (1966 Onward)

School and University Mass Shootings (from 1966)	Shooter	Event and Number of Deaths/Injuries
March 24, 1998 Jonesboro Jonesboro, Arkansas	Andrew Golden & Mitchell Johnson (AG & MJ)	Golden and Johnson dressed in camouflage, went to school, and shot 15 people at their school's playground. Five were killed.
May 21, 1998 Thurston High School Springfield, Oregon	Kip Kinkel (KK) Age 15	Kinkel killed two students in the hall and wounded 22 in the cafeteria firing 50 rounds from a semiautomatic pistol and two other guns. He had killed his parents before going to school.
April, 1998 James W. Parker School Edinboro, PA	Andrew Wurst (AW) Age 14	Wurst killed a teacher and wounded two students at an eighth-grade dance. Another teacher was grazed with a bullet but did not require medical treatment.
April 20, 1999 Columbine High School Littleton, Colorado	Eric Harris and Dylan Klebold (EDH & DK)	Harris and Klebold killed one teacher and 12 students. They wounded 24 others before committing suicide. They had two 9-mm firearms and two 12-gauge shotguns. Their 99 homemade bombs did not detonate.
May 20, 1999 Heritage High School Conyers, Georgia	Thomas Solomon Jr. (TJS)	Solomon went to school with a .22 rifle and began shooting at random. He injured 6 students.
December 6, 1999 Fort Gibson Middle School Fort Gibson, Oklahoma	Seth Trickey Age 13	Trickey shot a semiautomatic weapon into a crowd of about 70 students in front of the school. He wounded four students.
March 5, 2001 Santana High School Santee, California	Charles Andrew Williams (CAW) Age 13	Williams went to school with a .22 and began shooting in the men's bathroom where he killed 2 students. He proceeded to injure 13 others.

Date / School / Location	Name / Age	Description
March 22, 2001 Granite Hills High School Granite Hills, California	Jason Hoffman (JH) Age 18	Hoffman knelt next to a tree on the school grounds and fired at fellow students with a shotgun. He wounded one teacher and three students. He was wounded by a policeman.
September 24, 2003 Rocori High School Cold Spring, Minnesota	John Jason McLaughlin (JJM) Age 15	McLaughlin killed two students with a pistol.
September 4, 2004 Columbia High School White East Greenbush, NY	Jon William Romano Age 16	Referenced Columbine but only wounded one.
March 21, 2005 Red Lake High School, Red Lake, MN	Jeffrey Weise (JW) Age 16	Weise killed his grandfather and grandfather's companion, one teacher, a security guard, and five students. He then killed himself.
November 8, 2005 Campbell County High School Jacksboro, Tennessee	Kenneth Bartley Jr. (KB) Age 15	Bartley killed an assistant principal and seriously wounded two other administrators. May have been accidental weapon discharge.
March 14, 2006 Pine Middle School White Reno, Nevada	James Scott Newman Age 14	Studied Columbine. Wounded two.
August 30, 2006 Orange High School Hillsborough, North Carolina	Alvaro Rafael Castillo Age 18	Studied and referenced Columbine. Killed one.
September 29, 2006 Weston High School Cazenovia, Wisconsin	Eric Hainstock (EHa) Age 15	Hainstock, armed with two guns, killed the school principal in a struggle over one of the guns.

Continued

TABLE 1.1 (*Continued*) Completed U.S. School Shootings With Multiple Victims (1966 Onward)

School and University Mass Shootings (from 1966)	Shooter	Event and Number of Deaths/Injuries
April 16, 2007 Virginia Tech Blacksburg, Virginia	Seung-Hui Cho (S-HC) Age 23	Cho Seung-Hui killed two in a dorm; 2 hours later he killed 30 and wounded 15 in a classroom building. He then killed himself.
October 10, 2007 Success Academy White Cleveland, Ohio	Asa Coon Age 14	Killed one, wounded five.
February 14. 2008 Northern Illinois University DeKalb, Illinois	Steven Kazmierczak Age 27	A former NIU student stepped from behind a screen on a lecture hall stage; with four guns, he fired dozens of shots into a geology class, then shot himself; killed five; injured more than a dozen.

Note: This list may not be comprehensive. It is limited to cases occurring in the U.S. Listings are taken from newspaper stories (e.g., *New York Times, Chicago Sun Times*) and from texts and articles by Daniels et al., 2004; Davis, 2004; Larkin, 2009; Pollack, 2004; and Stearns, 2008.

among factors that are important to self-regulation. In general, bullying (e.g., relational or physical aggression) is associated with moral disengagement and lack of emotional understanding. However, the socially intelligent youth has the option to use this skill peacefully or aggressively; some social intelligence is needed in order to engage in concealed relational aggression (Peeters et al., 2010). Genetic predispositions may combine with parental modeling such that youth are prone to and learn to resolve interpersonal conflict with antagonism/aggression. In such cases, lack of social skills combined with coercive behaviors may lead to peer rejection, and noncompliance may lead to failure in school. In turn, these failures may exacerbate problems. Additionally, time of onset is a factor. Early onset patterns of aggression emerge before age 6 and may translate into adult criminality (Bennett, Elliot, & Peters, 2005). As early as kindergarten, elementary school teachers may assist the increase of social skills and self-control, as well as the reduction of social and behavioral problems.

School Shootings With Multiple Deaths and/or Injuries

In addition to school shootings aimed at one or two individuals because of disputes, power seeking, or gang activities, there are shootings aimed at multiple students. Such shootings, sometimes referred to as rampage or targeted school shootings/attacks or barricaded captive situations (depending on the circumstances), may be adult or youth perpetrated. Although full information about perpetrators of these events is usually not available (e.g., withheld for legal reasons; lack of thorough findings prior to events) and newspaper accounts are not always accurate (Borum et al., 2010; Lieberman, 2006), some information is provided in the psychological investigations that follow these events (see Chapter 2). As will be discussed in the pages to follow and in the chapters of this book, what is known underscores the need for, among other things, the treatment of traumas, complicated grief, and other mental disorders, as well as the reduction of bullying, teaching youth skills to deal with bullying and other adversities, and the provision of early interventions for faulty caretaker–youth attachments.

CHILD-RELATED VARIABLES THAT INFLUENCE DEVELOPMENT

Life provides numerous stressors for youth. Early attachment relationships (Chapters 6 and 10) help to shape a youth's ongoing ability to cope with stress and adversity. The nature of a youth's personality, neurobiology, social skills (e.g., perspective taking/empathy, social ease), and coping skills influence how they respond to stressors, including the likelihood of aggression or suicidality.

Neurobiology

As discussed in Chapter 2, genetic (e.g., low MAOA activity) and neurochemical characteristics are associated with aggression as well as with internalizing (e.g., serotonin system and depression) and other externalizing disorders (Nader, 2008). Changes in hormone levels, changes in reactivity to neurochemicals (such as cortisol reactivity), specific brain injury, and activation of the fight–flight neurochemistry have been linked to aggression (McBurnett, King, & Scarpa, 2003; Sapolsky, 1998). Serotonin deficiencies, for example, have been associated with low mood, lack of willpower, poor appetite control, and the dysregulation of aggression (Grigorenko, 2002; Schmidt & Fox, 2002). Although care must be taken in prescribing drugs for youth, the correction of deficits by use of serotonin reuptake inhibitors decreases aggression, ameliorates anxiety, and induces secure attachment phenomena. Additionally, even though from a neurobiological perspective most aggression is not associated with brain deficits, when the brain is implicated in the expression of aggression, a number of brain deficits, especially right hemispheric deficits, are found to be associated with aggression (Kaiser, 2005). Violence and antisocial behaviors have been linked to abnormal prefrontal circuitry, especially on the right side.

Previous traumatization has been among associations with behavioral problems including aggression and suicidality. Either over-activation (e.g., fear or fight-inducing traumas) or under-activation (e.g., neglect) of important neural systems during critical periods may profoundly affect child development (Perry, Pollard, Blakely, Baker & Vigilante, 1995). For example, extreme stress may disrupt the functioning of the cortex, which is critically involved in inhibiting the stress response as well as in attention, organization, self-regulation, and planning (Rothbart & Rueda, 2005; Stevens et al., 2007; Stein & Kendall, 2004) (see Trauma and Adversity, to come).

Social and Coping Skills

Social and coping skills deficits have been associated with adjustment problems and behavioral disorders (Chapter 5). Nonproductive coping strategies have moderated the relationship between personality characteristics and delinquency (Hasking, 2007; Chapter 5). Aspects of self-regulation are associated with social and coping competence—for example, the ability to delay gratification and to inhibit reactions is important to coping and social interaction (Posner & Rothbart, 2007). Research indicates that, compared to youth with poor self-regulation, youth with good self-regulation score higher on measures of social competence, as well as academic achievement, grades, and coping (Buckner, Mezzacappa, & Beardslee, 2009). They score lower on behavioral problems, anxiety, and depression. Youth high in self-regulation appear to respond in more adaptive manners to real past and hypothetical stressors. Buckner et al. (2009) suggest that self-regulation skills may help children cope with adversity in manners that help to alleviate distress and to resolve problems.

Evidence suggests that interventions can integrate prevention of suicide and violence by focusing on their joint risk and protective factors. Among these factors are coping skills and family functioning (Lubell & Vetter, 2006). Although it has been suggested that, under continued harassment, anyone might eventually erupt into violence, become self-destructive, or suffer other severe adverse emotional effects (see Daniels et al., 2010b), well-developed coping skills reduce the likelihood of aggression (Chapter 5).

Empathy

Empathy is a multidimensional concept that encompasses cognitive as well as emotional dimensions, including the ability to take the perspective of others, to correctly identify their subjective reality, and to experience appropriate affective responses to the perception of others' emotional states (e.g., empathic concern, sharing the emotions of the other; Grynberg, Luminet, Corneille, Grèzes, & Berthoz, 2010). Martin Henley suggests that lack of social skill development and inadequacies of emotional intelligence handicap disruptive youth, such as those who bully, talk back, or refuse to finish tasks (interview in Hopkins, 2004). These youth may have shortcomings in their abilities to understand the impact of their behaviors on others as well as to control impulses, anticipate consequences, and manage stress.

Alexithymia refers to a deficit in the ability to identify and describe one's own emotions, as well as a tendency to deal with superficial themes and to avoid emotional/affective thinking (such avoidance is referred to as *externally oriented thinking*) (Frewen et al., 2008; Grynberg et al., 2010). Alexithymia has been found in some traumatized individuals and in association with somatic and other mental illnesses (Frewen et al., 2008). Evidence suggests a correlation between empathy (e.g., perspective taking, empathic concern) and the ability to identify and describe personal emotions as well as a negative association between empathy and externally oriented thinking (i.e., when empathy is higher, externally oriented thinking is lower) (Grynberg et al., 2010; Guttman & Laporte, 2002). Youth who perpetrate social cruelty (e.g., relational or overtly aggressive bullying) tend to lack empathy, compassion, and perspective taking (Cunningham, 2007).

Processing of facial expressions and other indicators of emotion is important to human interaction (Douglas, & Porter, 2010). Traumatic or depressive reactions may interfere with components of empathy such as information processing (e.g., perspective taking and accurate recognition of others' emotions). For example, individuals who experience violence or exclusion may attribute malicious intent to others more often than their peers, even in ambiguous situations (Crick & Dodge, 1996). Depressive symptoms have been associated with negative interpersonal expectations and perceptions, biased information processing in interpersonal interactions, and maladaptive relationship-oriented beliefs (Hammen & Rudolph, 2003). For example, depressed individuals more often than others see sadness and less often see happiness in neutral faces (Douglas & Porter, 2010). Cognitive biases may contribute to aggression (Nader, 2008). Aggressive youth may have biases that endorse the value of aggression. Aggressive individuals tend more often to demonstrate a hostile attribution bias (Georgiou & Stavrinides, 2008). That is, they more often see hostile intent in ambiguous or neutral situations than others.

ENVIRONMENTAL FACTORS

Family, school, community, and national environments influence outcomes such as effective coping or aggression, exclusion or support, and risk or resilience in youth. For example, socioeconomic status (SES) and community violence have been implicated (Klein & Cornell, 2010). A number of school environmental factors have been linked to school violence (see Chapter 3; "The Caring School Community Project," Chapter 7; and "Peaceful Schools Project," Chapter 8). School size, climate or social atmosphere, connection, the cycle of victimization and aggression, bullying and an atmosphere that condones it, among other factors, have been linked to school outcomes (Gregory, Cornell, Fan, Sheras, Shih, & Huang, 2010). Creating a safe environment and enhancing rapport between adults and students is a part of prevention, as well as a part of averting potential aggression. As Chapters 2 and 8 elaborate, programs that reduce the acceptability of bullying behaviors, increase perceived adult responsiveness, and promote conflict resolution have been linked to reductions in bullying and other aggression. Providing youth with methods of coping with aggressors has also proven effective.

The School Environment—School Size

Among the multiple school-related factors that influence behavioral and mental health outcomes (Werblow, Robinson, & Duesbery, 2010), school size is associated with mixed findings influenced by differences in study methods (e.g., variable inclusion, source of data) and in school and community characteristics. For example, demographics such as SES (e.g., low SES), ethnic make-up of schools (e.g., ethnic diversity/homogeneity), and local crime rates (e.g., high crime) are associated with outcomes (e.g., antisocial aggressiveness, externalizing behaviors; see Klein & Cornell, 2010 for a summary). In addition, the frequency of problems must be distinguished from the percentage rate of their occurrence. That is, larger schools may have more reported behavior problems but may have a smaller percentage of problems for their population than smaller schools. For example, Klein and Cornell (2010) found a higher frequency but a lower rate of recorded bullying offenses in larger schools. More study is needed to discover the meaning of findings. For example, do increased bullying discipline violations reflect stricter enforcement in racially diverse schools or the impact of diversity? Is school size, location, or demographics the key factor in outcomes? In the case of physical attacks, Klein and Cornell (2010) found that the danger did not appear to be linked to urban location or school size, but instead to the proportion of low-income, minority students.

Although small and larger school-size are discussed here, some research suggests an optimal school size related to some outcomes. Six studies found an "inverted U" relationship between school size and achievement. Achievement increased with school size up to an optimum size then began to decline as school size exceeded the optimum (Leithwood & Jantzi, 2009).

Small Schools

Proponents of small schools suggest the following upper limits for schools: (a) for elementary schools, the recommended range is 300 to 400 students; and (b) for secondary schools, the range is 400 to 800 (Cotton, 1996; Leithwood & Jantzi, 2009; Werblow & Duesbery, 2009). Many investigators conclude that no school should have more than 400 or 500 students. Related to achievement and student attendance and retention rates, Leithwood and Jantzi (2009) concluded that especially struggling and economically disadvantaged students benefit from smaller schools. A body of research has demonstrated that small schools have greater parent participation, better student engagement in school (i.e., more participation, identification, and connection with school), more positive school climates, warmer relationships between adults and students, more opportunity for school involvement, better school achievement, and fewer behavioral problems (Abbott, Joireman, & Stroh, 2002; Cotton, 1996; Klein & Cornell, 2010; Leithwood & Jantzi, 2009; Werblow & Duesbery, 2009).

Larger Schools

Arguments in favor of large schools point out their economic and resource benefits. In addition to economical advantages (e.g., bulk purchasing; Klein & Cornell, 2010), large schools sometimes provide a greater variety of courses (Leithwood & Jantzi, 2009; Monk & Haller, 1993). Although findings are mixed for achievement, some research suggests higher scores for middle and high school students in larger schools (Klein & Cornell, 2010).

Some evidence suggests an absence of correlation between large school size and some externalizing problems (e.g., bullying; Klein & Cornell, 2010). In a large Virginia statewide study of high school size and victimization, according to school records, the relationship between school size and bullying, threat, and attack violations was negative (Klein & Cornell, 2010). That is, larger schools had a lower rate of violations than smaller schools. Because school principals and their assistants can only deal with a fixed number of discipline cases each day, it is possible that less serious cases were not recorded. Student reports of their own victimization showed no correlations with school size. In contrast, a nationally representative longitudinal study of 2,232 elementary schoolchildren demonstrated that school size was associated with an increased risk of being victimized by bullying (Bowes et al., 2009).

The School Environment—Peer Victimization

Vying for social status is among normal human behaviors. Vying for status is among forms of bullying and relational aggression as well. Victims, bullies, and bully-victims are at risk for a number of negative outcomes, such as absenteeism, alcohol abuse, antisocial behaviors, cigarette smoking, and use of other forms of violence, as well as poor psychosocial adjustment, poor academic achievement, loneliness, rejection, depression, anxiety, and poor self-esteem (Beran & Lupart,

2009; Hawker & Boulton, 2000; Nansel, Overpeck, Haynie et al., 2003; Nansel, Overpeck, Pilla et al., 2001; Phillips, 2007). Findings for prevalence of bullying are influenced by definitional criteria (Cornell & Bandyopadhyay, 2010). In a study of prevalence rates of bullying victimization reported for the 2 months prior to questioning, in a nationally representative sample of grades 6–10, Wang, Ionnatti, and Nansel (2009) stated that 12.8% of students reported being physically bullied, 36.5% were verbally bullied, 41.0% relationally bullied, and 9.8% cyber bullied. Bullying and the impact of humiliation and helplessness are discussed in more detail in Chapter 2.

Vying for Social Status

According to Kaiser (2005), all adolescent primates, especially males, strive for social status. For animals and humans, aggression has been linked to social status. *Rough and tumble* (R&T) play, for example, demonstrates this link (Nader, 2008). R&T behavior combines (1) gentle contact such as open-handed hitting, pushing, or teasing; (2) positive affect such as smiling or laughing; and (3) remaining together after the *rough* act (Pellegrini, 2003). *Aggressive* behavior, in contrast, combines (1) hard contact such as closed-handed hitting or kicking; (2) negative affect such as frowning or crying; and (3) separation after the *aggressive* act. Although, R&T and aggression are separate systems, and they appear to be linked to different neural and endocrine controls, Pellegrini (2003) demonstrated that R&T practices are used to establish dominance in adolescence. R&T permits youth to evaluate the strength of others or to establish their own dominance. In most mammalian species and cultures, males engage in more R&T than females (Pellegrini & Smith, 1998). Females, in contrast, primarily use verbal rather than physical means to gain or keep resources. For adolescents, the stronger boy may escalate the intensity of behaviors such as fighting if the weaker boy does not yield or show distress. Vying for status has been a part of bullying and relational aggression.

Peer Reinforcement and the Cycle of Violence

Aggressors and victims help to shape each other's behaviors, and peers reinforce the pattern (Nader, 2008; Chapter 8). In a longitudinal study, Schwartz et al. (1993) found that aggressive boys targeted youth who were not well regarded. The peer group environment fostered chronic victimization by offering positive regard to aggressors for agonistic behaviors towards victims but not for aggression toward nonvictims. Additionally, in the Schwartz et al. study, boys reinforced the aggressive behaviors of their attackers, for example, by permitting domination or giving up objects. As time progressed, peers rarely rewarded and frequently refused persuasion attempts by victim boys. The more boys were victimized, the less peers liked them. Thus, early victimization may result in additional or ongoing victimization by exclusion or other forms of relational aggression as well as overt aggression. In turn, repeated victimization may lead to humiliation and rage that ultimately erupts into violence. Chronically victimized boys have been among those who have committed school shootings (including targeted school shootings) or suicides (Seals & Young, 2003). Exposure to school shootings (or suicides) can traumatize youth. A history of trauma is among the factors associated with subsequent aggressiveness in youth (Greenwald, 2002; Nader, 2008).

Averted School Shootings

A number of targeted shootings (or shooting rampages) have been averted. An examination of schools where planned shootings have been averted has demonstrated some of the measures that can be taken to prevent in-school violence (O'Toole & Critical Incident Response Group, 2000). Methods used are elaborated in Table 1.2. *Zero tolerance* policies that impose severe sanctions (e.g., suspension or expulsion) even for minor offenses in hopes of preventing more serious ones have not proven effective in preventing school violence (Allen et al., 2008; APA Zero Tolerance Task Force, 2008; Borum et al., 2010). Threat assessment methods have received greater endorsement. Youth often communicate their plans for targeted acts of violence. High-level threats are specific and detailed; the individual has taken steps to carry out the plan (Daniels et al., 2010b). Creating a safe environment in which youth feel free to tell what they have been told or overheard is important. In addition to establishing a good rapport with all students, making an effort to establish a relationship with at-risk youth or those who have shown warning signs is also important. Responding immediately to any reports of potential rampages is essential. As documented by student reports and school records, Cornell, Sheras, Gregory, and Fan (2009) found that schools using the Virginia threat assessment method reported less bullying, greater willingness to seek help related to threats of violence or bullying, more positive perceptions of school climate, and fewer long-term suspensions than schools using other threat assessment approaches.

Home and Community Environments

A number of home and community issues influence aggressive and other outcomes in youth. When combined with adversity, parental mental health, parenting and attachment styles (Chung & Steinberg,

TABLE 1.2   Targeted School Violence Prevention

Method	Aspects of the Method
Safe climate	Maintaining a safe and positive school climate
	Mutual respect between adults and students
	Rapport building—developing positive connections with students, treating students with dignity and respect, compassionate interactions, accentuating students' strengths, open and trusting relationships with families
	The visible presence of school personnel throughout the school
	Encouragement for students to communicate rumors/concerns or weapons
	Use of a trained, uniformed school resource officer
Staff training	Watchfulness—ever-present awareness of conditions in and around the school
	• reporting any altercation, behavioral changes, indicators of mental illness, or suspect body language
	• taking all threats seriously
	Crisis planning
	• methods of response
	• planning and practice for worst case scenarios
	• planning for the aftermath of events
	Anticipating police and media response
Liaison	Clear communication and liaison with law enforcement and mental health professionals before, during, and after an event
Threat assessment (e.g., see Virginia Threat Assessment Model, Dallas Threat of Violence Risk Assessment)	Use of a threat assessment team (e.g., principal or assistant principal, school resource officer or law enforcement officer, and a psychologist, counselor, or social worker)
	Using a multidisciplinary approach—employment of all school personnel, law enforcement, and mental health professionals
	Using a problem-solving approach
	Maintaining order—looking for evidence
	Investigation, triggered by a student's threatening behavior or behaviors (not characteristics) that are of concern
	Assessment of youth's intent or ideas of attack—communication of intent, interest in other attacks or attackers, interest in and access to weapons, belief that violence is an acceptable way of dealing with things

Continued

TABLE 1.2 (*Continued*)   Targeted School Violence Prevention

Method	Aspects of the Method
	Assessment of youth's ability to carry out an attack
	Assessment of youth's mental state—hopelessness, desperation, and/or despair
	Cognizance of whether others are worried about the student's potential for violence
	Examination of circumstances that might influence the likelihood of attack
	Assessment of whether the case can be resolved as a transient threat
	Immediate security measures, if deemed appropriate—notification of law enforcement, warning potential victims, and/or other intervention
Bullying prevention	Teacher/staff awareness of bullying as a problem
	Teacher/staff willingness to intervene
	Equipping students to deal with bullying
Crisis intervention	Communicating with a suspected shooter in a calm, nonconfrontational manner to deescalate emotions of the assailant; use of good listening skills
	Trained negotiators negotiating the release of any hostages
	Restoring safety
	Deescalating the situation—assuring students that they are safe, enlisting mental health services
	Evaluating psychological trauma risk and responding to psychological needs

Note: From Allen, K., Cornell, D., Lorek, E., and Sheras, P., 2008; Borum, R., Cornell, D., Modzeleski, W., and Jimerson, S., 2010; Cornell, D., 2006; Cornell, D., & Sheras, P., 2006; Daniels, J., Royster, T., Vecchi, G., & Pshenishy, E., 2010; Daniels, J., Volungis, A., Pshenishy, E. Gandhi, P., Winkler, A., Cramer, D., & Bradley, M., 2010; see Chapter 9 this book.

2006; Fletcher, Steinberg, & Williams-Wheeler, 2004), family history and structure (Langenkamp & Frisco, 2008; Scaramella, Sohr-Preston, Callahan, & Mirabile, 2008), and peer and community influences (Chung & Steinberg, 2006; Laird et al., 2001) affect mental health outcomes. For example, across racial and economic demographic groups, the combination of strong supervision and positive parental involvement is protective against outcomes such as aggression and delinquency (Chung & Steinberg, 2006; Nader, in press). Discussions of attachment, adversity, and support follow.

Attachment

Research on parent–child/infant attachment has demonstrated the importance of early attachment relationships (Cassidy & Shaver, 1999). Caregiver–youth relationships evolve over time and continue to influence well-being and functioning. Infants and children who are valued and sensitively cared for develop qualities (e.g., good self-confidence and self-esteem, reasonable trust, empathy, and the capacity to self-reflect and to self-soothe) that enhance the ability to be productive, competent (personally and interpersonally), and resilient (i.e., the facility to do well in the face of adversity; see Fosha, 2003; Knox, 2003a,b; Main, 1995; Nader, 2008). Children with secure early and ongoing attachments are more resistant to stress and are less vulnerable to problem behaviors and other psychopathology (Fosha, 2003; Weinfield, Sroufe, Egeland, & Carlson, 1999; Chapter 6). They are more likely to rebound toward adequate functioning following a period of troubled behavior. In contrast, insensitive, frightening, or confusing care may result in the lack of resilience and in behavioral, temperamental, and emotional difficulties. Disorganized/disoriented attachments, for example, predict later chronic disturbances of affect regulation, stress management, hostile-aggressive behavior, a predisposition to relational aggression, and risk of a number of mental disorders (Lyons-Ruth & Jacobvitz, 1999; Schore, 2003). Notably, as will be discussed in Chapter 6, insecure or disorganized attachments have been associated with aggression, low self-esteem, depressive, anxiety, dissociative, somatic, externalizing, internalizing, and overall psychopathology in childhood, adolescence, and young adulthood, as well as to vulnerabilities to a number of disturbances including PTSD and being led into acts of violence (e.g., terrorism) (Hesse et al., 2003; Lyons-Ruth, Zeanah, & Benoit, 2003; Muller, Sicoli, & Lemieux, 2000; Scheff, 1997; Volkan, 2001; see Nader, 2008 for a summary). Adolescents' *insecure–dismissing* attachments also have been linked to externalizing problems (e.g., aggression or delinquency, conduct disorder, and substance abuse; Allen & Land, 1999).

Trauma and Adversity

Traumatic reactions are associated with a number of mental health problems including aggression or suicidality. Overt aggression (e.g., bullying and other assaults, childhood abuse), relational aggression (e.g., relational bullying, exclusion, depersonalizing gossip), and other traumas (e.g., witnessing domestic violence, traumatic deaths of loved ones) often are among the experiences of those who committed multiple shootings at schools (Henry, 2009; Nader, 2008). For example, the UT clock tower shooter's father abused him. Incarcerated violent adolescents significantly more often than not have histories of violent traumas (Ford, 2002). A number of clinicians have observed that severe, repeated, or varied traumas damage the core self or personal spirit (Ford, 2002; Kalsched, 1996; Knox, 2003a; Nader, 2008; Pearlman, 2001; Wilson, 2004). As noted, dysregulation of emotion and behavior may also result (Ford & Courtois, 2009; van der Kolk, 2005).

Support

Some individuals need more alone time than others. Some individuals have less regard for others than the average person. Nevertheless, all individuals need a good support system. For example, research suggests that mental health outcomes following adversities have been better with increased levels of social support (Kilpatrick et al., 2007; Scheeringa, in press). Research has now demonstrated that the combination of structure (consistent enforcement of school discipline) and support (availability of caring adults) in schools is associated with lower bullying and victimization rates (when school size, ethnicity, and low-income are controlled for; Gregory et al., 2010).

National Influences

Societies and religions differ in their emphasis on independence or connectedness–interdependence (Hofstede, 1980; Shiang, 2000). The importance of competitiveness and fame may be related to this orientation and/or to the media that influences their desirability. Pushing children to outdo their peers is sometimes motivated by a desire to give a child an advantage in life. If competition does not include a goal of enhancing each individual's personal talents and skills, some may benefit while others suffer from its effects. Emphases on, for example, competition and independence influence youth's motivations such as those related to rating their personal worth, valuing others, and committing or avoiding aggression. In addition to those values taught and modeled in the home, much of the national value system is shaped or reinforced by electronic media.

Media

Although entertainment media can have a positive (e.g., increasing helping behaviors) or a negative effect on youth, across studies, violent media, in TV, movies, video games, music, and comic books, have been linked to aggressive thoughts and behaviors, angry feelings, and arousal levels (Nader, 2010). Well-designed research has repeatedly shown that the effects of watching electronic media violence (i.e., the intentional injury or irritation of a person by another person or character) increases the risk of behaving aggressively right after viewing and years later (Anderson et al., 2010; Huesmann, 2007, 2010; Bushman & Huesmann, 2006). Even after controlling for early aggressiveness, habitual exposure to media violence in middle-childhood predicted increased aggressiveness 1, 3, 10, 15, and 22 years later (Huesmann, 2007).

IMPLICATIONS

Multiple factors influence aggressive behaviors and other mental health disturbances. A number of youth and environmental characteristics have been identified as relevant to the manifestation of aggression and other disturbances. In part, because children exhibiting persistent disruptive behaviors are more likely to become delinquents, and delinquents are more likely to become chronic, serious, or violent offenders, some observers believe that providing interventions as early as the preschool level is critical in preventing the emergence of disruptive behaviors and child delinquency (Loeber, Farrington, & Petechuk, 2003). In fact, prevention begins with the child's beginnings. Early and ongoing secure attachment relationships and other parenting practices may enable the skills and habits to live without resorting to aggression (Chapter 6). Additional interventions can be used in preschool and throughout the elementary school years to assist prevention.

A number of early interventions are associated with prevention of aggressive and other behavioral and mental health disturbances. Among them are teaching youth social skills, coping skills, and empathy, as well as creating environments that enhance support and secure attachments, do not tolerate bullying, provide skills for dealing with bullies, and instill healthy competition. To be effective, interventions must be aimed at both sides of the problem—would-be killers and the environments that produce them. Some of the well-known targeted/rampage shooters have been victims of bullies before lashing out in violence. As will be clear in the chapters of Section I, bullying in schools must be addressed early. Many of the interventions discussed in the chapters of Section II of this book may assist bullies and their victims who might become violent.

As discussed in Chapter 2, rejecting experiences such as early insecure attachments, bullying, and other humiliations may engender intense feelings of helplessness and hopelessness, rage, and vulnerability that lead to self-destructive behaviors, violence, or vulnerability to be manipulated by others who intend harm. Those who train terrorists often choose from those who have suffered severe or ongoing traumas, abandonment, or other repeated humiliations (Scheff, 1997; Volkan, 2001). Early interventions may reduce vulnerabilities and increase skills that provide choices other than aggression. As Chapter 9 will demonstrate, youth can learn to respond to aggressors in a way that makes their continued aggression less likely. Valuing of others and of uniqueness can be learned in and outside of schools. As will be shown (Chapters 3 and 10), increasing connection among and between youth and adults in schools and at home is an important aspect of prevention. To be most effective, interventions begin early and include parents, schools, and communities.

REFERENCES

Abbott, M., Joireman, J., & Stroh, H. (2002). The influence of district size, school size, and socioeconomic status on student achievement in Washington: A replication study using hierarchical linear modeling. Lynnwood, WA: Washington School Research Center Report #3. ED 470338.

Allen, K., Cornell, D., Lorek, E., & Sheras, P. (2008). Response of school personnel to student threat assessment training. *School Effectiveness and School Improvement, 19*(3), 319–332.

Allen, J. P., & Land, D. (1999). Attachment in adolescence. In J. Cassidy & P. R. Shaver (Eds.), *Handbook of attachment: Theory, research, and clinical applications* (pp. 319–335). New York: Guilford Press.

American Psychological Association Zero Tolerance Task Force (2008). Are zero tolerance policies effective in schools? An evidentiary review and recommendations. *American Psychologist, 63*(9), 852–862.

Anderson, C. A., Shibuya, A., Ihori, N., Swing, E. L., Bushman, B. J., Sakamoto, A., … Saleem, M. (2010). Violent video game effects on aggression, empathy, and prosocial behavior in Eastern and Western countries. *Psychological Bulletin, 136,* 151–173.

Angold, A., & Heim, C. (2007). A developmental perspective, with a focus on childhood trauma. In W. Narrow, M. First, P. Sirovatka, & D. Regier (Eds.). *Age and gender considerations in psychiatric diagnosis: A research agenda for DSM-V.*, (pp. 81–100). Arlington, VA: American Psychiatric Publishing, Inc.

Bennett, P., Elliott, M., & Peters, D. (2005). Classroom and family effects on children's social and behavioral problems. *The Elementary School Journal, 105*(5), 461–480.

Beran, T., & Lupart, J. (2009). The relationship between school achievement and peer harassment in Canadian adolescents: The importance of mediating factors. *School Psychology International, 30,* 75–91.

Borum, R., Cornell, D., Modzeleski, W., & Jimerson, S. (2010). What can be done about school shootings? A review of the evidence. *Educational Researcher, 39(*1), 27–37.

Bowes, L., Arseneault, L., Maughan, B., Taylor, A., Caspi, A., & Moffitt, T. (2009). School, neighborhood, and family factors are associated with children's bullying involvement: A nationally representative longitudinal study. *Journal of the American Academy of Child & Adolescent Psychiatry,* 2009 May; *48(*5): 545–53.

Brooks, K., Schiraldi, V., & Ziedenberg, J. (2000). *School house hype: Two years later.* Center on Juvenile and Criminal Justice (www.cjcj. org/schoolhousehype.html).

Buckner, J., Mezzacappa, E., & Beardslee, W. (2009). Self-regulation and its relations to adaptive functioning in low income youths. *American Journal of Orthopsychiatry,* 79(1), 19–30.

Bushman, B., & Huesmann, L. (2006). Short-term and long-term effects of violent media on aggression in children and adults. *Archives of Pediatric Adolescent Medicine, 160,* 348–352.

Cassidy, J., & Shaver, P. R. (Eds.). (1999). *Handbook of attachment: Theory, research, and clinical applications.* New York: Guilford Press.

Centers for Disease Control and Prevention (CDC) (2009b). Youth Violence: Facts at a Glance. Downloaded on 5/30/10 from www. cdc.gov/violenceprevention.

CDC (2008b). Youth risk behavioral surveillance—United States, 2007. MMWR 57 (No. SS–4).

Chung, H., & Steinberg, L. (2006). Relations between neighborhood factors, parenting behaviors, peer deviance, and delinquency among serious juvenile offenders. *Developmental Psychology, 42*(2), 319–331.

Cornell, D. (1990). Prior adjustment of violent juvenile offenders. *Law and Human Behavior, 14,* 569–578.

Cornell, D. (2006). *School violence: Fears versus facts.* Mahwah, NJ: Lawrence Erlbaum.

Cornell, D., & Bandyopadhyay, S. (2010). The assessment of bullying. In S. R. Jimerson, S. M. Swearer, & D. L. Espelage (Eds.), *The handbook of bullying in schools: An international perspective* (pp. 265–276). New York: Routledge.

Cornell, D., Benedek, E., & Benedek, D. (1987). Juvenile homicide: Prior adjustment and a proposed typology. *American Journal of Orthopsychiatry, 57,* 383–393.

Cornell, D., & Sheras, P. (2006). *Guidelines for responding to student threats of violence.* Longmont, CO: Sopris West.

Cornell, D., Sheras, P., Gregory, A., & Fan, X. (2009). A retrospective study of school safety conditions in high schools using the Virginia threat assessment guidelines versus alternative approaches. *School Psychology Quarterly, 24*, 119–129.

Cotton, K. (1996). Social Benefits of Small-Scale Schooling. ERIC DIGEST ED401088 1996-12-00 Retrieved 6/19/08 from http://www.eric.ed.gov/ERICDocs/data/ericdocs2/content_storage_01/0000000b/80/2a/27/0c.pdf

Crick, N., & Dodge, K. (1994). A review and reformulation of social information-processing mechanisms in children's social adjustment. Psychological Bulletin, 115, 74–101.

Crick, N., & Dodge, K. (1996). Social information-processing mechanisms in reactive and proactive aggression. *Child Development, 67*(3), 993–1002.

Cunningham, N. (2007). Level of bonding to school and perception of the school environment by bullies, victims, and bully victims. *The Journal of Early Adolescence 27(4)*, 457–478.

Daniels, J., Royster, T., Vecchi, G., & Pshenishy, E. (2010a). Barricaded captive situations in schools: Mitigation and response. *Journal of Family Violence, 25*, 587–594.

Daniels, J., Volungis, A., Pshenishy, E. Gandhi, P., Winkler, A., Cramer, D., & Bradley, M. (2010b). A qualitative investigation of averted school shooting rampages. *The Counseling Psychologist, 38*(1), 69–95.

Davis, C. (2004). *Children who kill: Profiles of preteen and teenage killers*. Croydon, Surrey, UK: Bookmarque Ltd.

Douglas, K., & Porter, R. (2010). Recognition of disgusted facial expressions in severe depression *The British Journal of Psychiatry, 197*, 156–157.

Fletcher, A., Steinberg, L., & Williams-Wheeler, M. (2004). Parental influences on adolescent problem behavior: Revisiting Stattin and Kerr. *Child Development, 75*(3), 781–796.

Ford, J. D. (2002). Traumatic victimization in childhood and persistent problems with oppositional-defiance. *Journal of Aggression, Maltreatment and Trauma, 6*(1), 25–58.

Ford, J., & Courtois, C. (2009). Defining and understanding complex trauma. In C. Courtois & J. Ford (Eds.), *Treating complex traumatic stress disorders* (pp. 13–30). New York: Guilford.

Fosha, D. (2003). Dyadic regulation and experiential work with emotion and relatedness in trauma and disorganized attachment. In M. Solomon & D. J. Siegel (Eds.), *Healing trauma* (pp. 228–281). New York: W. W. Norton.

Frewen, P., Dozois, D., Neufeld, R., & Lanius, R. (2008). Meta-analysis of alexithymia in Posttraumatic Stress Disorder. *Journal of Traumatic Stress, 21*(2), 243–246.

Georgiou, S., & Stavrinides, P. (2008). Bullies, victims and bully-victims: Psychosocial profiles and attribution styles. *School Psychology International, 29*(5), 574–589.

Gould, M., Greenberg, T., Velting D., & Shaffer, D. (2006). Youth suicide: A review. *Prevention Researcher, 13*(3), 3–7.

Greenwald, R. (Ed.). (2002). *Trauma and juvenile delinquency: Theory, research, and interventions.* New York: Haworth Press.

Gregory, A., Cornell, D., Fan, X., Sheras, P., Shih, T., & Huang, F. (2010). Authoritative school discipline: High school practices associated with lower student bullying and victimization. *Journal of Educational Psychology, 102,* 483–496.

Grigorenko, E. L. (2002). In search of the genetic engram of personality. In D. Cervone & W. Mischel (Eds.), *Advances in personality science* (pp. 29–82). New York: Guilford Press.

Grynberg, D., Luminet, O., Corneille, O., Grèzes, J., & Berthoz, S. (2010). Alexithymia in the interpersonal domain: A general deficit of empathy? *Personality and Individual Differences 49,* 845–850.

Guttman, H., & Laporte, L. (2002). Alexithymia, empathy, and psychological symptoms in a family context. *Comprehensive Psychiatry, 43,* 448–455.

Hammen, C., & Rudolph, K. D. (2003). Childhood mood disorders. In E. J. Mash & R. A. Barkley (Eds.), *Child psychopathology* (2nd ed., 233–278). New York: Guilford Press.

Hasking, P. (2007). Reinforcement sensitivity, coping, and delinquent behavior in adolescents. *Journal of Adolescence, 30*(5), 739–749.

Hawker, D., & Boulton, M. (2000). Twenty years' research on peer victimization and psychosocial maladjustment: A meta-analytic review of cross-sectional studies. *Journal of Child Psychology and Psychiatry, 41,* 441–455.

Henry, S. (2009). School violence beyond Columbine: A complex problem in need of an interdisciplinary analysis. *American Behavioral Scientist, 52*(9), 1246–1265.

Hesse, E., Main, M., Abrams, K. Y., & Rifkin, A. (2003). Unresolved states regarding loss or abuse can have "second-generation" effects: Disorganization, role inversion, and frightening ideation in the offspring of traumatized, non-maltreating parents. In M. Solomon & D. J. Siegel (Eds.), *Healing trauma* (pp. 57–106). New York: W. W. Norton.

Hofstede, G. (1980). Motivation, leadership, and organization: Do American theories apply abroad? *Organizational Dynamics, 9,* 42–61.

Hopkins, G. (2004). Teaching self-control. *National Education Association.* Retrieved June 18, 2008 from http://www.nea.org/classmanagement/ifc040629.html

28 Kathleen Nader

Huesmann, R. L. (2007). The impact of electronic media violence: Scientific theory and research. *Journal of Adolescent Health 41*, S6–S13.

Kaiser, D. A. (2005). School shootings, high school size, and neurobiological considerations. *Journal of Neurotherapy*, 9(3), 101–115.

Kalsched, D. (1996). *The inner world of trauma: Archetypal defenses of the personal spirit*. London: Brunner-Routledge.

Kaufman, P., Chen, X., Choy, S., Ruddy, S. A., Miller, A. K., Chandler, K. A., Chapman, C. D., Rand, M. R., & Klaus, P. (1999). *Indicators of school crime and safety, 1999*. Washington, D.C.: U.S. Department of Education (NCES 1999-057) and U.S. Department of Justice (NCJ-178906).

Kilpatrick, D., Koenen, K., Ruggiero, K., Acierno, R., Galea, S., Resnick, H. et al. (2007). Serotonin transporter genotype and social support and moderation of posttraumatic stress disorder and depression in hurricane-exposed adults. *American Journal of Psychiatry*, 164(11), 1–7.

Klein, J., & Cornell, D. (2010). Is the link between large high schools and student victimization an illusion? *Journal of Educational Psychology, 102*, 933–946.

Knox, J. (2003a). *Archetype, attraction, analysis: Jungian psychology and the emergent mind*. New York: Brunner-Routledge.

Knox, J. (2003b). Trauma and defenses: Their roots in relationship, an overview. *Journal of Analytical Psychology, 48*, 511–530.

Laird, R., Jordan, K., Dodge, K., Pettit, G., & Bates, J. (2001). Peer rejection in childhood, involvement with antisocial peers in early adolescence, and the development of externalizing behavior problems. *Development and Psychopathology, 13*, 337–354.

Langenkamp, A., & Frisco, M. (2008). Family transitions and adolescent severe emotional distress: The salience of family context. *Social Problems, 55*(2), 238–253.

Leithwood, K. & Jantzi, D. (2009). Review of empirical evidence about school size effects: A policy perspective. *Review of Educational Research, 79*(1), 464–490.

Lieberman, J. (2006). *The shooting game*. Santa Ana, CA: Seven Locks.

Loeber, R., Farrington, D., & Petechuk, D. (2003). Child delinquency: Early intervention and prevention. *Child Delinquency Bulletin Series*. U.S. Department of Justice.

Lubell, K. & Vetter, J. (2006). Suicide and youth violence prevention: The promise of an integrated approach. *Aggression and Violent Behavior, 11*(2), 167–175.

Lyons-Ruth, K., & Jacobvitz, D. (1999). Attachment disorganization: Unresolved loss, relational violence and lapses in behavioral and attentional strategies. In J. Cassidy & P. Shaver (Eds.), *Handbook of attachment* (pp. 469–496). New York: Guilford Press.

Lyons-Ruth, K., Zeanah, C. H., & Benoit, D. (2003). Disorder and risk for disorder during infancy and toddlerhood. In E. J. Mash & R. A. Barkley (Eds.), *Child psychopathology* (2nd ed., pp. 589–631). New York: Guilford Press.

Main, M. (1995). Recent studies in attachment: Overview with selected implications for clinical work. In S. Goldberg, R. Muir, & J. Kerr (Eds.), *Attachment theory: Social, developmental and clinical perspectives* (pp. 407–472). Hillsdale, NJ: Analytic Press.

McBurnett, K., King, J., & Scarpa, A. (2003). The hypothalamic-pituitary-adrenal system (HPA) and the development of aggressive, antisocial, and substance abuse disorders. In D. Cicchetti & E. Walker (Eds.), *Neurodevelopmental mechanisms in psychopathology* (pp. 324–344). Cambridge, UK: Cambridge University Press.

Monk, D. & Haller, E. (1993). Predictors of high school academic course offerings: The role of school size. *American Educational Research Journal, 30*(1), 3–21.

Muller, R., Sicoli, L., & Lemieux, K. E. (2000). Relationship between attachment style and posttraumatic stress symptomatology among adults who report the experience of childhood abuse. *Journal of Traumatic Stress, 13*(2), 321–332.

Nader, K. (2008). *Understanding and assessing trauma in children and adolescents: Measures, methods, and youth in context.* New York: Routledge.

Nader, K. (2010). Children and adolescents' exposure to the mass violence of war and terrorism: Role of the media. In N. B. Webb (Ed.), *Helping bereaved children* (3rd edition, pp. 215–239). New York: Guilford.

Nader, K. (2011). Trauma in children and adolescents: Issues related to age and complex traumatic reactions. *Journal of Child and Adolescent Trauma, 4*(3), 161–180.

Nansel, T., Overpeck, M., Haynie, D., Ruan, W., & Scheidt, P. (2003). Relationships between bullying and violence among US youth. *Archives of Pediatrics and Adolescent Medicine, 157*(4), 348–353.

Nansel, T., Overpeck, M., Pilla, R., Ruan, W., Simons-Morton, B., & Scheidt, P. (2001). Bullying behaviors among US youth. *Journal of the American Medical Association, 285*(16), 2094–2100.

National School Safety Center (NSSC, 2006). Review of school safety research. Westlake Village, CA: NSSC.

O'Toole, M., & the Critical Incident Response Group (2000). *The school shooter: A threat assessment perspective.* Quantico, VA: FBI Academy National Center for the Analysis of Violent Crime.

Pearlman, L. A. (2001). Treatment of persons with complex PTSD and other trauma-related disruptions of the self. In J. P. Wilson, M. Friedman, & J. Lindy (Eds.), *Treating psychological trauma and PTSD* (pp. 205–236). New York: Guilford Press.

Peeters, M., Cillessen, A., & Scholte, R. (2010). Clueless or powerful? Identifying subtypes of bullies in adolescence. *Journal of Youth Adolescence, 39*, 1041–1052.

Pellegrini, A. D. (2003). Perceptions and functions of play and real fighting in early adolescence. *Child Development, 74 (5)*, 1522–1533.

Pellegrini, A. D., & Smith, P. K. (1998). Physical activity play: The nature and function of a neglected aspect of play. *Child Development, 69*(3), 577–598.

Perry, B., Pollard, R., Blakely, T., Baker, W., & Vigilante, D. (1995). Childhood trauma, the neurobiology of adaptation and 'use-dependent' development of the brain: How 'states' become 'traits'. *Infant Mental Health Journal, 16*(4), 271–291.

Phillips, D. (2007). Punking and bullying strategies in middle school, high school, and beyond. *Journal of Interpersonal Violence, 22*(2), 158–178.

Pollack, W. (2004). Parent–child connections: The essential component for positive youth development and mental health, safe communities, and academic achievement. *New Directions for Youth Development, 103*, 17–30.

Posner, M., & Rothbart, M. (2007). *Educating the human brain.* Washington, DC: American Psychological Association.

Robers, S., Zhang, J., Truman, J., & Snyder, T. (2010). Indicators of school crime and safety: 2010. (NCES 2011-002/NCJ 230812). National Center for Education Statistics, U.S. Department of Education, and Bureau of Justice Statistics, Office of Justice Programs, U.S. Department of Justice. Washington, DC. Available from http://nces.ed.gov or http://bjs.ojp.usdoj.gov

Rothbart, M., & Rueda, M. (2005). The development of effortful control. In U. Mayr, E. Awh, & S. Keele (Eds.), *Developing individuality in the human brain: A Festschrift honoring Michael I. Posner* (pp. 167–188). Washington, DC: American Psycholological Association.

Sapolsky, R. M. (1998). *Biology and human behavior: The neurological origins of individuality* [Videotape series]. Chantilly, VA: The Teaching Company.

Scaramella, L., Sohr-Preston, S., Callahan, K., & Mirabile, S. (2008). A test of the family stress model on toddler-aged children's adjustment among Hurricane Katrina impacted and nonimpacted low-income families. *Journal of Clinical Child & Adolescent Psychology, 37*(3), 530–541.

Scheeringa, M. (2011). PTSD in children younger than age of 13: Towards developmentally sensitive assessment and management. *Journal of Child and Adolescent Trauma, 4*(3), 181–191.

Scheff, T. (1997). Deconstructing rage. Retrieved September 17, 2003, from http://www.soc.ucsb.edu/faculty/scheff/7.html

Schore, A. N. (2003). Early relational trauma, disorganized attachment, and the development of a predisposition to violence. In M. Solomon & D. J. Siegel (Eds.), *Healing trauma* (pp. 107–167). New York: W. W. Norton.

Schwartz, D., Dodge, K., & Coie, J. (1993). The emergence of chronic peer victimization in boys' play groups. *Child Development, 64*(6), 1755–1772.

Schmidt, L., & Fox, N. (2002). Individual differences in childhood shyness. In D. Cervone & W. Mischel (Eds.), *Advances in personality science* (pp. 83–105). New York: Guilford Press.

Seals, D., & Young, J. (2003). Bullying and victimization: Prevalence and relationship to gender, grade level, ethnicity, self-esteem, and depression. *Adolescence, 38*(152), 735–747.

Semrud-Clikeman, M., & Glass, K. (2010). The relation of humor and child development: Social, adaptive, and emotional aspects. *Journal of Child Neurology, 25,* 1248–1260.

Shiang, J. (2000). Considering cultural beliefs and behaviors in the study of suicide. In R. Maris, S. Canetto, J. McIntosh, & M. Silverman (Eds.), *Review of suicidology* (pp. 226–241). New York: Guilford.

Snyder, T., & Dillow, S. (2010). *Digest of Education Statistics 2009* (NCES 2010-013). National Center for Education Statistics, Institute of Education Sciences, U.S. Department of Education. Washington, DC.

Snyder, H., & Sickmund, M. (1999). Juvenile offenders and victims: 1999 national report (report no. NCJ 178257). Washington, DC: U.S. Department of Justice, Office of Justice Programs, Office of Juvenile Justice and Delinquency Prevention.

Stearns, P. (2008). Texas and Virginia: A bloodied window into changes in American public life. *Journal of Social History, 42*(2), 299–318.

Stein, P., & Kendall, J. (2004). *Psychological trauma and the developing brain: Neurologically based interventions for troubled children.* New York: Haworth Press.

Stevens, M., Kiehl, K., Pearlson, G., & Calhoun, V. (2007). Functional neural networks underlying response inhibition in adolescents and adults. *Behavioural Brain Research, 181*(1), 12–22.

Sutton, J., Smith, P. K., & Swettenham, J. (1999). Social cognition and bullying: Social inadequacy or skilled manipulation? *British Journal of Developmental Psychology, 17,* 435–450.

van der Kolk, B. (2005). Developmental trauma disorder: Toward a rational diagnosis for children with complex trauma histories. *Psychiatric Annals, 35*(5), 401–408.

van der Kolk, B. A., & Sapporta, J. (1991). The biological response to psychic trauma: Mechanisms and treatment of intrusion and numbing. *Anxiety Research, 4*, 199–212.

Volkan, V. D. (2001). September 11 and societal regression. *Mind and Human Interaction, 12*, 196–216.

Wang, J., Ionnatti, R., & Nansel, T. (2009). School bullying among adolescents in the United States: Physical, verbal, relational, and cyber. *Journal of Adolescent Health, 45*, 368–375.

Weinfield, N., Sroufe, L., Egeland, B., & Carlson, E. A. (1999). The nature of individual differences in infant-caregiver attachment. In J. Cassidy & P. R. Shaver (Eds.), *Handbook of attachment* (pp. 68–88). New York: Guilford Press.

Werblow, J., & Duesbery, L. (2009). The impact of high school size on math achievement and dropout rate. *The High School Journal, 92*, 14–23.

Werblow, J., Robinson, Q., & Duesbery, L. (2010). Regardless of school size, school climate matters: How dimensions of school climate affect student dropout rate regardless of high school size. In W. Hoy, & M. DiPaola (Eds.), *Analyzing school contexts: Influences of principals and teachers in the service of students* (pp. 191–208). Greenwich, CT: IAP Information Age Publishing.

Wilson, J. P. (2004). The broken spirit: Post-traumatic damage to the self. In J. P. Wilson & B. Drozdek (Eds.), *Broken spirits: Treating traumatized asylum seekers, refugees, war and torture victims* (pp. 107–155). New York: Brunner-Routledge.

CHAPTER 2

Youth at Risk

Targeted Shootings, Other School Violence, and Suicide

Kathleen Nader and Wallis Nader

The variables that influence mental disorders and problem behaviors likely contribute synergistically to outcomes (Cerda, Sagdeo, Johnson, & Galea, 2010; Nader, in press). Some of the youth-related factors associated with the expression of aggression and other problem behaviors also have been identified in individuals who do not commit aggression such as targeted school shootings or hostage takings. As this implies, it is unlikely that emotional and behavioral disturbances can be explained by individual risk factors such as a single temperamental, behavioral, or environmental characteristic (Nader, 2008; Rutter, 2003).

This chapter focuses on youth and, primarily, outcomes of aggression. It additionally addresses depression and suicide risk. The chapter first discusses perpetrators of targeted school shootings and hostage takings, and then examines issues related to aggression, aggressors, and victims. The possible role of shame and humiliation and a brief synopsis of personality and genetic influences are presented. Because bullying is a precursor to many of the targeted school shootings (Vossekuil, Fein, Reddy, Borum, & Modzeleski, 2002; see Chapter 8), and bullying is a form of aggression, bullies, victims, and bully–victims are described in this section as well. Finally, this chapter explores the need to belong, including validation support, rejection sensitivity, and attachment issues. Issues that are addressed elsewhere in this book as they relate to home and school environmental factors are discussed here in relationship to youth. For example, attachment, which involves issues of caretaking and interrelating, is discussed here specifically as it applies to youth interactional and personal styles.

THE PERPETRATORS OF TARGETED
SCHOOL SHOOTINGS

As noted in Chapter 1, although full information about perpetrators of targeted school shootings (sometimes referred to as rampage shootings) or hostage situations is usually not available (e.g., withheld for legal reasons; lack of thorough findings prior to events) and newspaper accounts are not always accurate (Borum et al., 2010; Lieberman, 2006), some information is provided in the psychological investigations that follow these events. Targeted school violence (or suicidality) may follow prolonged or repeated victimizations, such as bullying or abuse. Providing additional evidence for the link between traumatic victimization and delinquent behaviors, significant numbers of incarcerated youth have histories of trauma (Ford, 2002; Greenwald, 2002). Notably, trauma combined with other adversities (e.g., family dysfunction, parental marital discord; Anda et al., 2006) or multiple types of trauma exposure increase the likelihood of disordered behaviors including aggression and depression (Finkelhor, Ormrod, & Turner, 2007). As will be discussed, evidence of mental disturbances also has been present in some targeted school offenders. Similarly, a study of incarcerated juveniles suggest that around one third of them have mental disorders in addition to conduct disorder (Teplin, Abram, McClelland et al., 2002). Recognizing signs of risk permits school adults to engage youth who might otherwise emerge as aggressors and, yet, the prevalence of such signs among nonviolent youth complicates using risk factors to identify potential shooters.

Adult-Perpetrated Shootings

Adult-perpetrated shootings have included taking children hostage in an elementary school classroom (e.g., in Evanston, Illinois; Jackson Hole, Wyoming; a Pennsylvania Amish school) or shooting from off campus onto school grounds (e.g., a Los Angeles school on 49th street; Stockton, California; Bailey, Colorado; Daniels et al., 2010; Nader, 2008). As is true for incarcerated adolescents (Ford, 2002; Greenwald, 2002) and adults (Cima, Smeets, & Jelicic, 2008; Cuomo et al., 2008), unresolved traumas and/or traumatic grief are frequently found in the psychological histories of adult perpetrators of school shootings or hostage situations (Hough, Vega, Valle, Kolody, del Castillo, & Tarke, 1989; Nader, 2008; Pynoos et al., 1987; Seals & Young, 2003). For example, the young man who, in 1989, shot at children on the Stockton elementary school grounds had witnessed the spousal abuse of his mother. Additionally, the young man who, in 1984, shot at children on the playground at the

Los Angeles 49th Street elementary school had relatives who died in the Jonestown, Guyana, massacre (Nader, 2008; Pynoos et al., 1987). He suffered from untreated severe depression and complicated grief. Although also troubled by other thoughts (related to undocumented past behaviors and desires toward young girls), in 2006, the man who took children hostage in an Amish school had for years continued to be troubled by obsessive grief related to the loss of an infant daughter years earlier (Kasdorf, 2007). Loss of a child is significantly associated with a more complicated form of grieving (Lobb, Kristjanson, Aoun, Monterosso, Halkett, & Davies, 2010; Wijngaards-de Meij et al., 2007). Mental health disturbances also are among the histories of adult school shooters. For example, the young woman who took children hostage in an Evanston, Illinois, elementary school classroom had been a mental health inpatient. A woman who took an elementary classroom hostage in Orange, California, in the 1980s barely missed shooting a child when she accidentally fired her gun. She dictated a suicide note and then shot herself in front of the class. Her expressed complaint was that her doctors had not helped her, and she wanted to publicly expose them.

Youth-Perpetrated School Shootings

Among the most publicized school shootings are those described as rampage or targeted school shootings (see Table 2.1). Unless thwarted, they result in multiple deaths and injuries. Youth targeted school shooters have sometimes intended more deaths than they managed. In 1999, the Columbine shooters killed 12 students and one teacher, and wounded 24 others (Linedecker, 1999). Numerous handmade bombs planted around the school did not ignite successfully. The Columbine shootings served as a model for other shootings. Subsequent shooters and would-be shooters, in North America, Europe, Australia, and Argentina, have tried to match or exceed the Columbine rampage (Larkin, 2009). In 2007, at Virginia Tech, Cho Seung-Hui killed 33 students, including himself, and wounded at least 15 others.

Conditions and Traits Associated With Targeted Shootings

Before Columbine, targeted school shootings committed by youth were often linked to the settling of grudges against peers or teachers related to perceived injustices, petty hatreds, perceived rejection, misogyny, and/or revenge for bullying and public humiliation (Larkin, 2009). According to Larkin, after Columbine, in addition to personal revenge (e.g., for

TABLE 2.1   Family Circumstances of Shooters

Parent marital status	Intact marriage (AG, KK, MC)
	Troubled marriage (BL's father had an affair)
	Divorce (MJ, CAW, CJW)
	Acrimonious divorce (LW)
Parental mental health or prison status	No noted history of mental health disturbance
	Substance abuse (ER, mother; JR, father alcoholic and drug addicted)
	Depression (BL, in four generations of family; mother often spoke of suicide, saying BL would have to commit suicide with her)
	Incarcerated (ER, father; MJ, mother, a prison guard, remarried an inmate)
Parenting/parent–child relationship	Reported good relationship (AG, seemingly good relationship with parents and grandparents; they taught him to use a gun at age 6; DK, CAW, EH, MC, MJ)
	Child abuse (CJW, father beat and humiliated him, mother loved him; ER, multiple foster homes, said to be sexually abused; JD, mother abandoned him when he was a child, father had high expectations JD did not meet)
	Other (LW, conflicting reports of caring versus critical and neglecting parents; working single parent left him alone; KK, caring parents, father expected a lot of him)
Sibling relationships	Reported good relationship with sibling(s) (MJ)
	A more successful older sibling (KK, sister was a scholarship-winning cheerleader; MC, sister was valedictorian, others talked of her and not him)
	Problematic relationship with sibling (LW, older brother allegedly beat and picked on him)

Note: See Table 1.1 for names given by initials here. Some of the shooters in Table 1.1 are not represented here, because of insufficient available information. Information was not available for all categories in Table 2.1, column one, for all of the shooters in this table.

bullying, isolation, humiliation), shootings are linked to revenge for the collective, the desire to make a statement, memorialization of or to surpass Columbine in body count, or for notoriety. Such events also represent a failure of coping, support, and recovery (e.g., from insult, trauma). A number of school, home, and community environmental factors and youth traits have been found in some but not all of the youth who perpetrate school shootings (Tables 2.1, 2.2). Issues that have been identified as important in the backgrounds of targeted and other school shooters have also been linked to a number of other youth problems. For example, being a victim of bullying has been linked to depression, suicides, or suicidal ideation, low self-esteem, poor interpersonal relating, and disruptive behavioral disturbances (e.g., conduct disorder, oppositional defiance disorder; Harlow & Roberts, 2010; Klomek, Sourander, & Gould, 2010; Seals & Young, 2003). Trauma and traumatic grief have been linked to a number of disorders (e.g., conduct, anxiety, mood, personality) and disturbances (e.g., externalizing, internalizing, academic) (Nader, 2008).

Because characteristics of youth, home, and community environments, and school environments contribute to the possibility of school shootings, stabbings, or bombings with multiple victims, it is important to target these underlying difficulties in creating early interventions. Tables 2.1 and 2.2 elaborate some of the factors identified in the lives of school shooters targeting multiple victims. As noted, complete information is generally not available for shooters. Although diagnoses have sometimes been applied after school shootings, the information needed to make an accurate diagnosis is often unavailable, because information is not released or is withheld because of potential lawsuits (Cullen, 2007). Additionally, care must be taken in giving diagnoses such as personality disorders (including narcissistic personality disorder) to adolescents or assuming psychosis because of the nature of acts. A number of the symptoms of such disorders are within normal range during adolescence.

Identifying Shooters Who Plan Mass Violence

Lists of identifying factors for potential shooters as well as scales to measure them have been created by a number of agencies. Existing research does not support the use of warning signs or profiling for school shooters (Borum et al., 2010). Difficulties identifying students who are potentially mass killers are numerous. Lists of risk factors for such aggression also identify individuals who will not become mass killers. Even the most accurate prediction formula for identifying such youth would falsely identify a large number of students (Furlong, Sharkey, Bates, &

TABLE 2.2   Descriptors Applied to Some Shooters

Behaviors linked to aggression	Animal cruelty
	Movie, television, and/or video game violence (watched/mimicked)
	Music (e.g., death music, violent lyrics)
Interpersonal	Bullied others
	Girlfriend troubles
	Had friends
	Jokester
	Lacked empathy
	Negative peer influence
Mental health and well-being	Depression
	Paranoia or obsessive fears
	Medications
	Mental health disturbance
	Substance use
	Suicidal
	Emotionally immature
	Feeling helplessness/hopelessness
	Feeling isolated
	Hypersensitivity (e.g., to insult)
	Expressed rage
	Self-image—expressed self-loathing or low self-esteem
	Self-image—expressed superiority
	Nervous/fidgety or hyper
	Felt disliked, unloved, or shut out
	Physically small
	Poor or erratic coping skills
	Short temper
	Shy/withdrawn
	Unhappy or miserable
Previous victimization	Humiliated by relational aggression (e.g., teased, ridiculed, excluded; stories made up about them)
	Humiliated by physical aggression (e.g., bullying was physical such as pushing, hitting, throwing things, beating, or physical abuse was threatened)
	Humiliated by verbal aggression and/or exclusion

TABLE 2.2 (*Continued*) Descriptors Applied to Some Shooters

Previous problem behavior	Juvenile record
	In trouble for behavior
Plans for aggression	Access to weapons (e.g., guns)
	Desire for fame or recognition via media
	Hatred (anti-Semitic; homophobic; racist; humanity)
	Internet (visited hate sites; bombing instructions)
	Spoke to others about wanting to do violence and/or wrote about it
	Talked of killing to teach a lesson
	Thrill (talked of killing being gutsy or as though it would be exciting)
School	Academic or other failure
	Grades and intelligence above average
	Learning disability

Note: Descriptors obtained from professionals providing psychological autopsies of shooters, newspaper articles, and books are combined into this single list. Individual descriptors do not apply to all shooters and do apply to nonshooters as well.

Smith, 2004; Borum et al., 2010). In addition to potentially restricting their civil liberties, false accusations may increase the sense of humiliation and isolation of those with risk factors. Humiliation and isolation are among risk factors for psychopathology and aggression (Shanahan, Copeland, Costello, & Angold, 2008). Factors contributing to the eruption of a youth into a school mass killer are multiple, and the factors may be complexly interrelated (Nader, 2008). Much is yet to be learned about youth, risk factors (e.g., environment, personality, or genetic and emotional inheritance), and their interrelationships. In addition, the high number of false threats must be distinguished from threats that indicate danger (Cornell et al., 2009).

YOUTH AGGRESSION, DEPRESSION, AND SUICIDAL RISK

Aggressive behavioral development has been linked statistically to multiple factors that may occur in varied combinations (see Nader, 2008 for a summary and discussion). For example, aggression has been linked to specific temperament traits and/or genetic predispositions, neurobiology, information processing patterns, unacknowledged shame leading to increased frustration and anger, high levels of specific narcissistic traits combined with low self-esteem, early physical aggression, mental health problems, harsh physical experiences in early life, early conflict-ridden or insecure attachments, coercive discipline, domestic conflict or family instability, propaganda, group regression, modeling and imitation of others' behaviors, neighborhood quality, exposure to violent traumas (e.g., physical abuse; emotional abuse; nonfamilial violence), watching violent television and/or playing violent video games, rejection by peers, chronic goal-blocking, failure to succeed in school, and relations with deviant peers (Huesmann, 2007; Nader, 2008, 2010; Younge et al., 2010; Zurbriggen, Gobin, & Freyd, 2010). Similarly, depression is linked to multiple factors (e.g., genetics, neurobiology, environmental factors) (Rende, Slomkowski, Lloyd-Richardson, Stroud, & Niaura, 2006). Among variables linked to depression are low self-esteem, developing negative body image, low social support, having a parent with depression, a negative cognitive style, and ineffective coping as well as risk factors common to a number of negative outcomes such as exposure to violence (e.g., community, familial), social isolation, the burdens of poverty, and family instability (Gladstone, Beardslee, & O'Connor, 2011). Youth depression is common, is often associated with chronic and episodic depression, and is associated with long-term negative outcomes such as functional impairment (at school, work, and interpersonally), substance abuse, and suicide attempts (Gladstone & Beardslee, 2009). In addition to their association with depressive disorders, suicide attempts or ideation have been linked to alcohol abuse, disruptive disorders, panic attacks, family factors (e.g., divorce, family history of attempts, impaired parent–child relationships, parental psychopathology—particularly depression and substance abuse), life stressors (e.g., abuse trauma, interpersonal loss, bullying—victim or perpetrator), and contagion (Brent, Greenhill, Compton et al., 2009; Gould, Greenberg, Velting, & Shaffer, 2006). Hopelessness in combination with other factors, life stress combined with low problem-solving skills, or low problem-solving ability with aggressive–impulsive behavior are among combined risk factors for suicidal behavior (Gould et al., 2006). A history of suicidal behavior is a predictor of later attempts, and suicide attempts are a strong predictor of completions.

As noted, combinations of environmental, youth, and developmental factors influence the nature of outcomes such as aggression, depression, or suicidal risk. For example, when youth feel alienated and rejected by their families, they may develop antisocial attitudes, an affinity for violent media, and proneness to angry arousal (Ding, Nelson, & Lasonde, 2002). Such conditions may dispose them to react with aggression to events perceived as threatening or frustrating. Access to weapons may increase the potential for aggressive reactivity. Some perpetrators of violence are driven by feelings of low status and powerlessness or respond to humiliation by lashing out (Ding et al., 2002; Fuentes, 1998). Some school shooters have described humiliation among their complaints (Larkin, 2009). Serial murderers often experience a high number of humiliating situations during childhood, often perpetrated by one or both parents (Singer & Hensley, 2004). Conversely, youth may respond to trauma or humiliation with self-destructive rather than other-destructive thoughts and behaviors (Klomek et al., 2010).

Violence, in general, is not limited to one gender, ethnic group, or location (Douglas & Bell, 2011). Although perpetrators of violent crimes, including targeted school violence, most often have been male, the age and the nature of aggression may vary by gender. Evidence suggests that although girls are generally at lower risk levels (e.g., lower aggressive fantasies and lower hostile attribution biases) for aggression between ages 6 and 12½, by age 12½ their risk levels are almost equivalent to boys for both aggressive and competent interpersonal negotiation strategies and for conduct problems (Aber et al., 2003). Age of onset is a factor in the expression of aggression. Youth with early-onset violence tend to commit more crimes and more serious crimes than youth with late-onset violence, whose aggression tends to peak at age 16 and then decline (Douglas & Bell, 2011; McBurnett et al., 2003; Nader, 2008).

Victim Coping

Re-victimization is common among youth who have been traumatized, especially by violence (Finkelhor et al., 2007; Hanson et al., 2006). In addition to the possibility of aggression, repeatedly and complexly traumatized youth have sometimes been described as exhibiting "victim coping" with a view of self as damaged and living in a dangerous world (Nader, 2008; Tinnen, Bills, & Gantt, 2002). Such individuals feel weak and vulnerable as well as unacceptable, unworthy of love, and easily crushed by an indifferent or hostile world. Such an individual may develop an attitude of "safety first" and may believe that, in order to be safe from harm, distrust and defiance are necessary (Ford, 2002; Tinnen et al., 2002). Such a youth may put on a front of being fierce or present him- or herself as weak and harmless. Cognitively a youth may be spaced-out or disoriented, and unable to think logically or clearly (Ford, 2002; Nijenhuis, Spinhoven, Vanderlinden, van Dyck, & van der Hart, 1998). It is an exhausting way to live and may be accompanied by a sense

of entitlement because of suffering. Such coping affects school performance and interpersonal functioning.

SHAME OR HUMILIATION AND LASHING OUT OR IN

Humiliation and the resulting shame may follow victimizations such
as bullying or other traumas (Andrews et al., 2000; Fletcher, in press;
Leskela et al., 2002). Humiliation may be processed and overcome, or it
may continue to fester. In response to intense or repeated humiliation, a
youth's reactions may range from strong urges to self-destruct or to come
out fighting or may include varying levels of stress/distress. Humiliation
and shame represent failures that reflect on the self in an intensely negative way (Babcock & Sabini, 1990; Fletcher, in press; Tangney, 1992;
Tangney et al., 1996). A sense of self-directed disgust, anger, and/or
global *badness*, often with little hope of relief, is associated with shame or
humiliation (Fletcher, in press; Tangney, Wagner, Fletcher, & Gramzow,
1992). Negative self-attributions (particularly self-blame) and feelings of
shame are strongly predictive of negative outcomes (e.g., depression, dissociation) (Abramson et al., 2002; Coffey, Leitenberg, Henning, Turner,
& Bennett, 1996; Feiring & Cleland, 2007; Fletcher, in press; Whiffen
& MacIntosh, 2005).

Translation of Shame or Humiliation Into Aggression

Regardless of age or gender, the sense of being condemned by others
may lead to a kind of retaliatory anger that manifests as lashing out.
Thus shame may become "a humiliated rage that attempts to erase the
shame by removing the rejecting others or at least shifting the rejection
from the self to the other" (Fletcher, in press). Researchers, historians,
and forensic psychologists have found, among murderers, terrorists, and
youth with conduct disturbances, histories of repeated or severe humiliations such as occur in violent or other intense traumatic experiences
(Garbarino, 1999; Gilligan, 2003; Scheff, 1997). Like incarcerated violent adults, "youth may try to fight their way out of helplessness, fight for
respect, become self-destructive, or be functionally paralyzed by traumatic helplessness, humiliation, or rage" (Nader, 2006, p. 120). During
traumas, helplessness is among the subjective experiences associated
with PTSD. Rage, betrayal, resignation, fear, defeat, and shame are subjective experiences that, when trauma-related, may result in complicated
traumatic reactions that include disturbances in affect and behavioral

regulation among other symptoms (van der Kolk, 2005). These issues are relevant to victims of bullying who may emerge as aggressors, as well as to victims of targeted school and other violence.

YOUTH AGGRESSORS AND VICTIMS

Bullies, Victims, and Bully–Victims

Investigators have shown that high school students' *punking, ganging up,* aggressing, and/or labeling of selected individuals has resulted in extreme distress, suicide, or school violence (Klomek et al., 2010; Nader, 2008; Simmons, 2002). Whether relational aggression (e.g., exclusion, gossip, cyber bullying) or overt aggression (e.g., hitting, pushing, throwing things) is committed by a school's social elite in defense of their own social privilege or by individuals reacting to perceived threat, these behaviors that may instigate aggression or suicidality in the recipient must be addressed. Henry (2009) suggests that it is essential to "deconstruct hierarchies of power that exclude, and in the process create, a wasted class of teenagers who feel hopeless, whose escape from hopelessness is blocked, and whose only way out are violent symbolic acts of self-destruction and other destruction" (p. 1262). Youth need both the provision of safe environments and the skills to deal with aggression in order to function effectively. In Chapter 9 of this book, Kalman presents an alternative method for defusing bullying that teaches youth the skills to handle such situations. To follow is a discussion of forms of bullying as well as victims and victimizers.

Bullies and Victims

Whether referred to as bullying, peer victimization, peer harassment, or peer rejection, youth who suffer humiliation at the hands of their peers are likely to experience a variety of emotional and behavioral problems (Beran & Lupart, 2009; Chapter 8). As noted, in addition to the hurt, embarrassment, loneliness, and depression that may follow being physically or relationally aggressed (i.e., physically, verbally, or psychologically abused in and around school or via the Internet), youth may exhibit a number of difficulties (e.g., insecurity, low self-esteem, self-blame, cautiousness, impaired social skill development, poor academic performance, and absenteeism as well as externalizing behaviors including hyperactivity and aggression).

Bullies and other aggressive youth may display overt aggression (i.e., use threat of or actual physical aggression) or relational aggression (i.e., harm others through threat of or actual damage to their peer relationships) (Nader, 2008). They are likely to be proactive (i.e., goal-directed behavior to achieve outcomes such as position, domination, or acquisition), but may also be reactive (i.e., engage in retaliatory or defensive responses to provocation or frustration). Observers suggest that girls are more prone to relational aggression, and boys more prone to physical aggression. By middle adolescence, however, physical aggression is less tolerated, and relational aggression is more normal for both genders (Peeters, Cillessen, & Scholte, 2010). Putallaz et al. (2007) found that gender differences in physical and relational aggression are often minimal. Although girls are more inclined to harm others by indirect means, boys tend to use equal amounts of physical and relational aggression. Recent meta-analyses of research on antibullying programs suggest that the effects of such programs are modest at best (Graham, 2010). Only about a third of the studied school-based interventions showed any decrease in incidents of bullying. Graham (2010) noted that increased bullying followed a few programs. The need to address bullying in schools is clear. Negative findings underscore the need to employ effective intervention programs. Additionally, researchers suggest providing increased time for programs and the need for developing antibullying attitudes in the home as well as school (Cunningham et al. 2009; Graham, 2010; see Chapters 8 and 9). Chapter 8 describes programs that have proven successful in U.S. schools. As noted in Chapter 1, the Virginia Threat Assessment method is associated with decreased bullying as well (Cornell, Sheras, Gregory, & Fan, 2009).

Cyber bullying. Cyber bullying is the use of electronic media (e.g., Internet, texting) to send harmful or cruel information about a person or embarrassing images of a person. It is another method that is used to relationally aggress youth (e.g., malign, intimidate, exclude) and may include false information or images. Victims may keep silent about being cyber bullied, for example, because of fear of reprisal (Cassidy, Jackson, & Brown, 2009a). They often do not trust the school's ability to intervene. On the one hand, much cyber bullying occurs within friendship groups (Jackson, Cassidy, & Brown et al., 2009). On the other hand, like the victims of other bullying, some cyber bullying victims do not fit in, for example because of dress, ethnicity, physical appearance, or academic or athletic inability (Cassidy et al., 2009a). Cassidy et al. (2009a) found that approximately one-third of students report that they have been cyber bullied. The results of cyber bullying are similar to other bullying, including the possibilities of suicidality or retaliation. Cyber bullies explain their behaviors as fun, others do it, they were on the receiving end of it, or the recipient upset them.

Bullies. Peeters et al., (2010) identified three bully subtypes among boys and girls: a popular socially intelligent group, a popular moderate group, and an unpopular less socially intelligent group (see also Thunfors & Cornell, 2008). Many studies have compared bullies, victims, and bully victims (Cunningham, 2007; Graham, 2010; Table 2.3). As is true generally among humans, bullies often have friends who are like themselves (Graham, 2010). Compared to nonbullying youth and to bullies who cease bullying, persistent bullies have more aggressive attitudes (e.g., the expectation that aggressive behaviors result in positive social outcomes; hit first or be hit) and are more likely to get into trouble in school (Carlson & Carnell, 2008; Cunningham, 2007).

Bully–Victims. Bully–victims have some of the characteristics of both bullies and victims. Adolescents who are harassed or bullied by peers and exhibit disruptive behavior problems and poor peer interactions are at risk of experiencing poor school achievement as well. Bully–victims are more like bullies in their attributional biases (Georgiou & Stavrinides, 2008). Additionally, when victimized by others who are more powerful than they are, they often strike out at others perceived to be weaker than they are. Some evidence suggests that bully–victims are more aggressive than bullies (Salmivalli & Nieminen, 2002).

Victims. Among bullies, victims, and bully–victims, peers and teachers generally rate victims as lowest in social status (Cunningham, 2007; Table 2.3). Many studies suggest that youth who are victimized are both physically and relationally aggressed. While they are victims, usually no one comes to their aid (Graham, 2010). Adults and children normally incorporate perceived levels of support and approval from others into their assessments of their personal worth (Harter et al., 1998). Compared to aggressors, victims more often place the blame for outcomes on their own behavior or something inherent within them. Over time, some of the youth who are victimized cease to be so. Differences from mainstream traits, like shyness, being new at school, or delayed pubertal development, increase the likelihood of continued victimization.

GENETICS, TRAITS, AND STYLE

Personality

Personality traits are differentially associated with a youth's image among peers and adults and with behavioral tendencies. Mental health outcomes and personality traits may share genetic mechanisms (e.g., shyness/behavioral inhibition or negative emotionality [N] and depression) and may vary by age (Cisler et al., in press; Harro et al., 2009). In general, emotionally positive youth are more likely than emotionally negative children to experience more positive social interactions (Eisenberg et al., 2001).

TABLE 2.3   Bully Types and Victims

Categorization	Subtypes	Characteristics
Popularity and social intelligence status (Peeters et al., 2010)	Popular socially intelligent group	Have high social status accompanied by social intelligence
		Use relational aggression (e.g., gossip)
		May use their skills to gain dominance (i.e., power and influence)
		Compared to nonbullies, they scored significantly higher on physical aggression, verbal aggression, leadership, social rejection (the number of dislike nominations from peers), and network centrality (the number of reciprocal friendships and the power of friends)
	Popular moderate group	Less aggressive than other bullies and more aggressive than nonbullies
		Lower than popular-socially intelligent bullies on leadership, social rejection, and network centrality scores but scored higher than nonbullies on leadership and network centrality
	Unpopular less socially intelligent group	Use relational aggression (e.g., exclusion)
		Use direct rather than covert relational aggression methods
		May perceive ambiguous cues as hostile
		Their aggressive methods may be more reactive
Bully or victim status	Bullies	Tend to be secure, sure of themselves, and to lack empathy (Cunningham, 2007); may be described as having an inflated view of themselves
		May have high status and many friends (Graham, 2010)
		In a school where bullying is tolerated, bullies were the most comfortable in the school environment among bullies, victims, and bully–victims (Cunningham, 2007).

	Bullies may demonstrate aggressive and antisocial behavior in adulthood and/or may report depression (Georgiou, 2008).
	Often report loneliness, anxiety, and depression as well as fewer friends.
Bully–Victims	Tend to be highly emotional, impulsive, and anxious (Cunningham, 2007).
	Display poor social skills and are consequently unpopular with peers.
	Are often identified as having conduct problems, have poor school adjustment, and lack bonding to their school
	Tend to have friends who bully
	Research suggests that bully-victims suffer from more severe psychological and social problems than bullies or victims (Cunningham, 2007)
Victims	Likely to have low social status (Cunningham, 2007)
	More often tend to be introverted, insecure, lonely, and quiet
	More likely to appear vulnerable and to have poorer peer relationships (Georgiou, 2008).
	May have better academic achievement than others
	May experience internalizing (e.g., anxiety, depression), increased somatic complaints, and may exhibit posttraumatic stress symptoms and suicidality (Georgiou, 2008; Graham, 2010)

Research suggests that children perceived as happy are better liked and have more successful outcomes (Lyubomirsky, King, & Diener, 2005). Additionally, among positive traits, higher levels of effortful self-control are associated negatively with levels of externalizing and internalizing problems (Eisenberg et al., 2009; Eisenberg, Spinrad, & Eggum, 2010). Although shared genetics may play a role, N is associated with depression and with vulnerability to traumatic reactions (Carrion et al., 2002; Kendler, Health, Kessler, Heath, and Eaves, 1993). Research indicates that heightened N is linked to a tendency to avoid or control internal experiences rather than accept them, which, in turn, prevents effective processing of painful emotions (Borkovec, Alcaine, & Behar, 2004; Cassidy, Shaver et al., 2009b; Roemer, Salters, Raffa, & Orsillo, 2005).

Low resting salivary cortisol levels are associated with personality traits of impulsivity and insensitivity to punishment (Nader & Weems, in press; Rothbart & Bates, 1998; Shoal et al., 2003). Accordingly, high resting cortisol levels predict later reflectiveness and caution, whereas low levels predict impulsiveness and carelessness and the aggressive behavior associated with them (Shoal et al., 2003; Nader, 2008). Low cortisol levels are found in early onset conduct disorder and may be a later and long-term consequence of trauma (Nader & Weems, in press).

A youth's mannerisms or behaviors may elicit different responses—types of discipline, degrees of validation, and levels of nurturance from others (Caspi, 1998). For example, conduct-disordered boys evoke more negative responses than nonproblem boys from mothers of both types of boys (Anderson, Lytton, & Romney, 1986; Caspi, 1998). An extravert's positive emotions may elicit more positive reactions in others. Youths with negative emotional styles may create situations that lead to rejection or reciprocation and thus reinforce negative emotionality.

Early traits as well as early experiences (e.g., victimizations) may enhance the likelihood of anticipatory attitudes that influence behaviors (Caspi, 1998; Nader, 2008). Information processing research has consistently shown that aggressive youths exhibit attributional biases; they perceive, interpret, and make decisions about social interactions that increase the likelihood of their aggressive acts (Crick & Dodge, 1996; de Castro et al., 2003; Schippell et al., 2003). For example, compared to depressive youths, aggressive youths search situations for fewer cues before making an attributional decision, tend to make more hostile attributions (i.e., see hostile intent whether or not it exists), generate more aggressive responses, and more frequently expect rewards from aggressive problem solving (Crick & Dodge, 1996; see Nader, 2008). When biases lead to aversive behavioral, nonverbal, or verbal expressions, they are likely to elicit reactions that, in turn, reinforce them (Crick, 1995).

Genetic Vulnerability

Genetic factors are an important focus of attention in the study of mental health outcomes. Environmental adversity (e.g., trauma, nonsupportive parenting) is a key element in the expression of genetic vulnerability factors that may manifest differently at different developmental periods (Dahl & Gunnar, 2009). Without a trigger, such as trauma or other adversity, the effect of genetic factors on the emergence of gene-related specific dysfunction is reduced (Lau & Pine, 2008). Although it is likely that genetic factors, like other variables, contribute synergistically to psychiatric outcomes (Cerda, Sagdeo, Johnson, & Galea, 2010), a few genetic factors have been linked to specific types of disorders (Nader, in press). A short allele serotonin transporter gene interaction with high environmental risks has been linked to depression but not to antisocial behavior (Rutter, Moffit, & Caspi, 2006). A monoamine oxidase A (MAOA) gene has been linked to externalizing disorders such as antisocial personality (Kim-Cohen et al., 2006). Low MAO activity in platelets is associated with suicidal behavior, impulsive aggression, bipolar disorder, and alcoholism as well as with monotony avoidance, sensation seeking, and impulsiveness (Byrnes, 2001; Nader, 2008). A dopamine polymorphism has been associated with alcoholism and impulsiveness (Cerda et al., 2010; Limosin et al., 2005) but may be related to a nonspecific vulnerability to a wide range of impulsive and reward-inducing behaviors rather than specifically to alcoholism (Cerda et al., 2010; Hoenicka et al., 2007; Nader, in press).

THE NEED TO BE ACCEPTED/VALUED

When a youth is respected and personally valued by self and others, the youth and her/his community are more likely to increase protection and the meeting of the youth's physical, emotional, and spiritual needs (Nader, 2006). Thus, like a child's attachment behaviors, the human need for respect and a sense of personal value may be based in biological survival needs. It is unbearable for humans to feel that they are of no or of little value to others, unlovable, or the object of hatred (Gilligan, 2003; Knox, 2003a; Nader, 2008). The fear, humiliation, and profound sense of helplessness that result are powerful emotions that may translate into information processing conducive to aggression, eruptive rage, or self-destructive attitudes and behaviors (Crick et al., 2001; Knox, 2003b; Nader, 2006, 2008). Studies of cortisol levels suggest that shame and humiliation stressors may be more potent than other stressors for individuals over the age of 4 (Gunnar, Talge, Herrera, 2009). Threats to one's sense of being valued or respected can increase arousal symptoms (Gilligan, 2003; Nader, 2006, 2008; Scheff, 1997; Wilson, 2006). If added to additional stressors across life, such threats may undermine resilience in a number of undesirable ways, disrupting life and health.

Validation Support

The opinions of others form an important initial basis on which children judge themselves (Harter et al., 1998). Harter et al. (1998) found that validation from a specific group of significant others is most strongly associated with sense of self-worth with those particular others. Well before adolescence, a youth's value to his peers is important to her/him. As early as preschool, relational victimization is associated with serious adjustment problems such as problematic friendships, depression, loneliness, low self-esteem, and emotional distress (Crick, Werner, Casas, O'Brien, Nelson, Grotpeter, & Markon, 1998). Gilligan (2003) states, "It appears to be difficult if not impossible for a child to gain the capacity for self-love without first having been loved by at least one parent, or parent-substitute. And when the self is not loved, by itself or by another, it dies, just as surely as the body dies without oxygen" (p. 1154; see section "Attachment and Relationship Style," following).

Rejection Sensitivity

> People's fears and doubts about whether others will meet their needs for acceptance and belonging can cause them to behave in ways that erode their relationships and their sense of well-being ... (Ayduk, Mendoza-Denton, Mischel, Downey, Peak, & Rodriguez, 2000, p. 776)

In contrast to those who expect acceptance, individuals who expect rejection behave in more hostile, aggressive ways in relationships (Ayduk et al., 2000). People who expect rejection have more troubled, dissatisfying, quicker to end relationships as well as increased susceptibility to social anxiety, loneliness, and depression in response to rejection. Being bullied or otherwise traumatized may increase the likelihood of expecting rejection. Ayduk et al. (2000) found that adults who as children scored low on the ability to delay gratification, and currently rated high on rejection sensitivity, had lower education levels and rated lower than others in self-esteem, self-worth, and coping ability. As studies suggest, an early ability to delay gratification may moderate negative outcomes for those who are rejection sensitive.

ATTACHMENT AND RELATIONSHIP STYLE

Attachment relationships are originally forged from a parent's value of a child and the related sensitive care. In addition to the associations of parent–child attachment bonds, youth attachment styles are linked to specific aspects of personality, behavior, and interrelating. Children's confidence in their relationships with caregivers or others permits them to explore away from a secure base and to successfully master their school and other environments (Aviezer et al., 2002). This is reflected in school competence and indicators of emotional maturity. Importantly, attachments to school and peers as well as to parents influence the emergence of delinquent behaviors (Anderson, Holmes, & Ostresh, 1999; see Chapter 6).

As discussed in Chapter 6, across racial and SES groups, combinations of strong supervision and positive parental involvement provide protection against outcomes such as aggression and delinquency (Chung & Steinberg, 2006; Gorman-Smith et al., 2000; Pollack, 2001, 2004). Adolescent drinking attitudes, the severity of delinquency, scholastic skills and achievement, emotional maturity (e.g., ability to work independently and to cope with frustrations and criticisms), task persistence, and positive affect are associated with the strength of attachment to parents (Anderson et al., 1999; Aviezer, Sagi, Resnick, & Gini, 2002). Pollack (2001) suggests that it is the "potency of connection" of family relationships that protects youth from emotional harm and others from being harmed by them.

Creation of Attachment Styles/Classifications

When a child's intentions and behaviors are consistently misread, misperceived, or distorted by a parent, and responses to the child are overly shaped by a caregiver's own needs, perceptions, or difficulties, the child is forced to adapt to these expectations and behaviors in order to maintain a sense of connection to the parent (Crittenden, 2008; Svanberg, Mennet, & Spieker, 2010). Attachment classification results from the patterning of these adaptations over time. *Secure* attachment is associated with a caregiver's sensitive responsiveness, warmth, and interactive synchrony as well as the repair of disturbances in caregiver–infant interactions (De Wolff & Van IJzendoorn, 1997; Schore, 2003; Svanberg, Mennet, & Spieker, 2010). In contrast, withdrawn (e.g., failure to respond to distress) and under-stimulating or intrusive caregiving is associated with *avoidant* attachment, reflected in an infant's inhibited use of the caregiver as a secure base and diminished signaling for close contact, Moss et al., 2009). Inconsistent caregiving (e.g., of comfort and safety) corresponds to *ambivalent* attachment, reflected in an infant's exaggerated cues for contact, conveying heightened helplessness and anger in attachment relationships (Svanberg, Mennet, & Spieker, 2010). Parents of *avoidant* insecure children appear to emphasize independence and minimize attachment behavior; parents of *ambivalent* insecure children appear to emphasize dependence and exaggerate attachment (Berlin & Cassidy, 2003).

Attachment Representations

Attachment theory (Bowlby, 1969/1982; Chapter 6) suggests that, from infancy, individuals build experience-based "representational or working models" of the world and of self in the world that influence personality development, emotional well-being, and psychosocial adjustment across the lifespan. In accordance with these representations, the individual perceives experiences/events, predicts the future, develops plans, and selects strategies for interacting with others (Feeney, Cassidy, Ramos-Marcuse, 2008). Attachment representations influence many aspects of children's personal and interactional styles (Tables 2.4–2.6), such as their styles of emotional expression, ability to self-soothe, their self-concept, tendency to suppress or express anger, attentional focus, ability to trust, expectations of support, support-seeking and support-giving behaviors exhibited during conversations with others, and more (Broussard & Cassidy, 2010; Dykas & Cassidy, 2007; Feeney et al., 2008; Nader, 2008). The Granot & Mayseless (2001) findings suggest that children with *disorganized* and *avoidant* attachment classifications may be more likely to have serious adjustment problems, while *ambivalent* children may be more likely to have problematic social relations with peers and have an expectation of rejection. Especially disorganized and also other insecure attachments have been linked to a number of problematic mental health outcomes including aggression (Chapter 6, this volume).

Attachment representations influence self-perception, which in turn influences behavior and psychosocial health. For example, a mother's negative perception of a newborn, which may be reflected in the parent's ongoing behavior toward the child, is a powerful predictor of psychosocial difficulties in childhood and adolescence and of adult insecure attachment (Broussard & Cassidy, 2010). Individuals tend to seek information that confirms their beliefs about themselves. These beliefs are influenced by attachment and feedback from others. Cassidy, Ziv, Mehta, & Feeney (2003) found that children and adolescents who had a positive self-perception (i.e., perceptions of personal competence) in one domain

TABLE 2.4 Parent, Peer, and Self-Perception

Perception by	Securely Attached Youth	Insecurely Attached Youth
Parental perception of infant	More likely to have had parent's positive perception of them (Broussard & Cassidy, 2010)	Negative perception by parent increased the risk of infant's later adult insecure attachment status (Broussard & Cassidy, 2010)
Peer acceptance versus rejection	Most likely to be accepted by peers (Dykas, Ziv, & Cassidy, 2008)	*Dismissing/avoidant* were less likely than secure adolescent peers to be socially accepted (Dykas, Ziv, & Cassidy, 2008)
		Avoidant and *disorganized* youth had highest levels of peer rejection (Granot & Mayseless, 2001)
		Ambivalent receive less acceptance than secure youth (Granot & Mayseless, 2001)
Self-perception	Attachment security is associated with positive self-worth (Cassidy, Ziv et al., 2003)	*Ambivalent* children were more rejected by their peers than secure children, but perceived themselves as rejected or unwanted by peers to a greater extent than corroborated by actual peer rejection (Granot & Mayseless, 2001)
	Seek more positive feedback (Cassidy, Ziv et al., 2003)	Insecure children do not seek more positive feedback than others and may lack the tendency to seek positive feedback (Cassidy, Ziv et al., 2003)

TABLE 2.5 Personal Style

Trait	Securely Attached Youth	Insecurely Attached Youth
Personal Style	(see also, "Support seeking and support giving" in column 1) More likely to be perceived by adolescent peers as behaving prosocially than insecure youth (Dykas, Ziv, & Cassidy, 2008) Less likely to be perceived by adolescent peers as aggressive, shy/withdrawn, or victimized by peers (Dykas, Ziv, & Cassidy, 2008)	Insecurity is related to more hostile behavior toward peers (Allen et al., 2005) *Ambivalent* children, show "busy" representations in the absence of stressful life-events but not in stressful circumstances (Bureau & Moss, 2010) *Ambivalent/attachment anxiety* exhibit less constructive reactions and more intense feelings of rejection, crying, and negative emotions (Cassidy, Shaver, Mikulincer, & Lavy, 2009) *Ambivalent* children are more likely to have an expectation of rejection in relationships (Granot & Mayseless, 2001) *Avoidant* children were more likely to minimize indices of danger and distress in stories (may reflect a representation of caregivers as unavailable and rejecting) (Bureau & Moss, 2010) *Avoidant*, when thinking about a hurtful event, tend to dismiss events, suppress distress, and react hostilely. *Disorganized/controlling* children, despite tentative efforts to adopt a controlling strategy to regulate distressful emotions and parental behavior, produced stories that were chaotic, violent, and unresolved or constricted in the face of the task (Bureau & Moss, 2010)

		Dismissing/avoidant were more likely to be seen as aggressive and shy-withdrawn by peers than secure youth; more likely to be perceived as victimized by peers (Dykas et al. 2008)
		Adolescents with high *attachment anxiety* (which corresponds to insecure ambivalent attachments; reflects a concern of being rejected by others) exhibit increased support seeking, but also demonstrate more negativity/hostility in care-seeking role with a stranger; demonstrate high levels of negativity in relation to negative peer behavior and high levels of positivity in relation to peer acceptance (Feeney, Cassidy, Ramos-Marcuse, 2008)
Support seeking and support giving	Securely attached youth are more likely to seek and accept support (Feeney, Cassidy, Ramos-Marcuse, 2008)	Adolescents with *attachment avoidance*: although less frequent, findings were consistent with expectations that they would interact in ways that reflect discomfort with expressions of distress, a desire to mute attachment behaviors, and a generally unresponsive and controlling style of responding to others' needs; did not exhibit negative/hostile affect in response to peers' provision of instrumental/controlling support, but exhibited less warmth/friendliness in such situations (Feeney, Cassidy, Ramos-Marcuse, 2008)

TABLE 2.6   Attachment-Related Outcomes

Outcome Variable	Results
Autonomy and interpersonal relatedness with parent	Adolescent autonomy and relatedness behavior (e.g., listening, inquiring, and responding versus hostility and interrupting) was related to attachment quality as rated in infancy, in childhood, and in adolescence; securely attached youth rated higher on autonomy and relatedness in a plan-a-vacation task (Becker-Stoll et al., 2008)
	In a disagreement-task, secure attachment appeared to enable adolescents to more openly and cooperatively express nonverbal communication pattern towards mothers—positive and vivid nonverbal expression as well as signs of tension (Becker-Stoll et al., 2008)
Externalizing behavior problems	*Avoidant* and *disorganized* children had the highest rates of behavioral problems (externalizing and internalizing), poorest emotional, scholastic, and social adjustment, and highest level of peer rejection (Granot & Mayseless, 2001)
	Ambivalent children had an intermediate level of scholastic, emotional, and behavioral adjustment levels (between the secure and the avoidant and disorganized groups); were less socially adept (teacher report) (Granot & Mayseless, 2001)
	Disorganized attachments (at ages 6 and 8) corresponded to significantly higher teacher-reported externalizing scores than secure or avoidant children (at age 8; Bureau & Moss, 2010)
	Both increased conflict representations (see "Narrative themes" in column 1) and disorganized/controlling attachment patterns contributed to the prediction of both externalizing and overall problem behaviors (Moss et al., 2009)
Internalizing problems	*Disorganized/controlling* profiles significantly predicted internalizing symptoms (Moss et al., 2009)
Narrative themes	*Ambivalent* children's narratives were less organized and less likely to lead to problem resolution than those of securely attached children (Moss et al., 2009)
	Avoidant children's narratives contain fewer discipline themes and are less likely to depict themselves as submissive to parents than securely attached 8-year-olds (Moss et al., 2009)

TABLE 2.6 (*Continued*)   Attachment-Related Outcomes

Outcome Variable	Results
	Disorganized/controlling children were more likely to represent conflict themes in their narratives than secure or avoidant children (Moss et al., 2009)
Scholastic achievement/ school adjustment	Early adolescent school adaptation (teacher and self-rated school competence and emotional maturity) was linked to current and early secure attachment relationships, beyond currently assessed IQ and self-perceived competence (Aviezer et al., 2002)
	Securely attached youth exhibit better school adjustment as indicated in teachers' reports of behavioral adjustment and scholastic, emotional, and social ratings, as well as in peer-rated social status (Granot & Mayseless, 2001)

(e.g., scholastic, athletic, artistic, social) and a negative self-perception in another domain sought confirming feedback for these perceptions. Children with positive self-worth sought significantly more positive feedback than expected by chance. Children with negative self-worth did not seek more positive feedback. Similarly, depressed adolescents sought less positive feedback than nondepressed adolescents. Although attachment security is a robust predictor of risk or resilience, severe and repeated victimizations may undermine resilience (Wilson, 2006).

Securely Attached Youth

Secure attachment is associated with resilience—the ability to function and feel well despite adversity (see Nader, 2008). For example, *securely attached* youth are more likely to have a positive self-image, to seek more positive feedback, to offer and accept more support, and to be seen as behaving prosocially (Cassidy et al., 2003; Feeney, Cassidy, Ramos-Marcuse, 2008). They are less likely to be seen as aggressive, shy or withdrawn, or as victims by peers than insecure youth (Dykas, Ziv, & Cassidy, 2008). Securely attached youth demonstrate higher levels of conscience (Kochanska & Clark, 1997) and competence in developmental tasks (Masten & Powell, 2003). Attachment security is a general protective factor against general risk and against traumatization (see Nader, 2008). Securely attached youth are more resistant to stress and more likely to rebound toward adequate functioning following a period of troubled behavior (Weinfield, Sroufe, Egeland, & Carlson, 1999; Yates et al., 2003).

Insecure Ambivalent Youth

Attachment insecurity is a risk factor for low-self-esteem and a variety of negative outcomes. Children classified with insecure *ambivalent* attachments are more likely to appear "busy" in nonstressful circumstances (Bureau & Moss, 2010), to have an expectation of rejection (Granot & Mayseless, 2001), to seek more support but to be more negative in a care-seeking role than secure youth (Feeney, Cassidy, Ramos-Marcuse, 2008), and to be highly positive in response to positive behaviors from peers and highly negative in response to negative behaviors from peers (Feeney et al., 2008). When thinking about a hurtful event, these youth with *attachment anxiety* exhibited less constructive reactions and higher levels of intense feelings of rejection, crying, and negative emotions (Cassidy et al., 2009b).

Insecure Avoidant and Disorganized Youth

Avoidant youth are more likely to be seen as aggressive or shy/withdrawn than peers (Dykas, Ziv, & Cassidy, 2008). They often minimize indicators of danger or distress and demonstrate discomfort with expressions of distress (Bureau & Moss, 2010). Cassidy et al. (2009b) found that children with *avoidant* attachment styles tended to dismiss hurtful events, inhibit expressions of distress, and react hostilely. Some research suggests that *avoidant* youth appear to desire to mute attachment behaviors and are generally unresponsive and controlling when responding to others' needs (Feeney et al., 2008). Although they may not exhibit negativity or hostility in response to peers' provision of controlling supportive behaviors, they may exhibit less warmth/friendliness in such situations (Feeney et al., 2008).

Some data demonstrate that *avoidant* youth are more often victimized and victimizers (Dykas et al., 2008). Both *avoidant* and *disorganized* youth exhibit higher levels of externalizing behavior problems and experience high levels of peer rejection (Bureau & Moss, 2010; Granot & Mayseless, 2001). Some evidence suggests that, despite attempts at controlling parents, *disorganized/controlling* children demonstrate chaotic and violent behavior or behavioral constriction in stressful circumstances (Bureau & Moss, 2010).

CONCLUSIONS

Although a number of child-specific and environmental factors have been identified or inferred for youth who commit targeted school shootings, existing research does not support the use of warning signs or profiling for school shooters (Borum et al., 2010). Lists of risk factors for targeted school aggression also identify individuals who will not commit mass or other aggression. Nevertheless, as will be clear in the chapters that follow, a number of youth as well as family and environmental factors can be addressed in the prevention of school aggression and other negative outcomes such as depression and suicidal behavior. For example, the behaviors of children with particular attachment styles may be shaped by teachers and their styles and relationships assisted by assisting their parents.

Aggression, depression, and suicidal behavior/risk have been linked statistically to multiple factors that may occur in varied combinations. Given the high prevalence and costs of youth disorders such as aggression or depression, prevention is warranted (Gladstone, Beardslee, & O'Connor, 2011). Aggressive victimization has multiple deleterious outcomes (Nader, 2008). Early-onset depression is usually recurrent in adulthood, difficult to treat, and, the longer the duration of a depressive episode, the less likely it is to respond to proven treatments (Gladstone et al., 2011). Substance abuse and suicide are possible outcomes of depression. Among the factors common to many negative outcomes are low support, low self-esteem, poor coping, and faulty attachment relationships.

Protective factors for a number of youth disturbances include the presence of supportive adults and strong family relationships, strong peer relationships, effective coping skills, and emotion regulation skills (Beardslee et al., 2011; Pollack, 2004). Attachment security, for example, influences multiple aspects of a youth's life, including the way that individuals deal with painful experiences. After subliminally viewing a security-based word (e.g., love, secure, affection) for 22 minutes, *avoidant* youth demonstrated more openness to the pain of a hurtful experience, which is necessary to processing such emotions (Cassidy et al., 2009b). Repair is possible (Pollack, 2004; Chapter 6). After exposure to security priming words, youth with *attachment anxiety* showed less negative behavior. That is, security priming resulted in behavior more like securely attached youth in response to psychological pain. If even subliminal exposure to security-related words can change behaviors, then enhancing overt connections between adults and youth and between youth and parents, other adults, and peers holds even greater promise for changing or preventing negative youth behaviors and interactions. In addition to identifying vulnerabilities (e.g., faulty coping skills, traits), eliminating bullying in the form of overt aggression, humiliation, or exclusion as well as increasing school and inter-human connection are important aspects of repair.

REFERENCES

Aber, J. L., Brown, J. L., & Jones, S. M. (2003). Developmental trajectories toward violence in middle childhood: Course, demographic differences, and response to school-based intervention. *Developmental Psychology, 39*(2), 324–348.

Abramson, L. Y., Alloy, L. B., Hankin, B. L., Haeffel, G. J., MacCoon, D. G., & Gibb, B. E. (2002). Cognitive vulnerability-stress models of depression in a self-regulatory and psychobiological context. In I. H. Gotlib & C. L. Hammen (Eds.), *Handbook of depression* (pp. 268–294). New York, NY: Guilford Press.

Anda, R., Felitti, V., Bremner, J., Walker, J., Whitfield, C., Perry, B., Dube, S., & Giles, W. (2006). The enduring effects of abuse and related adverse experiences in childhood: A convergence of evidence from neurobiology and epidemiology. *European Archives of Psychiatry and Clinical Neuroscience, 256*, 174–186.

Anderson, B., Holmes, M., & Ostresh, E. (1999). Male and female delinquents' attachments and effects of attachments on severity of self-reported delinquency. *Criminal Justice and Behavior, 26*, 435–452.

Anderson, K., Lytton, H., & Romney, D. (1986). Mothers' interactions with normal and conduct-disordered boys: Who affects whom? *Developmental Psychology, 22*, 604–609.

Andrews, B., Brewin, C. R., Rose, S., & Kirk, M. (2000). Predicting PTSD symptoms in victims of violent crime: The role of shame, anger, and childhood abuse. *Journal of Abnormal Psychology, 109*, 69–73.

Aviezer, O., Sagi, A., Resnick, G., & Gini, M. (2002). School competence in young adolescence: Links to early attachment relationships beyond concurrent self perceived competence and representations of relationships. *International Journal of Behavioral Development, 26*(5), 397–409.

Ayduk, O., Mendoza-Denton, R., Mischel, W., Downey, G., Peake, P., & Rodriguez, M. (2000). Regulating the Interpersonal Self: Strategic Self-Regulation for Coping With Rejection Sensitivity. *Journal of Personality and Social Psychology, 79*(5), 776–792.

Babcock, M. K., & Sabini, J. (1990). On differentiating embarrassment from shame. *European Journal of Social Psychology, 20*, 151–169.

Beardslee, W., Chien, P., & Bell, C. (2011). Substance abuse and problem behaviors: A developmental perspective. *Psychiatric Services, 62*(3), 247–254.

Beran, T., & Lupart, J. (2009). The relationship between school achievement and peer harassment in Canadian adolescents: The importance of mediating factors. *School Psychology International, 30*, 75–91.

Berlin, L., & Cassidy, J. (2003). Mothers' self-reported control of their preschool children's emotional expressiveness: A longitudinal study of associations with infant-mother attachment and children's emotional regulation. *Social Development, 12*(4), 477–495.

Borkovec, T., Alcaine, O., & Behar, E. (2004). Avoidance theory of worry and generalized anxiety disorder. In R. G. Heimberg, C. L. Turk, & D. S. Mennin (Eds.), *Generalized anxiety disorder: Advances in research and practice* (pp. 77–108). New York: Guilford Press.

Borum, R., Cornell, D., Modzeleski, W., & Jimerson, S. (2010). What can be done about school shootings? A review of the evidence. *Educational Researcher, 39*(1), 27–37.

Bowlby, J. (1969, 1982). *Attachment and loss. Volume 1: Attachment.* New York: Basic Books.

Brent, D., Greenhill, L., Compton, S. et al., (2009). The Treatment of Adolescent Suicide Attempters Study (TASA): Predictors of suicidal events in an open treatment trial. *American Academy of Child and Adolescent Psychiatry, 4*(10), 1–10.

Broussard, E., & Cassidy, J. (2010). Maternal perception of newborns predicts attachment organization in middle adulthood. *Attachment & Human Development, 12*(1–2), 159–172.

Bureau, J-F., & Moss, E. (2010). Behavioural precursors of attachment representations in middle childhood and links with child social adaptation. *British Journal of Developmental Psychology, 28*, 657–677.

Byrnes, J. P. (2001). *Minds, brains, and learning.* New York: Guilford Press.

Carlson, L. & Cornell, D. (2008). Differences between persistent and desistent middle school bullies. *School Psychology International, 29*(4): 442–451.

Carrion, V., Weems, C., Ray, R., & Reiss, A. (2002). Toward an empirical definition of pediatric PTSD: the phenomenology of PTSD symptoms in youth. *Journal of the American Academy of Child and Adolescent Psychiatry, 41*(2), 166–173.

Caspi, A. (1998). Personality development across the life course. In W. Damon & N. Eisenberg (Eds.), *Handbook of child psychology (5th ed., Vol. 3). Social, emotional, and personality development* (pp. 311–388). New York: Wiley & Sons.

Cassidy, W., Jackson, M., & Brown, K. (2009a). Students' experiences with cyber-bullying: Sticks and stones can break my bones, but how can pixels hurt me? *School Psychology International, 30*(4), 383–402.

Cassidy, J., Shaver, P., Mikulincer, M., & Lavy, S. (2009b). Experimentally induced security influences responses to psychological pain. *Journal of Social and Clinical Psychology, 28*(4) 463–478.

Cassidy, J., Ziv, Y., Mehta, T., & Feeney, B. (2003). Feedback seeking in children and adolescents: Associations with self-perceptions, attachment representations, and depression. *Child Development, 74*(2), 612–628.

Cerda, M., Sagdeo, A., Johnson, J., & Galea, S. (2010). Genetic and environmental influences on psychiatric comorbidity: A systematic review. *Journal of Affective Disorders, 126,* 14–38.

Chung, H.,& Steinberg, L. (2006). Relations between neighborhood factors, parenting behaviors, peer deviance, and delinquency among serious juvenile offenders. *Developmental Psychology, 42*(2), 319–331.

Cima, M., Smeets, T., & Jelicic, M. (2008). Self-reported trauma, cortisol levels, and aggression in psychopathic and non-psychopathic prison inmates. *Biological Psychology, 78*(1), 75–86.

Cisler, J., Amstadter, A., & Nugent, N. (in press). Genetic influences on post-trauma adjustment in children and adolescents: The role of personality constructs. *Journal of Child and Adolescent Trauma.*

Coffey, P., Leitenberg, H., Henning, K., Turner, T., & Bennett, R. (1996). Mediators of the long-term impact of child sexual abuse: Perceived stigma, betrayal, powerlessness, and self blame. *Child Abuse & Neglect, 20,* 447–455.

Cornell, D., Sheras, P., Gregory, A., & Fan, X. (2009). A retrospective study of school safety conditions in high schools using the Virginia threat assessment guidelines versus alternative approaches. *School Psychology Quarterly, 24,* 119–129.

Crick, N. (1995). Relational aggression: The role of intent attributions, feelings of distress, and provocation type. *Development and Psychopathology, 7,* 313–322.

Crick, N., & Dodge, K. (1996). Social information-processing mechanisms in reactive and proactive aggression. *Child Development, 67*(3), 993–1002.

Crick, N., Nelson, D., Morales, J., Cullerton-Sen, C., Casas, J., & Hickman, S. (2001). Relational victimization in childhood and adolescence: I hurt you through the grapevine. In J. Juvonen & S. Graham (Eds.), *Peer harassment in school: The plight of the vulnerable and victimized* (pp.196–214). New York: Guilford Press.

Crick, N., Werner, N., Casas, J., O'Brien, K., Nelson, D., Grotpeter, J., & Markon, K. (1998). Childhood aggression and gender: A new look at an old problem. In D. Bernstein et al. (Eds.), *Gender and motivation. Nebraska symposium on motivation* (Vol. 45, pp. 75–141). Lincoln, NE: University of Nebraska Press.

Crittenden, P. M. (2008). *Raising parents: Attachment, parenting, and child safety.* Collumpton, UK: Willan Publishing.

Cullen, D. (April 27, 2007). Talk to the Chos. *New York Times.* Downloaded 6/30/10 from http://www.nytimes.com/2009/08/20/us/20vtech.html.

Cunningham, N. (2007). Level of bonding to school and perception of the school environment by bullies, victims, and bully victims. *The Journal of Early Adolescence 27(4)*, 457–478.

Cunningham, C., Vaillancourt, T., Rimas, H., Deal, K., Cunningham, L., Short, K., & Chen, Y. (2009). Modeling the bullying prevention program preferences of educators: A discrete choice conjoint experiment. *Journal of Abnormal Child Psychology, 37(7)*, 929–943.

Cuomo, C., Sarchiapone, M., Giannantonio, M., Mancini, M., & Roy, A. (2008). Aggression, Impulsivity, Personality Traits, and Childhood Trauma of Prisoners with Substance Abuse and Addiction. *American Journal of Drug & Alcohol Abuse, 34(3)*, 339–345.

Dahl, R., & Gunnar, M. (2009). Heightened stress responsiveness and emotional reactivity during pubertal maturation: Implications for psychopathology. *Development and Psychopathology, 21,* 1–6.

Daniels, J., Volungis, A., Pshenishy, E. Gandhi, P., Winkler, A., Cramer, D., & Bradley, M. (2010). A qualitative investigation of averted school shooting rampages. *The Counseling Psychologist, 38(1)*, 69–95.

de Castro, B., Slot, N., Bosch, J., Koops, W., & Veerman, J. (2003). Negative feelings exacerbate hostile attributions of intent in highly aggressive boys. *Journal of Clinical Child and Adolescent Psychology, 32(1)*, 56–65.

De Wolff, M. S., & Van IJzendoorn, M. H. (1997). Sensitivity and attachment: A meta-analysis on parental antecedents of infant attachment. *Child Development, 68(4)*, 571–591.

Ding, C., Nelsen, D., & Lassonde, C. (2002). Correlates of gun involvement and aggressivness among adolescents. *Youth & Society, 34(2)*, 195–213.

Douglas, K., & Bell, C. (2011). Youth homicide prevention. *Psychiatry Clinics of North America, 34,* 205–216.

Dykas, M. & Cassidy, J. (2007). Attachment and the processing of social information in adolescence. *New Directions for Child and Adolescent Development, 117,* 41–56.

Dykas, M., Ziv, Y., & Cassidy, J. (2008). Attachment and peer relations in adolescence. *Attachment & Human Development, 10(2)*, 123–141.

Eisenberg, N., Gershoff, E., Fabes, R., Shepard, S., Cumberland, A. J., Losoya, S. et al. (2001). Mother's emotional expressivity and children's behavior problems and social competence: Mediation through children's regulation. *Developmental Psychology, 37,* 475–490.

Eisenberg, N., Spinrad, T., & Eggum, N. (2010). Emotion-related self-regulation and its relation to children's maladjustment. *Annual Review of Clinical Psychology, 6,* 495–525.

Eisenberg, N., Valiente, C., Spinrad, T., Cumberland, A., Liew, J., Reiser, M. et al. (2009). Longitudinal relations of children's effortful control, impulsivity, and negative emotionality to their externalizing, internalizing, and co-occurring behavior problems. *Developmental Psychology, 45,* 988–1008.

Feeney, B., Cassidy, J., & Ramose-Marucuse, F. (2008). The generalization of attachment representations to new social situations: Predicting behavior during initial interactions with strangers. *Journal of Personality and Social Psychology, 95*(6), 1481–1498.

Feiring, C., & Cleland, C. (2007). Childhood sexual abuse and abuse-specific attributions of blame over 6 years following discovery. *Child Abuse & Neglect, 31,* 1169–1186.

Finkelhor, D., Ormrod, R., & Turner, H. (2007). Poly-victimization: A neglected component in child victimization, *Child Abuse & Neglect, 31,* 7–26.

Fletcher, K. (in press). Understanding and assessing guilt, shame, and anger among children, adolescents, and young adults. *Journal of Child and Adolescent trauma.*

Ford, J. D. (2002). Traumatic victimization in childhood and persistent problems with oppositional-defiance. *Journal of Aggression, Maltreatment and Trauma, 6 (1),* 25–58.

Fuentes, A. (1998, June 15). The crackdown on kids. *Nation, 266,* 20–23.

Furlong, M., Sharkey, J., Bates, M., & Smith, D. (2004). An examination of the reliability, data screening procedures, and extreme response patterns for the Youth Risk Behavior Surveillance Survey. In M. Furlong, G. Morrison, D. Cornell, & R. Skiba (Eds.), *Issues in school violence research* (pp. 109–130). New York: Haworth.

Garbarino, J. (1999). *Lost boys: Why our sons turn violent and how we can save them.* New York: The Free Press.

Georgiou, S., & Stavrinides, P. (2008). Bullies, victims and bully-victims: Psychosocial profiles and attribution styles. *School Psychology International, 29*(5): 574–589.

Gilligan, J. (2003). Shame, guilt, and violence. *Social Research, 70(4),* 1149–1180.

Gladstone, T., & Beardslee, W. (2009). The prevention of depression in children and adolescents: A review. *Canadian Journal of Psychiatry, 54*(4), 212–221.

Gladstone, T., Beardslee, W., & O'Connor, E. (2011). The prevention of adolescent depression. *Psychiatric Clinics of North America, 34,* 35–52.

Gorman-Smith, D., Tolan, P., & Henry, D. (2000). A developmental– ecological model of the relation of family functioning to patterns of delinquency. *Journal of Quantitative Criminology, 16*, 169–198.

Gould, M., Greenberg, T., Velting D., & Shaffer, D. (2006). Youth suicide: A review. *Prevention Researcher, 13*(3): 3–7.

Graham, S. (2010). What educators need to know about bullying behaviors. *Kappan, 92*(1), 66–69.

Granot, D., & Mayseless, O. (2001). Attachment security and adjustment to school in middle childhood. *International Journal of Behavioural Development, 25*(6), 530–541.

Greenwald, R. (Ed.). (2002). *Trauma and juvenile delinquency: Theory, research, and interventions.* New York: Haworth Press.

Gunnar, M., Talge, N., & Herrera, A. (2009). Stressor paradigms in developmental studies: What does and does not work to produce mean increases in salivary cortisol. *Psychoneuroendocrinology, 34*, 953–967.

Hanson, R., Self-Brown, S., Fricker-Elhai, A., Kilpatrick, D., Saunders, B., & Resnick, H. (2006). The relations between family environment and violence exposure among youth: Findings from the national survey of adolescents. *Child Maltreatment, 11*(1), 3–15.

Harlow, K., & Roberts, R. (2010). An exploration of the relationship between social and psychological factors and being bullied. *Children & Schools, 32*(1), 15–26.

Harro, J., Merenakk, L., Nordquist, N., Konstabel, K., Comasco, E., & Oreland, L. (2009). Personality and the serotonin transporter gene: Associations in a longitudinal population-based study. *Biological Psychiatry, 81*, 9–13.

Harter, S., Waters, P., & Whitesell, N. R. (1998). Relational self-worth: Differences in perceived worth as a person across interpersonal contexts among adolescents. *Child Development, 69*(3), 756–766.

Henry, S. (2009). School violence beyond Columbine: A complex problem in need of an interdisciplinary analysis. *American Behavioral Scientist, 52*(9), 1246–1265.

Hoenicka, J., Ponce, G., Jimenez-Arriero, M., Ampuero, I., Rodriguez-Jimenez, R., Rubio, G., Aragues, M., Ramos, J., Palomo, T. (2007). Association in alcoholic patients between psychopathic traits and the additive effect of allelic forms of the CNR1 and FAAH endocannabinoid genes, and the 3′ region of the DRD2 gene. *Neurotoxicity Research, 11*, 51–59.

Hough, R. L., Vega, W., Valle, R., Kolody, B., del Castillo, R. G., & Tarke, H. (1989). Mental health consequences of the San Ysidro McDonald's massacre: A community study. *Journal of Traumatic Stress, 3*, 71–92.

Huesmann, R. (2007). The impact of electronic media violence: Scientific theory and research. *Journal of Adolescent Health 41*, S6–S13.

Jackson, M., Cassidy W., & Brown, K. N. (2009). "You were born ugly and you'll die ugly too": Cyber-bullying as relational aggression, submitted to the *Journal of School Violence.*

Kasdorf, J. (2007). The pasture. *CrossCurrents, 328*–347.

Kendler, K., Health, M., Kessler, R., Heath, A., & Eaves, L. (1993). A longitudinal twin study of personality and major depression in women. *Archives of General Psychiatry, 50*, 853–862.

Kim-Cohen, J., Caspi, A., Taylor, A., Williams, B., Newcombe, R., Craig, I., & Moffitt, T. (2006). MAOA, maltreatment, and gene–environment interaction predicting children's mental health: New evidence and a meta-analysis. *Molecular Psychiatry, 11*, 903–913.

Klomek, A., Sourander, A., & Gould, M. (2010). The association of suicide and bullying in childhood to young adulthood: A review of cross-sectional and longitudinal research findings. *Canadian Journal of Psychiatry, 55*(5), 282–288.

Knox, J. (2003a). *Archetype, attraction, analysis: Jungian psychology and the emergent mind.* New York: Brunner-Routledge.

Knox, J. (2003b). Trauma and defenses: Their roots in relationship, an overview. *Journal of Analytical Psychology, 48*, 511–530.

Kochanska, G., & Clark, L. (1997). Implications of mother's personality for their parenting and their young children's developmental outcomes. *Journal of Personality, 65*(2), 387–420.

Leskela, J., Dieperink, M., & Thuras, P. (2002). Shame and posttraumatic stress disorder. *Journal of Traumatic Stress, 15*, 223–226.

Larkin, R. (2009). The Columbine legacy: Rampage shootings as political acts. *American Behavioral Scientist, 52*(9), 1309–1326.

Lau, J., & Pine, D. (2008). Elucidating risk mechanisms of gene–environment interactions on pediatric anxiety: Integrating findings from neuroscience. *European Archives of Psychiatry and Clinical Neuroscience, 258*, 97–106.

Lieberman, J. (2006). *The shooting game.* Santa Ana, CA: Seven Locks.

Limosin, F., Romo, L., Batel, P., Adès, J., Boni, C., Gorwood, P. (2005). Association between dopamine receptor D3 gene ball polymorphism and cognitive impulsiveness in alcohol-dependent men. *European Psychiatry, 20*, 304–306.

Linedecker, C. (1999). *Babyface killers.* New York: St. Martin's.

Lobb, E., Kristjanson, L., Aoun, S., Monterosso, L., Halkett, G., & Davies, A. (2010). Predictors of complicated grief: A systematic review of empirical studies. *Death Studies, 34*, 673–698.

Lyubomirsky, S., King, L., & Diener, E. (2005). The benefits of frequent positive affect: Does happiness lead to success? *Psychological Bulletin, 131*(6), 803–855.

Masten, A. S., & Powell, J. L. (2003). A resilience framework for research, policy and practice. In S. S. Luthar (Ed.), *Resilience and vulnerability: Adaptation in the context of childhood adversities* (pp. 1–25). New York: Cambridge University Press.

McBurnett, K., King, J., & Scarpa, A. (2003). The hypothalamic-pituitary-adrenal system (HPA) and the development of aggressive, antisocial, and substance abuse disorders. In D. Cicchetti & E. Walker (Eds.), *Neurodevelopmental mechanisms in psychopathology* (pp. 324–344). Cambridge, UK: Cambridge University Press.

Moss, E., Bureau, J.-F., Béliveau, M.-J., & Lépine, S. (2009). Links between children's attachment behavior at early school-age, their attachment-related representations, and behavior problems in middle childhood. *International Journal of Behavioral Development, 1*, 1–12.

Nader, K. (2006). Childhood trauma: The deeper wound. In J. P. Wilson (Eds.), *The posttraumatic self: Restoring meaning and wholeness to personality* (pp. 117–156). New York: Routledge.

Nader, K. (2008). *Understanding and assessing trauma in children and adolescents: Measures, methods, and youth in context.* New York: Routledge.

Nader, K. (2010). Children and adolescents' exposure to the mass violence of war and terrorism: Role of the media. In N. B. Webb (Ed.), *Helping bereaved children* (3rd edition, pp. 215–239). New York: Guilford.

Nader, K. (in press). Assessing exposure and reactions to trauma in children and adolescents. In P. Clements & S. Seedat (Eds.), *Mental health issues of child maltreatment*, St. Louis, MO: STM Learning, Inc.

Nader, K., & Weems, C. (in press). Understanding and assessing cortisol levels in children and adolescents. *Journal of Child and Adolescent Trauma.*

Nijenhuis, E., Spinhoven, P., Vanderlinden, J., van Dyck, R., & van der Hart, O. (1998). Somatoform dissociative symptoms as related to animal defensive reactions to predatory imminence and injury. *Journal of Abnormal Psychology, 107*(1), 63–73.

Peeters, M., Cillessen, A., & Scholte, R. (2010). Clueless or powerful? Identifying subtypes of bullies in adolescence. *Journal of Youth Adolescence, 39*, 1041–1052.

Pollack, W. (2001). The importance of family: Preventing violence through family connection. *The Brown University Child and Adolescent Behavior Letter, 17*(12), 1, 3–4.

Pollack, W. (2004). Parent-child connections: The essential compo-
    nent for positive youth development and mental health, safe com-
    munities, and academic achievement. *New Directions for Youth
    Development, 103*, 17–30.
Putallaz, M., Grimes, L., Foster, J. K., Kupersmidt, J., Coie, J., & Dearing,
    K. (2007). Overt and relational aggression and victimization:
    Multiple perspectives within the school setting. *Journal of School
    Psychology, 45*, 523–547.
Pynoos, R., Frederick, C., Nader, K., Arroyo, W., Eth, S., Nunez, W.,
    Steinberg, A., & Fairbanks, L. (1987). Life threat and posttraumatic
    stress in school age children, *Archives of General Psychiatry, 44*,
    1057–1063.
Rende, R., Slomkowski, C., Lloyd-Richardson, E., Stroud, L., Niaura,
    R. (2006). Estimating genetic and environmental influences on
    depressive symptoms in adolescence: Differing effects on higher and
    lower levels of symptoms. *Journal Of Clinical Child And Adolescent
    Psychology, 35*(2), 237–43.
Roemer, L., Salters, K., Raffa, S., & Orsillo, S. (2005). Fear and avoidance
    of internal experiences in GAD: Preliminary tests of a conceptual
    model. *Cognitive Therapy and Research, 29*, 71–88.
Rothbart, M. K., & Bates, J. E. (1998). Temperament. In W. Damon
    (Series Ed.) & N. Eisenberg (Vol. Ed.), *Handbook of child psychol-
    ogy: Vol. 3. Social, emotional, and personality development* (5th ed.,
    pp. 105–176). New York: Wiley.
Rutter, M. (2003). Commentary: Causal processes leading to antisocial
    behavior. *Developmental Psychology, 39*(2), 372–378.
Rutter, M., Moffitt, T., & Caspi, A. (2006). Gene–environment interplay
    and psychopathology: Multiple varieties but real effects. *Journal of
    Child Psychology and Psychiatry, 47*(3/4), 226–261.
Salmivalli, C., & Nieminen, E. (2002). Proactive and reactive aggres-
    sion among school bullies, victims and bully-victims. *Aggressive
    Behavior, 28*, 30–44.
Scheff, T. (1997). Deconstructing rage. Retrieved September 17, 2003,
    from http://www.soc.ucsb.edu/faculty/Scheff/7.html.
Schippell, P. L., Vasey, M. W., Cravens-Brown, L. M., & Bretveld, R. A.
    (2003). Suppressed attention to rejection, ridicule, and failure cues:
    A unique correlate of reactive but not proactive aggression in youth.
    Journal of Clinical Child and Adolescent Psychology, 32(1), 40–55.
Schore, A. (2003). Early relational trauma, disorganized attachment, and
    the development of a predisposition to violence. In M. Soloman &
    D. J. Siegel (Eds.), *Healing trauma* (pp. 107–167). New York: W.
    W. Norton.

Seals, D., & Young, J. (2003). Bullying and victimization: Prevalence and relationship to gender, grade level, ethnicity, self-esteem, and depression. *Adolescence, 38 (152)*, 735–747.

Shanahan, L., Copeland, W. Costello, E., & Angold, A. (2008). Specificity of putative psychosocial risk factors for psychiatric disorders in children and adolescents. *Journal of Child Psychology and Psychiatry, 49*(1), 34–42.

Shoal, G., Giancola, P., & Kirillova, G. (2003). Salivary cortisol, personality, and aggressive behavior in adolescent boys: A 5-year longitudinal study. *Journal of the American Academy of Child and Adolescent Psychiatry, 42*(9), 1101–1107.

Simmons, R. (2002). *Odd girl out.* New York: Harcourt.

Singer, S., & Hensley, C. (2004). Applying social learning theory to childhood and adolescent firesetting: Can it lead to serial murder? *International Journal of Offender Therapy and Comparative Criminology, 48*(4), 461–476.

Svanberg, P., Mennet, L., & Spieker, S. (2010). Promoting a secure attachment: A primary prevention practice model. *Clinical Child Psychology and Psychiatry, 15*(3) 363–378.

Tangney, J. (1992). Situational determinants of shame and guilt in young adulthood. *Personality and Social Psychology Bulletin, 18*, 199–206.

Tangney, J., Hill-Barlow, D., Wagner, P. E., Marschall, D. E., Borenstein, J. K., Sanftner, J., Mohr, T., & Gramzow, R. (1996). Assessing individual differences in constructive versus destructive responses to anger across the lifespan. *Journal of Personality and Social Psychology, 50*, 780–796.

Tangney, J., Wagner, P., Fletcher, C., & Gramzow, R. (1992). Shamed into anger? The relation of shame and guilt to anger and self-reported aggression. *Journal of Personality and Social Psychology, 62*, 679–675.

Teplin, L., Abram, K., McClelland, G. et al. (2002). Psychiatric disorders in youth in juvenile detention. *Archives of General Psychiatry, 59*(12), 1133–1143.

Thunfors, P., & Cornell, D. (2008). The popularity of middle school bullies. *Journal of School Violence, 7*, 65–82.

Tinnen, L., Bills, L., & Gantt, L. (2002). Short-term treatment of simple and complex PTSD. In M. B. Williams & J. Sommer (Eds.), *Simple and complex posttraumatic stress disorder* (pp. 99–118). New York: Haworth Maltreatment and Trauma Press.

van der Kolk, B. (2005). Developmental trauma disorder: Toward a rational diagnosis for children with complex trauma histories. *Psychiatric Annals, 35*(5), 401–408.

Vossekuil, B., Fein, R. A., Reddy, M., Borum, R., & Modzeleski, W. (2002). The final report and findings of the Safe School Initiative: Implications for the prevention of school attacks in the United States. Washington, DC: U.S. Secret Service and U.S. Department of Education.

Whiffen, V., & MacIntosh, H. (2005). Mediators of the link between childhood sexual abuse and emotional distress: A critical review. *Trauma, Violence and Abuse, 6*, 24–39.

Weinfield, N., Sroufe, L., Egeland, B., & Carlson, E. A. (1999). The nature of individual differences in infant-caregiver attachment. In J. Cassidy & P. R. Shaver (Eds.), *Handbook of attachment* (pp. 68–88). New York: Guilford Press.

Wijngaards-de Meij, L., Stroebe, M., Schut, H., Stroebe, W., van den Bout, J., van der Heijden, P. & Dijkstra, I. (2007). Patterns of attachment and parents' adjustment to the death of their child. *Personality and Social Psychology Bulletin, 33*, 537.

Wilson, J. P. (Ed.). (2006). *The posttraumatic self: Restoring meaning and wholeness to personality*. New York: Routledge.

Yates, T. M., Egeland, B., & Sroufe, A. (2003). Rethinking resilience: A developmental process perspective. In S. S. Luthar (Ed.), *Resilience and vulnerability: Adaptation in the context of childhood adversities* (pp. 243–266). New York: Cambridge University Press.

Younge, S., Salazar, L., Sales, J., DiClemente, R., Wingood, G., & Rose, E. (2010). Emotional victimization and sexual risk-taking behaviors among adolescent African American women, *Journal of Child & Adolescent Trauma, 3*(2), 79–94.

Zurbriggen, E., Gobin, R., & Freyd, J. (2010). Childhood emotional abuse predicts late adolescent sexual aggression perpetration and victimization. *Journal of Aggression, Maltreatment & Trauma, 19*, 204–223.

CHAPTER 3

The School Environment, School Rampage Killings, and Other Forms of School Violence

John Eller

INTRODUCTION

An atmosphere of solid intellectual safety, emotional safety, and physical safety and the related reduction in a sense of emotional, intellectual, and physical danger is conducive to learning and a sense of well-being (Bucher & Manning, 2005; Cohen et al. (2009). Schools should be safe places for both children and adults (Robers, Zhang, & Truman, 2010). When this perception of safety is broken by school violence and rampage killings, they command the attention of the public, school officials, and parents. Public concern over school discipline (and school violence) seems to have diminished over recent years (Bushaw and Lopez, 2010). Gallop Polls related to education conducted in the United States from 1970 to 2010 show that public concern in the area of lack of discipline and control has diminished from a high of approximately 27% in 1980 to approximately 10% in 2010 (Bushaw & Lopez, 2010). Despite this drop in concern related to discipline and control, school violence is still an area of concern for schools (Robers, Zhang, & Truman, 2010). Each year the US Department of Education and the US Department of Justice Office of Justice Programs develop a comprehensive report that details the state of schools in relation to violence. In the 2010 report, "Preliminary data show that among youth ages 5–18, there were 38 school-associated violent deaths from July 1, 2008, through June 30, 2009" (Robers, Zang,

& Truman, pg. iii). This number includes both homicide and suicide-related deaths. The actual number of deaths by homicide was reported as 24 (Robers, Zhang, & Truman, 2010). In the 2008–09 school year, an estimated 55.6 million students were enrolled in prekindergarten through grade 12 (Snyder & Dillow, 2010 as reported in Robers, Zhang, & Truman, pg. iii). The number of homicides during this period equates to 1 in about 2.3 million students.

Even though the odds are relatively low for high profile incidents involving deaths (Robers, Zhang, & Truman, 2010), these high profile events can cause widespread fear and increased public outcries for tougher rules and questions around gun control and the way schools deal with seemingly disturbed students. The author has been personally involved in two institutions where school rampage killings have occurred. In both cases the impact was widespread and left a permanent mark on the climate and culture of these schools. One only has to say the names Columbine or Red Lake, Minnesota, and visions of seemingly evil, out-of-control adolescent boys come to mind. Residents of these and other locations where school killing rampages have occurred ask questions like, "How could this happen here?" or "Why didn't we notice this problem?" or "What caused the deep emotional problems that allowed this situation to fester and finally boil over?"

Since the Columbine incident many institutions and researchers have examined the issue of rampages by students against their schools and peers. This chapter discusses school climate, school culture, and school connectedness. Studies suggest that school climate, culture, and connectedness may help to prevent or at least minimize the chances of school rampage incidents from occurring.

SCHOOL CLIMATE, CULTURE, AND CONNECTEDNESS

School climate and culture are foundational elements that define operating aspects of schools and are often seen as the same even though each is unique (Robers, Zhang, & Truman, 2010; Brunner & Lewis, 2006; Holtappels & Meier, 2000). It is important to review both school climate and culture to understand their relationship to each other and their combined impact on the school and the school community.

School Climate

A number of definitions of school climate have been presented in the literature. This section will focus on those offered in relation to educational leadership. School climate is a relatively enduring quality of a school's environment that is based on school participants' collective behaviors in schools. It is both experienced by participants and affects their behavior (Hoy, 1990). School climate is essentially the school's "personality." It includes the immediate day-to-day feel or tone (atmosphere) of the school (Eller & Eller, 2009). School climate may be one of the most important ingredients of a successful instructional program (Hoyle, 1982). Climate can be immediately impacted because of its moment-to-moment nature (Eller & Eller, 2009). Since the climate of a school has some fluidity to it, it would then make sense that climate is an aspect that can be influenced or changed. As will be discussed later in this chapter, individuals' perceptions of school climate may inadvertently create conditions for negative ideas to breed (Peterson and Skiba, 2001).

The Dimensions of School Climate

Understanding that school climate can be impacted and changed, it is helpful to examine and understand a framework that outlines some of the dimensions of climate. A clear framework enables a school leader to use the information it contains to analyze various aspects of school climate and possibly make adjustments in them or even develop interventions and strategies to ensure they are positive and contributing to the positive climate of the school. Cohen, McCabe, Michelli, and Pickeral (2009) have integrated information from a variety of sources to develop a clear description of school climate centered on four major dimensions. The dimensions they offer seem to be comprehensive and measurable by school leaders. These dimensions include safety, teaching and learning, relationships, and environmental–structural and appear below.

1. Safety—physical and social–emotional safety for students, staff, and school community members as well as rules and norms.
2. Teaching and Learning—high expectations for students and high quality of instruction, with respect for all learning styles and intelligences; social, emotional, and civic learning. opportunities for students; pertinent professional development; and leadership with clear vision, accessibility, respect for individuals, and support giving.
3. Relationships—respect for diversity in background and thoughts and good relationships among and between adults and students; school and community collaborations and mutual support; high morale and a student sense of "connectedness" to the school and one or more adults.

4. Environmental–Structural—a clean, well-organized, appropriately sized, and inviting physical plant; varied curricular
and extracurricular offerings. (Cohen, McCabe, Michelle, &
Pickeral p. 184)

As Cohen et al. (2009) point out, an awareness of and focus on these
attributes can be helpful for school leaders (see also National School
Climate Council, 2007). For example, the school environment benefits
when the members of the school community (parents, students, teachers,
community members, etc.) share in the success of the school, understand
and appreciate their individual differences, have some internal locus of
control in relation to their own lives, and engage in behaviors where
they see the benefits of collaborating rather than always competing.
Enhancing respect, communication, participation, and connectedness
(cf. (3) Relationships) are likely to decrease the chances that school community members feel isolated. When the four attributes from Table 3.1
become a focus of the school community, positive climate conditions
may take on a foundational role in the operation and leadership of the
school. When the four attributes are part of the school mission, then
school leaders can look for and assess the presence of them in classrooms and other aspects of the school. For example, under the sub-
section related to morale and connectedness, a school leader might be
looking for observable evidence that staff members truly engage in two-
way communication (speaking and listening) with students, that there
are opportunities for student participation in decision-making (possibly
school site councils, venues to allow for student participation in relation to decisions on policies, discipline processes, and other aspects of
the school's operation that directly impact them. If engagement vehicles
are in place, their effectiveness can be assessed; if they are not in place,
plans can be made to start such programs. Because of the apparent fluid
nature of the school climate, the implementation of strategies can have
an immediate impact on its tone. Impacting the deeper, more permanent
structure of the school, the school culture may require more effort. It's
important to look more closely at the concept of school culture.

School Culture

A positive school climate can eventually become a part of the deeper foundation of a school—that is, its culture. Sergiovanni (2007) describes school
culture as "the normative glue that holds a particular school together"
(pg. 145). A group's culture can be defined as "a pattern of shared basic
assumptions that the group learned as it solved its problems of external

adaptation and internal integration" (Schein, 1997, p. 12). Such assumptions are considered valid by the group, are woven into the inner fabric of a school or organization, become almost automatic, and are, therefore, taught to new members as the correct way to perceive, think, and feel in relation to problems. Accordingly, these assumptions define how a school operates, how decisions are made, and what norms the school uses to operate. School culture may be seen as a pattern of shared orientations that bind the school together and give it a distinctive identity (Hoy & Miskel, 2009). School culture is generally stable and consistent over time (Eller & Eller, 2009). Changing a school's culture can be difficult "like changing the course of a large ship moving in a certain direction" (Eller & Eller, p. 3)

The culture of a school becomes the permanent, unifying force that determines how things are done, how students are treated, and what behavior norms are promoted (or tolerated). It governs the relationships within a building. Within a particular school setting there may be many interrelated connections and patterns. Professionals studying the culture or the administrator leading a school may need to step back and take a more global look at the patterns of relationships (Wheatley, 2006), in order to effect any needed change.

Attributes of School Culture

Based on the earlier work of Schein (1997), Kruse and Seashore Louis (2009) identified three attributes important for consideration, when evaluating school culture—artifacts, espoused values, and basic underlying assumptions. *Artifacts* include observable components or evidence that demonstrate the presence or absence of cultural conditions. For example, in a school where the culture outlines accepting everyone regardless of background, race, or ethnicity, an observer may see posters in the school talking about this value. *Espoused values* are the values that people say they believe in when asked. In a school culture where students are encouraged to feel connected, a researcher might find a majority of people would share this value openly. *Basic underlying assumptions* are the unwritten rules or norms that guide the actions of its members. For example, in a school where the culture is such that inclusiveness is valued, new students might be welcomed by others and made to feel welcome. In other words, a school's culture is demonstrated in concrete evidence, communications, and behaviors.

School Connectedness

Researchers suggest that good-quality school climates cultivate a connection to the school, and in this way protect youth from negative outcomes ... adolescents who establish social bonds to their school are more likely to strive to meet society's expectations and therefore, are less likely to engage in deviant behavior. (Loukas, Suzuki, & Horton, 2006, pg. 492)

School connectedness is reflected in a sense of connection to the school. School connectedness influences school climate (Blum, Gates, & Carr, 2010; Waters, Cross, & Shaw, 2010; Loukas, Suzuki, & Horton, 2006). In a study of 36,000 7th through 12th grade students, Blum, Gates, and Carr (2010) reported that school connectedness, as well as parent–family connectedness and high parental expectations for academic achievement, were protective against a range of adverse behaviors. School-related factors that impact connectedness include adult support, belonging to a positive peer group, commitment to education, and school environment. A positive school environment/climate is characterized by caring and supportive interpersonal relationships (e.g., respect from adults to students and vice versa), opportunities to participate in school activities and decision-making, and shared positive values, goals, and norms. In contrast, research indicates (Blum, Gates, & Carr, 2010), student connectedness is lower in schools with harsh and punitive discipline. Students with good school connectedness typically engage in fewer problem behaviors (Waters, Cross, & Shaw, 2010). Structural factors such as size, grade configuration, and others were also related to school climate and had a positive influence on student connectedness (Waters et al., 2010; see Chapter 1).

SCHOOL CLIMATE AND CULTURE AND ITS RELATIONSHIP TO SCHOOL VIOLENCE

A safe school is one in which the total school climate allows students, teachers, administrators, staff, and visitors to interact in a positive, nonthreatening manner that reflects the educational mission of the school while fostering positive relationships and personal growth. The decisions of individual teachers about classroom management theories or their choices of management practices and strategies have significant effects on the school climate and the ways in which students resolve problems. (Manning & Bucher, 2003)

Positive climates and cultures encourage positive student attitudes and behaviors while negative climates and cultures promote uncomfortable situations for students and negative behaviors (Peterson & Skiba, 2001). Negative climates and cultures can become factors that cause some students to begin to disconnect from the school.

Findings Related to School Rampages

Two reports outlining studies conducted by the US Secret Service and the US Department of Education related to school violence and rampage killings—*The Final Report and Findings of the Safe Schools Initiative: Implications for the Prevention of School Attacks in the United States* (available online at www.secretservice.gov/ntac/ssiJinaLreport.pdf) and *Threat Assessment in Schools: A Guide to Managing Threatening Situations and to Creating Safe School Climates* (available online at www. secretservice.gov/ntac/ssi_guide.pdf)—include case studies of school sites that recently experienced rampage killings. In these case studies, investigators interviewed people at schools where rampage killings had occurred. They also analyzed documents and communications, observed the schools in operation, and recreated some of the situations and events that contributed to the violent incident. Since the Secret Service was involved, they had unprecedented access to people and records held by law enforcement officials that other researchers would not have had. They generated extensive reports based on the case studies that contained much information about the conditions and outcomes of these violent incidents.

Brunner and Lewis (2006) conducted an in-depth analysis of these two reports and elaborated the following 10 key findings:

1. Incidents of targeted violence, which take place at school are usually not sudden or impulsive
2. In most of these incidents, the student had made some type of either verbal or else written threat to others
3. Most of the attackers did not directly threaten or target an individual
4. There is no accurate profile of students who are likely to commit violence
5. Prior to the actual incident itself, most perpetrators of the events exhibited some type of behavior that indicated that there was a need for help
6. Many of the attackers had considered or attempted suicide
7. Many of these students believed that they had been bullied
8. Weapons were readily available to the students
9. In most of these cases, other students were involved
10. Most shootings were stopped by someone other than law enforcement officers (Brunner & Lewis, p. 35)

Several of the key findings (attributes 2, 5, 6, 7, and 9) have at least some connection to the school climate and culture. For example, in attribute 7, most students had experienced some form of bullying (see

Chapters 2 and 8). Attribute 9, other students' involvement in some manner in the violent incident can also be a reflection of a negative school culture where students engage in negative behavior as a way to belong to a group because they may feel less connected to the school. Holtappels and Meier (2000) found a connection between negative school climate and student violent behavior. They also found that students became more disconnected and likely to engage in violent actions if they thought their teachers were not interested in them as students and people. Although actors outside of the school, such as the lack of future vocational opportunities, problems with family upbringing, or violence-approving values in a youth clique may contribute to violence, the school itself and its climate and culture can have an effect on school-related negative events.

Another impact of connectedness to the school involves students reporting potential violent acts to school officials or other adults. Pollack, Modzeleski, and Rooney (2008) shared that school climate and connectedness are important factors in determining whether students who have knowledge of a potential attack come forward to report this knowledge. A sense of connectedness helped students feel comfortable in reporting and feeling that their story would be taken seriously and believed.

PRELIMINARY RECOMMENDATIONS FOR RESEARCHERS, SCHOOL LEADERS, AND SCHOOL COMMUNITY MEMBERS

What can be learned from the incidents that have been so violent and shocking in the past? How can educators, parents, and community members work together to develop school climates and cultures that nurture the commitment and connections necessary to help students to get their emotional needs met and minimize the chances that rampages of killing and violence will be their outlet for attention? How might educators develop the climates and cultures that teach students how to productively work through issues and conflicts in support rather than try to gain power over others? One recommendation relates to the improvement of school climate and the eventual operating culture of the school.

Improving School Climate and Culture

There are lessons from the analysis of school climate and culture and school violence incidents that school leaders should consider.

Peterson and Skiba (2001) suggest several areas in which schools can improve the climate and culture and minimize the potential for violent student behavior. They are

- Parent and community involvement
- Character education
- Violence prevention and conflict resolution curricula
- Peer mediation
- Bullying prevention

Parent involvement within the school, such as attending school programs, has been linked to a host of beneficial student outcomes, including increased academic achievement and improved youth behavior (Brookmeyer, Fanti, & Henrich, 2006, p. 505). Parental participation by all parents, tended to increase student perceptions of school connectedness (Brookmeyer et. al, 2006). Parent and community involvement can be enhanced using a variety of strategies. Strategies such as increasing parent-teacher organization participation, hosting whole-school parental involvement events, and helping parents to feel welcome at the school may hold promise for increasing total parental involvement.

Programs that are designed to provide character education, peer mediation, and foster violence prevention and design conflict resolution curricula are highly variable and should be carefully selected to meet the unique needs of the school and the students (Breunlin, Cimmarusti, Hetherington, & Kinsman 2006). In light of this obvious recommendation, each school leader would need to assess the specific needs of their school and the unique nature of the potential violence it may encounter before selecting programs and interventions to mediate these challenges (see Section II of this book).

Bucher and Manning (2005) point out that creating a safe school requires more than eliminating fights, knifings, and shootings. Name calling; ridiculing; teasing; offensive touching; racial, ethnic, cultural, or sexual slurs; and other bullying are also violent acts (Hernandez & Seem, 2004). As Stephens (2003) notes, "a safe school is a place where the business of education can be conducted in a welcoming environment free of intimidation, violence, and fear. Such a setting provides an educational climate that fosters a spirit of acceptance and care for every child. It is a place free of bullying where behavior expectations are clearly communicated, consistently enforced, and fairly applied" (Mabie 2003, as reported in Bucher & Manning, 2005, pg. 57). Bucher and Manning (2005) contend that most school violence incidents do not come up all of a sudden. Many of the students involved in the worst killings and violent acts against their peers and school officials may have taken years to develop and grow before they exploded into the catastrophic events that we read and hear about in the news. In light of the fact that these violent acts may take years of influence from a negative school climate (and obviously other factors) to develop, early and ongoing interventions may hold some promise in changing the negative cycles and minimizing the chances of a violent act from erupting in a school.

CONCLUSIONS

School community members can help to develop climates and cultures that minimize the potential for negative student experiences that can lead to catastrophic events. Helping students to learn skills related to their ability to work through conflict and issues is important to creating a positive school climate and culture. Providing emotional, intellectual, and physical safety for students is conducive to helping students learn and grow rather than become isolated and disconnected. Finally, developing a framework using the work of Cohen, McCabe, Michelle, and Pickeral (2009) will help schools to put a comprehensive and observable plan in place. Its major dimensions of safety, teaching, learning, relationships, and environmental-structural provide a clear and straightforward structure for school leaders to follow in planning and implementing school climate and ultimately school culture changes that will enhance connectedness for all members of the school community.

Positive school climate and culture will be evidenced in, for example, the school's artifacts, espoused values, and basic underlying assumptions (Kruse & Seashore-Lewis, 2009; Schein's (1997). Artifacts (i.e., concrete evidence) will appear that enhance connectedness, a sense of respect between individuals (among and between adults and youth), and other positive school values. School community members and leaders will talk about operating a school that cares for students and how much they value their efforts to make this a reality. Espoused values will reflect caring, respect, and connection. Finally, positive underlying assumptions based on these values will be evident in communication, behaviors, overall school environment, and connection to helping individuals outside of the school community. When this happens, the small, day-to-day interventions and interactions so crucial to student relationship development will be in place.

REFERENCES

Breunlin, D. C., Cimmarusti, R. A., Hetherington, J. S., & Kinsman, J. (2006). Making the smart choice: A systemic response to school-based violence. *Journal of Family Therapy, 28*(3), 246–266.

Blum, R., Gates, W., & Carr, D. (2010). School connectedness: Strategies for increasing protectedness factors among youth. Center for Disease Control. *Reclaiming Children and Youth.* www.reclaimingjournal.com.

Brookmeyer, K., Fanti, K., & Henrich, C. (2006). Schools, parents, and youth violence: A multilevel, ecological analysis. *Journal of Clinical Child and Adolescent Psychology, 35*(4), 504–514.

Brunner, J., & Lewis, D. (2006). Telling a "red flag" from the real threat with students of today. *Education Digest, 72*(4), 33–36.

Bucher, K. T., & Manning, M. (2005). Creating safe schools. *Clearing House, 79*(1), 55–60.

Bushaw, W. J., & Lopez, S. J. (2010). A time for change. *Phi Delta Kappan, 92*(1), 9–26.

Cohen, J., MCCabe, E. M., Michelli, N. M., & Pickeral, T. (2009). School climate: Research, policy, practice, and teacher education. *Teachers College Record, 111*(1), 180–213.

Dinkes, R., Kemp, J., and Baum, K. (2009a). *Indicators of school crime and safety: 2008* (NCES 2009–022/NCJ 226343). Washington, DC: National Center for Education Statistics, Institute of Education Sciences, U.S. Department of Education, and Bureau of Justice Statistics, Office of Justice Programs, U.S. Department of Justice.

Dinkes, R., Kemp, J., and Baum, K. (2009b). *Indicators of school crime and safety: 2009* (NCES 2010–012/NCJ 228478). Washington, DC: National Center for Education Statistics, Institute of Education Sciences, U.S. Department of Education, and Bureau of Justice Statistics, Office of Justice Programs, U.S. Department of Justice.

Eller, S., & Eller J. (2009). *Creative strategies to transform school culture.* Thousand Oaks, CA: Corwin Press.

Holtappels, H., & Meier, U. (2000). Violence in schools. *European Education, 32*(1), 66–79.

Hoy, W. K. (1990). Organizational climate and culture: A conceptual analysis of the school workplace. *Journal of Educational & Psychological Consultation, 1*(2), 149–168.

Hoyle, J.(1982). *Guidelines for the preparation of school administrators.* Alexandria, VA: American Association of School Administrators.

Kruse, S., & Seashore-Louis, K. (2009). *Building strong school cultures: A guide to leading change.* Thousand Oaks, CA: Corwin Press.

Loukas, A., Suzuki, R., & Horton, K. D. (2006). Examining school connectedness as a mediator of school climate effects. *Journal of Research on Adolescence (Blackwell Publishing Limited)*, 16(3), 491–502.

National School Climate Council (2007). The school climate challenge: Narrowing the gap between school climate research and school climate policy, practice guidelines and teacher education policy. Available online at: http://nscc.csee.net/ or http://www.ecs.org/school-climate

Peterson, R. L., & Skiba, R. (2001). Creating school climates that prevent school violence. *Social Studies*, 92(4), 167–175. Retrieved from EBSCO*host*.

Pollack, W., Modzeleski, W., & Rooney, G. (2008). *Prior knowledge of potential school-based violence: information students learn may prevent a targeted attack*. Washington DC: United States Secret Service and United States Department of Education.

Robers, S., Zhang, J., and Truman, J. (2010). *Indicators of School Crime and Safety: 2010* (NCES 2011-002/NCJ 230812). Washington, DC: National Center for Education Statistics, U.S. Department of Education, and Bureau of Justice Statistics, Office of Justice Programs, U.S. Department of Justice.

Schein, E. (2004). *Organizational culture and leadership*. San Francisco, CA: Jossey-Bass.

Sergiovanni, T. (2007). *Rethinking leadership: A collection of articles* (2nd ed.). Thousand Oaks, CA: Corwin Press.

Waters, S., Cross, D., & Shaw, T. (2010). Does the nature of schools matter? An exploration of selected school ecology factors on adolescent perceptions of school connectedness. *British Journal of Educational Psychology. 80*, 381–402.

Wheatley, M. (2006). *Leadership and the new science: Discovering order in a chaotic world*. San Francisco, CA: Berrett-Koehler Publishers.

CHAPTER 4

A Continuum of Youth Violence

Edmund Bruyere and James Garbarino

Teenagers are involved in millions of incidents of "ordinary" aggression each year (U.S. Department of Health and Human Services, 2001). Hundreds of thousands commit serious acts of violence. More than a hundred thousand are arrested for assault. More than one thousand commit lethal assaults. A handful engaged in "rampage shootings," most infamously the Columbine School Shooting of April 1999, committed by Eric Harris and Dylan Klebold. How are the various points along this continuum of violence (from small aggressions to mass shootings) related to each other? What are the developmental and social foundations for this continuum of violence? These are questions with which this chapter will wrestle.

At the outset, we can observe that most research clusters at the lower end of this continuum of youth violence (U.S. Department of Health and Human Services, 2001). Thousands of studies have examined issues of physical aggression in adolescents; only hundreds have investigated lethal assaults. And only a handful have studied school rampage shootings. This complicates and even compromises the task of understanding the full range of youth violence. In this chapter we attempt to make the best of the existing evidence to address the developmental origins of youth violence by employing Bronfenbrenner's ecological perspective on human development as a framework.

AN ECOLOGICAL PERSPECTIVE ON HUMAN DEVELOPMENT

To understand the developmental origins of youth violence we use Bronfenbrenner's ecological perspective on human development (1979,

2005) as a framework. The ecological perspective argues that development depends on the interplay between biology and context (conceived of in terms of multiple levels of social systems). This reciprocal transaction between the biology of youth (and infants and children) and their environments influences the way they perceive the world around them. It places development along a complicated continuum (Rutter, 1989).

An underlying assumption of the ecological perspective is this: rarely is there a simple direct causal association between variables that are universal and comparable across contexts (Bronfenbrenner, 1979; Garbarino, 1999). This can be expressed as follows: "When the question is, does X cause Y? The best answer is almost always, "It depends." It depends upon a number of indirect causal variables including, the values and beliefs of a nation, policy, culture, biology, developmental history, perception, as well as peer influence. In short, it depends upon the net effect of the accumulation of risk as well as developmental assets.

Risk Accumulation

One of the essential concepts in understanding development is "risk accumulation" (Rutter, 1987; Sameroff, Seifer, Barocas, Zax, & Greenspan, 1987). Rarely, if ever, do two risk factors (e.g., attachment difficulties and abandonment) predict severe negative developmental outcomes. Rather, it is the accumulation of risk factors beyond these initial two that predict a high level of negative average outcomes. Why?

For one, children differ temperamentally and these differences will dictate how and to what degree they will react to different experiences. For example, two children exposed to similar traumatic events, with two distinct temperaments may react differently. A child who is more prone to internalizing may become depressed and isolated and even engage in self-directed violence; a child prone to externalizing may respond with aggression towards others. Traditionally it was thought that these temperamental differences mirrored underlying gender differences, with boys being more prone to externalizing aggression and girls to internalizing problems. However, recent trends have mostly reduced or eliminated whatever differences along these lines that may have existed in the past. Indeed, the role of gender in predicting aggression has declined in recent decades (Garbarino, 2006).

Despite these differences, when the nature of trauma is severe, pervasive, and prolonged enough, the psychological and behavioral costs may be profound. For example, a New Zealand study found that after controlling for confounding variables (e.g., social and family factors that in our terms might be considered additional risk factors) those children who experienced severe and prolonged sexual abuse were 2.7 to 11.9 times more likely to suffer from mental health problems at age 18 (e.g., major depression, anxiety disorder, *conduct disorder*, alcoholism, drug abuse, and suicide) than children not sexually abused (Fergusson, Horwood, & Lynskey, 1996). However, any attempt to isolate the effects of one form of trauma or abuse may well be misguided, since children usually experience multiple experiences of this sort, what is called *poly-victimization*. Poly-victimization refers to the experience of at least four types of victimization from a list of more than 30 types (e.g., assault, sexual molestation, witnessing violence, being robbed). Studies have demonstrated that poly-victimization accounts for much of the variance in symptoms such as depression, anxiety, and aggression (Finkelhor, Ormrod, & Turner, 2007). Finkelhor and his colleagues report that poly-victimization rather than single forms of victimization accounts for variance in outcomes (greatly reducing or even eliminating the association between individual types of victimization and symptomatology).

Without sufficient compensatory assets, cumulative risk can and usually does dictate problems with a child's cognition and social behavior. In a longitudinal study evaluating the influence of social risk factors (socio-economic status, race, maternal occupation and education, family size, family support, life events, parenting perspectives, anxiety, mental health, and parental interaction) on the intelligence of a sample (N = 152) of boys across two time points (age 4 and 13), Sameroff and colleagues (1993) found risk accumulation to negatively effect cognitive development. Little to no effect was found for intelligence scores (112–118) of boys with 0–2 risk factors. However, boys exposed to 3–10 risk factors experienced a significant reduction in intelligence scores, ranging from 112–85. Additionally, evaluating the influence of living in a high-risk neighborhood (i.e., high rates of crime and poverty) on the academic and mental health (measures of resilience) of a sample of minority males (ages 12–14) who were also dealing with racism and abusive families, not one of the boys was found to be unaffected (Tolan, 1996).

Watson and colleagues (2004) sought to answer this question: Does cumulative risk predict increased levels of aggression in boys over time? Evaluating the influence of 11 risk factors (gender, playing with toy guns, carrying weapons, parental physical abuse, parental verbal abuse, peer victimization, high-conflict at home, high-risk neighborhood, medical problems, believing aggression is justified to solve problems, and using aggression to solve problems) on the aggressive behavior of a sample (N = 371) of school children they found 0–5 risk factors to have little to no influence on escalating patterns of aggressive behavior. However, eight or nine (or more) risk factors significantly increased the likelihood that boys would use aggression (the most aggressive boy had 11). These studies demonstrate the power of cumulative risk to undermine cognitive competence and pro-social behavior. Resilience has been shown to counter these negative effects.

Resilience

Which positive factors protect children and youth from adversity? The following strengths are notable in their impact: at least average intelligence, a positive and likeable disposition, responsiveness to positive environments and social cues, strong attachment relationships with family members, as well as positive and supportive relationships with non-related adults (Bonanno, 2004; Werner, 2000). Fortunately, even amid an environment filled with social risk factors these positive factors are present for most children and youth.

AN ECOLOGICAL PERSPECTIVE ON GUNS

To illustrate the ecological perspective consider the question, Do guns cause youth to commit violence? It depends on the extent to which the social organization, belief systems, and lifestyles of any given culture influence the level of risk in the lives of children and youth. Gun policies can add the first lethal risk factor to our continuum, particularly when considered in the context of cultural support for gun ownership and use, as mediated by the mass media (Garbarino, 1999; Huessman, 2007; Nader, 2010).

In the United States, gun policies derive their meaning and application from the Second Amendment of the U.S. Constitution's Bill of Rights (1789). The Second Amendment is the foundation for an intergenerational belief system that provides social and legal coherence for a thriving gun culture (Hofstadter, 1970). This belief system is common among the general population, but particularly among those living in rural communities (particularly in Southern states where many, if not most, young men are raised to believe that owning and using a gun is normative). The efforts of parents to include children in this culture promote tradition in the form of sport and hunting as well as self-protection. Rarely has the goal been for children to commit any form of violence.

While most school rampage shooters grew up within a gun culture, the contrasting belief systems and behaviors between two fathers warrants discussion. The fathers of Dylan Klebold (Colorado) and Evan Ramsey (Alaska) sent two contrasting messages to their sons. Dylan's father was an antigun advocate (Garbarino, 2010). So much so that he was ready to leave Colorado if the state legislature passed a conceal-and-carry law (around the same time as the Columbine shootings). Thus, his explicit feelings about guns should have sent Dylan an antigun, antiviolence message. Dylan's lethal actions suggest that this message was not well received.

In contrast, Evan's father sent a progun and proviolence message (Langman, 2009). Armed with two loaded guns and over 200 rounds of ammunition, he entered a local newspaper to force the printing of an article he submitted to the paper that was rejected. His actions were thwarted, and he was subsequently adjudicated and imprisoned, leaving Evan without his support and guidance. His behavior sent the lethal message: "Evan, I believe guns and violence should be used to achieve a goal." Sadly, Evan's behavior mirrored this very sentiment, only he took it to another level as he killed two people and wounded two others at his high school in Bethel, Alaska.

However, for us, this issue is not so much about guns per se. Rather, our issue is with the social and psychological availability of guns within a society that continues to traumatize as well as send toxic messages (i.e., glamorize violence in its media) to boys biologically, socially, and psychologically vulnerable to committing any form of lethal violence (Garbarino, 1999).

CHILDREN AND AGGRESSION

Another way to illustrate the ecological perspective is to ask, Does genetic vulnerability cause children to be more aggressive? The answer, of course, is "It depends." It depends upon the attachment relationship, trauma and biology, historical trauma, parental emotional or physical absence and abandonment, as well as how boys perceive rejection (Bronfenbrenner, 2005).

Attachment

To answer the question in the previous paragraph we must move beyond blaming children and/or their parents for violence, and look deeper at early experience. These early experiences often take place during the attachment relationship (Ainsworth, Blehar, Waters, & Wall, 1978; Garbarino, 1999). The great Russian psychologist Lev Vygotsky (1978) proposed that learning and development occur best in the zone of proximal development, the point between what can be learned on one's own and what can be learned with the intervention of the "teacher." The attachment relationship is a child's first zone of proximal development.

Attachment relationships (secure, anxious-resistant, anxious-attached, and disorganized-disoriented; Ainsworth, Blehar, Waters, & Wall, 1978; Main and Solomon, 1990) reflect the type of trust, responsiveness, and sensitivity shown to infants by caregivers. They are reciprocal in nature, meaning the level of trust, responsiveness, and sensitivity shown to an infant is reflected by his behavior. A secure infant whose needs are met with patience, and is loved, nurtured, and accepted, over time typically responds to others in the same manner. On the other hand, infants raised by caregivers who show less attention and sensitivity, respond harshly, and show unpredictable affection are at risk for developing mental health and social problems (e.g., hyperactivity, anxiety, cognitive delays, depression, failed relationships, poor educational attainment, and criminality).

The type of care giving a child received predicts aggressive behavior. Sroufe and colleagues (2005) found that anxiously-attached and disorganized-disoriented children who had a history of early abuse and neglect showed a steady pattern of conduct problems from childhood through adolescence; failure to establish a strong bond with a primary caregiver indirectly influenced child abuse and out of control behavior, as well as conduct problems. What this research illustrates is that parental behavior influences behavior. In addition to guns, it adds another risk factor, predicting vulnerability to lethal violence. These are compounded by two other risk factors—chronic exposure to trauma and biological vulnerability.

Trauma and Biology

Research in neuroscience suggests that chronic trauma influences the functioning of neurobiological processes, in turn sensitizing the brain to patterns of reacting and responding that become maladaptive in the larger society (no matter how adaptive they are for survival within the dysfunctional family or community). For example, among other adaptive styles, some boys adapt and respond through dissociation, while others develop hyper-aroused fear responses and act out with aggression (Baker, Blakley, Perry, Pollard, & Vigilante, 1993). Without early intervention, these responses may crystallize into conduct disorder and persist over the life course.

Conduct Disorder

Conduct disorder refers to "a repetitive and persistent pattern of behaviors in which the basic rights of others or major age-appropriate norms or rules of society are violated" (American Psychiatric Association,

1994, p. 90). It is a multifaceted diagnosis covering behaviors like violence (to include aggression directed at animals), destroying property,
lying and stealing, and failing to obey societal rules. For some children
who develop conduct disorder in the first 18 years of life, it will predict
a developmental pathway leading to adult criminality.

The question of when conduct disorder develops is important to our
discussion. Adolescent-onset conduct disorder is relatively common for
youth in America. Teenagers defy authority, break rules, get into fights,
abuse drugs, and engage in vandalism; some extend this to more serious
forms of juvenile delinquency. Fortunately, most children who develop
adolescent conduct disturbances are able to draw upon the competencies learned in early and middle childhood to mature into law-abiding
citizens as adults (American Psychiatric Association, 2000). In contrast,
Rutter (1989) reports that roughly one third of children who develop
early onset conduct disorder (before age 8) carry this behavior into adulthood and become career criminals—a figure that is four times greater in
high-risk neighborhoods than in low-risk neighborhoods.

The earlier the aggressive behavioral disturbance begins, the more
likely it is to crystallize into an ongoing and general pattern of interaction (Farrington, 2007; Loeber, 1982). Furthermore, early conduct
disturbances suggests a history of difficult temperament, parental abandonment, family violence, child maltreatment (Sroufe et al., 2005), and/
or neurobiological deficits (Baker et al., 1993; Rutter et al., 2006). As a
result, some children will not develop the social and emotional competencies necessary to regulate pro-social behavior.

A Façade of Fearlessness

Some chronically traumatized children develop a pattern of responding
to the world through social and psychological withdrawal; this leads to
hidden (i.e., they do not openly express their emotions) depression and
anxiety (Baker et al., 1993). Especially for those who are living in violent
environments, dissociation may appear to others to be fear—a physical
and psychological liability.

Children—perhaps particularly boys—who show fear in violent
environments invite victimization (Garbarino, 1999). As a result, some
children and youth (again, particularly males) bury their fear and replace
it with a façade of fearlessness. Of course, because of temperament some
children are temperamentally predisposed to be fearless. However, others, like those displaying a façade of fearlessness, learn to suppress their
fear. Thus, rather than internalize the consequences of the experience of
fear, they learn to strike back. The point is that the façade of fearlessness

is emotionally, psychologically, and socially toxic. Such children and youth bury their true feelings and have limited options for managing their feelings as well as behaviors.

Biologically Vulnerable Children

Which traumatized children are prone to developing conduct disorder in the face of social risk? The MAO-A gene is responsible for metabolizing specific neurotransmitters. Normal metabolizing occurs during high gene activity or when the gene is turned on. Problems arise when the gene is turned off (low levels; Foley et al., 2004; Frezzato et al., 2007; Rutter et al., 2006). Studying the relation between MAO-A activity and child maltreatment to conduct disorder, Caspi and colleagues (2002) found that children (N = 1,037) with the MAO-A gene turned off are three times more likely to develop conduct disorder than non-maltreated children with this same genotype; they are ten times more likely to be convicted of a violent crime in adulthood. Maltreated children with the MAO-A turned on showed no significant signs of conduct disorder or violent arrests. Thus, children with the MAO-A gene turned off are less able to cope with stress (Caspi et al., 2002). When there are deficits in information processing they tend to overreact and act out with aggression. These effects are compounded by the risk factor, parental absence (Dodge & Sherrill, 2007). The "elephant in the room" in this research is that only boys were included in the Caspi study, since the MAO-A gene is located on the X chromosome and thus while all boys who get it show the effect, girls, in general, who have the MAO-A gene "off" on one X chromosome almost certainly have it "on" on their other X chromosome, thus protecting them from its effects.

Historical Trauma

For Native American youth there is an additional risk factor which to date has not been addressed, and that is historical trauma. The parents of two school shooters (Jeffrey Weise [Red Lake, Minnesota] and Evan Ramsey [Alaska]) are Native American; as such, historical trauma should not be discounted as a risk factor for Native youth who commit school rampage shootings (Byrd, 2007; Thurman, 2010).

Historical trauma involves massive group trauma (e.g., war, murder, death due to sickness, loss of relatives [land and animals], forced adoptions, legalized kidnapping and subsequent internment in residential schools where child abuse was rampant) that has cumulative effects on the mental health (psychological and behavioral well-being) of a traumatized people (e.g., Jews, African Americans, the Aboriginals of Australia, and Native Americans) across generations (e.g., suicide, homicide, domestic violence, child abuse, alcoholism, and early mortality; Brave Heart & DeBruyn, 1998). While research is scant, Whitbeck and his colleagues (2004) found a significant relation between historical trauma and perceived historical loss and grief manifested in anxiety, depression, anger, and isolation across generations. These emotions and behaviors undermine mental health (i.e., psychological and behavioral health).

In one form or another, historical trauma and its effects influenced the lives of Evan Ramsey and Jeffrey Weise (Thurman, 2010). The effects of historical trauma on the parents of Jeff Weise exposed him to paternal suicide, alcoholism, instability, foster care, child abuse, poverty, maternal incarceration, and perceived abandonment. Moreover, Jeff, who committed suicide after his rampage, lived in a community where the suicide rate for Native youth was four times higher than then the state average (Minnesota Department of Health, 2007). Likewise, Evan Ramsey (his mother was Native Alaskan) was exposed to alcoholism, instability, foster care, sexual and physical abuse, domestic violence, and poverty. The influence these negative intergenerational experiences had on their mental health were revealed through their lethal actions.

Parental Abandonment/Rejection

The second author (Garbarino) serves as an expert witness in capital murder cases. After numerous interviews of men sitting on death row or doing life for murder, Garbarino (2008) concludes that parental abandonment (i.e., maternal psychological and paternal physical abandonment) is a common risk factor among these men. According to Dodge and Sherrill (2007), failing to bond to a caregiver subsequently leads to feelings of rejection as well as the onset of conduct disorder. Crossculturally, Rhoner, Khaleque, and Cournoyer (2005) found perceived parental rejection to account for 25% of the variance in mental health problems. Thus, rather than learn to trust, to be sensitive, and to cooperate with others, some children learn to distrust, to be insensitive, to reject and be oppositional. Yet, even when psychologically abandoned by mothers, fathers can compensate and teach boys the prosocial mores and norms of good behavior (Flanders, Leo, Paquette, Pihl, & Sequin, 2009).

One of the primary responsibilities of fatherhood involves teaching children how to manage and control their aggression (Peterson & Flanders, 2005). Rough and tumble play (RTP) is a tool used by fathers to socialize boys (and girls) into the mores and norms (self-control and sensitivity to others) of aggression (Flanders et al., 2009). Ultimately, most children will show a persistent pattern of prosocial behavior (respect the basic rights of others, manage major age-appropriate norms or rules of society, treat others with kindness, respect others' property, and tell the truth). In contrast, children (and particularly boys) who are abandoned by their fathers may be left to their own for learning the mores and norms of aggression. Chronic behavioral disturbances that may mirror conduct disorder may result (Dodge & Sherrill, 2007).

Peers are another source of socialization but they too can be problematic. In many urban settings divorce and poverty leave single parents little choice but to seek affordable housing in impoverished and violent neighborhoods. Here, the rate of fatherless children is high. They often congregate together to form violent street gangs, as a means of protection as well as acceptance (National Fatherhood Initiative, 2007).

Chronic Peer Rejection

Chronic peer rejection can be just as psychologically cancerous as parental rejection (Dodge & Sherrill, 2007). Children are rejected because of their skin color, social status, income, academic and athletic abilities, traits or personalities, and disabilities. Still others are rejected because they lack the social competencies to interact appropriately or assertively with peers (Sroufe et al., 2005).

Functioning in peer groups, following its rules, and maintaining close friendships are the hallmark of most adolescent peer relationships (Vitaro, Boivin, & Tremblay, 2007). Youth who display normative emotions and behaviors are likely to be accepted by peers. Consequently, they experience more satisfying friendships, greater self-esteem and self-worth, school success, positive emotions, and participation in social activities than rejected youths.

Chronic peer rejection compromises strong self attitudes and healthy peer relationships (Vitaro et al., 2007). Ladd and Troop-Gordon (2003) found chronic peer rejection to predict negative self-competence, depression, and anxiety, as well as juvenile delinquency. Other research has found chronic peer rejection to undermine social competence or the ability to understand the intentions, motivations, and desires of others and cooperate and work with others.

To cope with the psychological consequences of rejection, some children socially withdraw and face perpetual victimization while others (particularly boys) act out with aggression and rage. In either case, some vulnerable youth will reach a boiling point where lethal violence becomes an option for dealing with their pain, especially when combined with distorted social maps (Garbarino, 1999; Vitaro et al., 2007).

Distorted Social Maps

For maltreated and rejected children, an accumulation of negative social experiences often results in the development of distorted perceptions and behaviors or distorted social maps (i.e., they fail to see the positive, are hypersensitive to the negative, believe aggression is successful, and respond with aggression as a first response; Dodge, 1993). They develop distorted social maps which influence how and to what degree they will interact in the world around them. Dodge and colleagues (1997) found that maltreated and rejected children who developed distorted social maps are eight times more likely to develop conduct disorder than nonmaltreated boys.

In this section we illustrated that cumulative risk (e.g., maltreatment, abandonment, rejection, attachment difficulties, and distorted social maps) contributes to a child's aggressive behavior as well as conduct disorder. When added to this risk model, dehumanization and desensitization take boys from ordinary aggression to lethal violence (Garbarino, 1999).

WHEN ORDINARY AGGRESSION BECOMES LETHAL VIOLENCE

Moral development is nurtured through relationships with caring, supportive, and moral adults (Garbarino & Bronfenbrenner, 1976). Most children who develop relationships with moral adults learn to act upon the expectations, values, and principles modeled for them. Over time, a steady pattern of moral decision making and prosocial behavior protect them from engaging in aggressive behavior as well as lethal violence. However, when caring, supportive, and moral adults are absent, children and youth become vulnerable to immoral decision making and antisocial behavior, particularly under negative peer influence. Thus, moral leadership provides the foundation for constraining immoral lethal violence. In this context, dehumanization and desensitization comprise the second level of our continuum, lethal violence.

Dehumanization

Dehumanization involves psychologically, emotionally, and morally disconnecting from the worth of other human beings (Kelman, 1973). Training in a U.S. Army boot camp provides an interesting example of the social process of dehumanization (Lankford, 2009). An element of basic training that stands out for the first author (who is an army veteran) is the use of cadence (a song or chant), a powerful tool used for psychologically, emotionally, and morally separating soldiers from the worth of enemies as human beings, breaking down the moral restraint that prevents most civilians from killing, and indoctrinating recruits into the mores and norms of army culture (Britt, Adler, & Castro, 2005).

Two distinct lines of cadence stand out. The first begins with a prompt by a drill sergeant. He shouts, "Airborne ranger, airborne ranger, what did you do?" to which we replied in unison, "We killed the *women* and the *children, too*." The other includes the unison response, "...we pushed '*em* (Chinese or Koreans), we shoved '*em*, we threw '*em* in the river and laughed as *they* drowned. We don't need no *commies*..." What does this mean? The message is this: In combat it is U.S. soldiers against, "all enemies both foreign and domestic," including women and children, as well as those living in nations with different political beliefs. The torturing of Iraqi civilians (or enemy combatants) at Abu Ghraid illustrates the dehumanizing capacity of U.S. military training (Lankford, 2009).

Early experiences (e.g., trauma, abandonment, violence, and rejection) can be dehumanizing experiences. Suffering assists youth with emotionally disconnecting themselves from seeing others as human beings deserving of empathy and compassion; they develop a repertoire of emotional coping mechanisms to assist them with overcoming the moral restraint preventing lethal violence (Haslam, 2006; Kelman, 1973).

Desensitization

Desensitization refers to being exposed to stimuli that assists in overcoming the mores and norms preventing lethal violence. Desensitization is socially learned through interactions with role models, repetitive exposure, as well as stimulus-response (Grossman, 2001; Jensen, 2007). Exposure to early and ongoing trauma, as well as engaging in or witnessing violence, may teach youth to be brutal to others as well as desensitizing them to the effects associated with brutalization. Trauma and violence moderates the fear and moral restraint preventing lethal violence (Garbarino, 1999). Moreover, evidence suggests that repetitive exposure to violent television, as well as movies, may desensitize children and youth to lethal violence as well as facilitating the enjoyment of seeing brutal and/or lethal violence; violent video games may condition them to take pleasure in killing, reducing empathy, and facilitating their expertise with guns (Funk, Baldacci, Pasold, & Baumgardner, 2004; Huessman, 2007). Many youths are living in a socially toxic society that is brutalizing and desensitizing them to the human reality of lethal violence. To make matters worse, they are living in environments devoid of the adult moral leadership known to prevent lethal violence (Garbarino, 1999).

PREVENTION: MORAL AND SPIRITUAL DEVELOPMENT

Even among genetic and biological risk, most youth possess the potential to be as good as the social environment around them allows them to be. This highlights the issue of "social health," the presence of social and cultural "nutrients" that promote the moral and spiritual development of youth, particularly those who are vulnerable to lethal violence (Garbarino, 1999). This crisis in moral and spiritual development requires special attention (Garbarino & Bedard, 1996).

There are many strategies for preventing aggression, lethal violence, and school rampage shootings. Daniels et al. (2009) suggest that early attachment difficulties, parental abandonment, mental illness, personality disorders, child maltreatment, peer rejection, and the availability of guns are undermining the moral and spiritual development of children and youth. Mentoring is one method of assisting students found to be "at risk." The *Cooperative Learning Program* is another method.

Cooperative learning is a teaching method that nurtures the growth of empathy (Aronson, 2000). This highly structured teaching method brings students from diverse backgrounds and learning styles into 3–5 person teams. Each team is assigned a similar project. Within each team members are assigned individual tasks to complete. Thus, individual success is based on team success, and vice versa. Success comes by cooperating, listening and engaging other teammates. In addition to improving academic achievement *cooperative learning* has been shown to enhance empathy (Aronson, 2000; Cartledge & Johnson, 2004; Slavin & Cooper, 1999). By exposing students from diverse cultures, ethnicities, and learning abilities to each other, they learn a number of social and individual competencies shown to counter the aggression that may lead to lethal behavior (Cartledge & Johnson, 2004). They learn to respond, support, and engage each other with compassion. Through this they begin to like each other; some develop friendships. Aronson (2000) reports that these outcomes are likely due to students developing the capacity to take the perspective of other students. Moreover, peer support and encouragement, as well as group and individual success has been shown to enhance self-esteem.

Spiritual development activities can also be useful in an effort to prevent violence (Garbarino & Bedard, 1996). With adequate adult supervision, involving youths in care-giving activities (e.g. with plants, animals, and other dependent beings) can enhance a sense of meaningfulness.

For youth at risk for aggression and juvenile delinquency, community gardening projects like Portland Oregon's Cultivating Community have been shown to enhance a sense of meaningfulness (Boyd, Fontaine, & Ledue, 1999). Similarly, pet care-giving activities, like equine therapy, also have been shown to increase a sense of meaningfulness (McCormick & McCormick, 1997).

SUMMARY

In this chapter we illustrated the developmental pathways that lead to youth violence. The task of understanding the full range of youth violence is complicated by a host of risk factors, including, developmental history, biology and genetic vulnerability, attachment problems, trauma, historical trauma, gender, culture, and distorted social maps, as well as a host of other risk factors. Interventions on behalf of boys walking this continuum of lethal violence require addressing the crises of moral and spiritual development.

REFERENCES

Ainsworth, M. D., Blehar, M. C., Waters, E., & Wall, S. (1978). *Patterns of attachment: A psychological study of the strange situation.* Hillsdale, NJ: Erlbaum.

American Psychiatric Association (1994). *Diagnostic and statistical manual of mental disorders* (4th ed.). Washington, DC: Author.

American Psychiatric Association (2000). *Diagnostic and statistical manual of mental disorders, Fourth edition, Text revision (DSM-IV-TR).* Washington, DC: Author.

Aronson, E. (2000). *Nobody left to hate: Teaching compassion after Columbine.* New York: W.H. Freeman and Company.

Baker, W. L., Blakley, T. L., Perry, B. D., Pollard, R. A., & Vigilante, D. (1993). Childhood trauma, the neurobiology of adaptation, and "use-dependent" development of the brain: How "states" become "traits." *Infant Mental Health Journal, 16*, 271–286.

Bonanno, G. A. (2004). Loss, trauma, and human resilience: Have we underestimated the human capacity to thrive after extremely aversive events? *American Psychologist, 59*, 20–28.

Boyd, M., Fontaine, R., & Ledue, B. (1999). Cultivating community. Available at http://scholar.google.com/scholar?cluster=1221178487 3556380009&hl=en&as_sdt=400000

Byrd, J. (2007). Living my native life deadly: Red Lake, Ward Churchill, and the discourses of competing genocides. *American Indian Quarterly, 31*, 310–332.

Brave Heart, M. Y. H., & DeBruyn, L. M. (1998). The American Indian holocaust: Healing historical unresolved grief. Retrieved from www.uchsc.edu/ai.

Britt, T. W., Adler, A. B., & Castro, C. A. (2005). *Military life: The psychology of serving in peace and combat (Vol. 4): Military culture.* Westport, CT: Praeger Security International.

Bronfenbrenner, U. (1979). *The ecology of human development: Experiments by nature and design.* Cambridge, MA: Harvard.

Bronfenbrenner, U. (2005). *Making human beings human: Bioecological perspectives on human development.* Thousand Oaks, CA: Sage.

Cartledge, G., & Johnson, C. T. (2004). School violence and cultural sensitivity. In J. C. Conoley & A. P. Golstein (Eds.), School Violence Intervention: A practical handbook (2nd ed., pp. 441–482). New York: Guildford Press.

Caspi, A., McClay, J., Moffitt, T. E., Mill, J., Martin, J. et al., (2002). Role of genotype in the cycle of violence in maltreated children. *Science, 297*, 851–855.

Daniels, J., Volungis, A., Pshenishny, E., Winkler, A., Cramer, D., Bradley, M. et al. (2010). A qualitative investigation of averted school shooting rampages. *The Counseling Psychologist, 38*, 69–95.

Dodge, K. (1993). Social-cognitive mechanisms in the development of conduct disorder and depression. *Annual Review of Psychology, 44*, 559–584.

Dodge, K., & Sherrill, M. R. (2007). The interaction of nature and nurture in antisocial behavior. In D. J. Flannery, A. T. Vazsonyi, & I. D. Waldman (Eds.), *The Cambridge handbook of violent behavior and aggression* (pp. 215–244). New York: Cambridge University Press.

Dodge, K., Petit, G., & Bates, J. (1997). How the experience of early physical abuse leads children to become chronically aggressive. In D. Cicchetti, & S. L. Toth (Eds.), *Rochester symposium on developmental psychopathology: Trauma: Perspectives on theory, research, and intervention.* Rochester, NY: Univ. Rochester Press.

Farrington, D. P. (2007). Origins of violent behavior over the life span. In D. J. Flannery, A. T. Vazsonyi, & I. D. Waldman (Eds.), *The Cambridge handbook of violent behavior and aggression* (pp. 19–48). New York: Cambridge University Press.

Fergusson, D.M., Horwood, M.T., & Lynskey, L.J. (1996). Childhood sexual abuse and psychiatric disorder in young adulthood: II psychiatric outcomes of childhood sexual abuse. *Journal of the American Academy of Child and Adolescent Psychiatry, 35*, 1365–74

Finkelhor, D., Ormrod, R. K., & Turner, H. A. (2007). Poly-victimization: A neglected component in child victimization trauma. *Child Abuse & Neglect, 31*, 7–26.

Flanders, J., Leo, V., Paquette, D. Pihl, R., & Seguin, J. (2009). Rough-and-tumble play and the regulation of aggression: An observational study of father–child play dyads. *Aggressive Behavior, 35*, 285–295.

Foley, D., Eaves, L., Wormley, B., Silberg, J., Maes, H., Kuhn, J. et al. (2004). Childhood adversity, Monoamine Oxidase A genotype, and risk for conduct disorder. *Archives of Genetic Psychiatry, 61*, 738–744.

Frazzetto, G., Lorenzo, G.D., Carola, V., Proietti, L., Sokolowska, E., Siracusano, A. et al. (2007). Early trauma and increased risk for physical aggression during adulthood: The moderating role of MAOA Genotype. *PLoS ONE, 2*, 1–5.

Funk, J. B., Baldacci, H. B., Pasold, T., & Baumgardner, J. (2004). Violence exposure in real-life, video games, television, movies, and the internet: Is there desensitization? *Journal of Adolescence, 27*, 23–39.

Garbarino, J. (2008). *Children and the dark side of human experience: Confronting global realities and rethinking child development*. New York: Springer.

Garbarino, J. (1999). *Lost boys: Why our sons turn violent and how we can save them*. New York: The Free Press.

Garbarino, J. (*Personal communication, June 25, 2010*).

Garbarino, J., & Bedard, C. (1996). Spiritual challenges to children facing violent trauma. *Childhood, 3*, 467–478.

Garbarino, J. (2006). *See Jane hit: Why girls are turning more violent and what we can do about it*. London: The Free Press.

Garbarino, J., & Bronfenbrenner, U. (1976). The socialization of moral judgment and behavior in cross-cultural perspective. In T. Lickona (Ed.), *Moral development and behavior*. New York: Holt, Rinehart, and Winston.

Grossman, D. (2001). Trained to kill. *Professorenforum Journal, 2*, 1–8.

Haslam, N. (2006). Dehumanization: An integrative review. *Personality and Social Psychology Review, 10*, 252–264.

Hofstadter, R. (1970). America as a gun culture. *American Heritage, 21*, 4–11.

Huesmann, R. L. (2007). The impact of electronic media violence: Scientific theory and research. *Journal of Adolescent Health, 41*, S6–S13.

Jensen, G. F. (2007). Social learning and violent behavior. In D. J. Flannery, A. T. Vazsonyi & I. D. Waldman (Eds.), *The Cambridge handbook of violent behavior and aggression* (pp. 636–646). New York: Cambridge University Press.

Kelman, H. C. (1973). Violence without moral restraint: Reflections on the dehumanizing of victims and victimizers. *Journal of Social Issues, 29*, 25–61.

Ladd, G., & Troop-Gordon, W. (2003). The role of chronic peer difficulties in the development of children's psychological adjustment problems. *Child Development, 74*, 1344–67.

Langman, P. (2009). *Why kids kill: Inside the mind of school shooters.* New York: Palgrave Macmillan.

Lankford, A. (2009). Promoting aggression and violence at Abu Ghraib: The U.S. military's transformation of ordinary people into torturers. *Aggression and Violent Behavior, 14*, 388–395.

Loeber, R. (1982). The stability of antisocial and delinquent behavior. *Child Development, 52*, 1431–1446.

Main, M., & Solomon, J. (1990). Procedures for identifying infants as disorganized/disoriented during the Ainsworth Strange Situation. In M. T. Greenberg, D. Cicchetti, & E. M. Cummings (Eds.), *Attachment in the preschool years: Theory, research, and intervention* (pp. 121—160). Chicago: University of Chicago Press.

McCormick A, & McCormick M. (1997). Horse sense and the human heart: What horses can teach us about trust, bonding, creativity and spirituality. *Deerfield Beach, Florida: Health Communications, Inc.*

Minnesota Department of Health (2007). New report available on suicide in Beltrami County. Available at http://www.health.state.mn.us/news/pressrel/suicide091707.html.

Nader, K. (2010). Children and adolescent's exposure to the mass violence of war and terrorism: Role of the media. In Webb, N. B. (Ed.), *Helping Bereaved Children* (3rd ed., pp. 215–239). New York: Guilford.

National Fatherhood Initiative (2007). *Father facts* (5th ed.). National Fatherhood Initiative. Gathersburg, MD: Author.

Peterson, J. B., & Flanders, J. L. (2005). Play and the regulation of aggression. In R. E. Tremblay W. W. Hartup & J. Archer (Eds), *Developmental origins of aggression* (pp. 133–157). New York: Guilford Press.

Primary Documents in American History: The Bill of Rights. The Library of Congress. Retrieved from http://www.loc.gov/rr/program/bib/ourdocs/billofrights.html.

Rhoner, R., Khaleque, A., & Cournoyer, D. (2005). Parental acceptance-rejection: Theory, methods, cross-cultural evidence, and implications. *Ethos, 33*, 299–334.

Rutter, M. (1987). Continuities and discontinuities from infancy. In J. Osofsky (Ed.), *Handbook of infant development* (2d ed., pp. 1256–1296). New York: Wiley.

Rutter, M. (1989). Pathways from childhood to adult life. *Journal of Child Psychology and Psychiatry, 30,* 23–51.

Rutter, M., Moffitt, T., & Caspi, A. (2006). Gene-environment interplay and psychopathology: Multiple varieties but real effects. *Journal of Child Psychology and Psychiatry, 47,* 226–261.

Sameroff, A., Seifer, R., Baldwin, A., & Baldwin, C. (1993). Stability of intelligence from pre-school to adolescence: The influence of social and family risk factors. *Child Development, 64,* 80–97.

Sameroff, A., Seifer, R., Barocas, R., Zax, M., & Greenspan, S. (1987). Intelligence quotient scores of 4-year-old children: Social environmental risk factors. *Pediatrics, 79,* 343–350.

Slavin, R. E., & Cooper, R. (1999). Improving intergroup relations: Lessons learned from cooperative learning programs. *Journal of Social Issues, 55,* 647–663.

Sroufe, L. A., Egeland, B., Carlson, E. A., & Collins, W. A. (2005). *The development of the person: The Minnesota study of risk and adaptation from birth to adulthood.* New York: Guilford Press.

Thurman, P. J. (*Personal communication, June 5, 2010*).

Tolan, P. (1996). How resilient is the concept of resilience? *Community Psychologist, 4,* 12–15.

U.S. Department of Health and Human Services. (2001). Youth violence: a report of the surgeon general. Rockville, MD: U.S. Department of Health and Human Services.

van IJzendoorn, M. H., Euser, E. M., Prinzie, P., Juffer, F., & Bakermans-Kranenburg, M. J. (2009). Elevated risk of child maltreatment in families with stepparents but not with adoptive parents. *Child Maltreatment, 14,* 369–375.

Vitaro, F., Boivin, M., & Tremblay, R. E. (2007). Peers and violence: A two-sided developmental perspective. In D. J. Flannery, A. T. Vazsonyi, & I. D. Waldman (Eds.), *The Cambridge handbook of violent behavior and aggression* (pp. 361–387). New York: Cambridge University Press.

Vygotsky, L. S. (1978). *Mind and society: The development of higher psychological processes.* Cambridge, MA: Harvard University Press.

Watson, M. W., Fischer, K. W., Andreas, J. B., & Smith, K. W. (2004). Pathways to aggression in children and adolescents. *Harvard Educational Review, 74,* 404–430.

Werner, E. E. (2000). Protective factors and individual resilience. In R. Meisells & J. Shonkoff (Eds.), *Handbook of early intervention* (2nd ed., pp. 115–132). New York: Cambridge.

Whitbeck, L. B., Adams, G. W., Hoyt, D. R., & Chen, X. (2004). Conceptualizing and measuring historical trauma among American Indian people. *American Journal of Community Psychology, 33,* 119–130.

Early Preventive Interventions

CHAPTER 5

Teaching Coping and Social Skills to Elementary School Children

Christine Mello and Kathleen Nader

In the dynamic interplay between person and environment, coping skills are an important factor in adaptational outcomes such as subjective well being, social functioning, and physical and emotional health (Lazarus & Folkman, 1987). Deficits in social skills and social competence, as well as in coping and adaptability, can lead to adjustment problems and behavioral disorders in childhood, adolescence, and adulthood (Elliott & Gresham, 1993; Kolbe, Collins, Cortese, 1997; Zins & Wagner, 1997, Spence, 2003). The Safe School Initiative (Vossekuil, Fein, Reddy, Borum, Modzeleski, 2002) examined 37 incidents of targeted school violence and, while they did not find any specific profile that fit a student likely to act out in this manner, they did find that most of the students had been victims of bullying, persecution, or injury by others prior to the attack. Although most had not received formal mental health evaluations they did exhibit suicidal attempts or thoughts, and had difficulty coping with significant losses or personal failure (Vossekuil et al., 2002, Leary, Kowalski, Smith, Phillips, 2003). The findings of the Safe School Initiative have prompted schools to look at social skills and coping skills as areas to address within the school curriculum in order to provide a safer school environment.

As discussed in other chapters, issues such as personality, attachment, and peer relationships influence youth's developing skills, sometimes in a complex manner. For example, children characterized by behavioral inhibition or shyness or by negative emotionality may be excluded by their peers, which in turn may exacerbate these qualities and deter the development of effective social and coping skills (Miller & Coll, 2007). Lack of social and coping skills may add to withdrawal and/or negativity.

Interventions are available to assist youth in the development of these skills. As will be discussed, the most effective programs, while sometimes more difficult to implement, are those that are implemented school-wide over long periods of time. Long-term coordinated efforts that involve parents are more effective than short-term isolated efforts (Cohen, 2006; Conoley & Goldstein, 2004; Zins, Weissberg, Wang, Walberg, 2004).

Research examining the prevalence of risk factors in children suggests that children's aggressive and oppositional behaviors are starting earlier and escalating in intensity (Patterson, Capaldi, & Bank, 1991; Snyder, 2001; Webster-Stratton & Reid, 2010). Some problems (e.g., aggressive behavior and reading difficulties) during early elementary school years are risk factors for adolescent problem behaviors (e.g., delinquency, academic failure, and substance use) (Barrera et al., 2002). Among the important areas of children's social–emotional development are (a) emotional self-regulation (e.g., identification and management of strong emotions such as anger, excitement, and frustration); (b) social competence (e.g., prosocial problem solving, sharing, helping, cooperation, positive peer interactions); and (c) compliance to school rules and cooperation with adults' requests (Webster-Stratton & Reid, 2010). A number of training programs combine coping, social, school, and/or self-control skills in an effort to reduce risk factors and strengthen protective factors associated with children's social emotional development and school success. Some of these programs are described.

RISK FACTORS AND TARGETS OF INTERVENTION

Learning social and coping skills begins with the parent–child relationship. Initially through interactively regulating the infant's positive and negative states and then through ongoing caregiver-child transactions, the sensitive parent directly influences development of the child's brain and stress response system (Nader, 2008; Schore, 2003; Siegel, 1999). Accordingly, a number of family risks factors reflect parental/family influence on children's emotional, behavioral, and cognitive difficulties. Among them are inconsistent and harsh discipline, low parental monitoring of children, low parental school involvement, and poor cognitive stimulation at home, as well as poverty, parent's low education, high family stress or isolation, single-parent family status, low English proficiency, marital discord or abuse, maternal depression, or drug abuse (Hawkins, Catalano, & Miller, 1992; Snyder, Schrepferman, & St. Peter, 1997; Webster-Stratton & Reid, 2010). School environmental factors such as exclusion, failure or lack of support, teacher dislike, and/or poor classroom management have been identified in association with child behavior problems (Birch & Ladd,

1997; Webster-Stratton & Reid, 2010). For example, social exclusion may be a result of or may contribute to depression, aggression, and/or association with deviant peers (Dodge, Coie, Pettit, & Price, 1990; Patterson, Reid, & Dishion, 1992). Child factors such as temperamental negative emotionality, disruptive disorders, impulsivity, language and academic delays, and poor social-cognitive skills contribute to poor emotional regulation (Galen & Underwood, 1997), compliance problems, and aggressive peer interactions (Dodge & Price, 1994).

COPING SKILLS

Coping strategies or effective habituated reactions to stress or challenge are important to all aspects of life, including situations of mild and severe stress (Nader, 2008). They influence social relationships as well as personal accomplishments. According to Compas (1998), coping is a subset of the ways that individuals respond to stress, including effortful and volitional responses and involuntary responses. The latter may be learned and repeatedly practiced reactions or may reflect aspects of temperament.

Whether human relationships are harmful or beneficial depends, on the one hand, on social and cultural environmental conditions and, on the other hand, on personal characteristics such as personality, skills, sense of control, trust, and self-esteem. In situations of stress or when there are obstacles to goals, individuals may appraise harm, threat, and challenge (the potential for mastery; primary appraisal; Lazarus & Folkman, 1987). In addition, individuals evaluate whether the situation can be changed, must be accepted, requires additional information, or requires self-regulation (e.g., holding oneself back) (secondary appraisal). When there is confidence in the ability to cope with a situation and/or to prevent harm or other detrimental outcomes, the sense of threat is likely to be minimal or absent. Moreover, emotional reaction is unlikely if a person has no stake in an encounter (i.e., considers it irrelevant to her or his well-being). Lazarus and Folkman suggest that the intensity and quality of emotion is likely to vary with what and how much is at stake. As Lazarus and Folkman (1987) put it, coping may "change the terms of the actual troubled person–environment relationship" (problem-focused coping) or "regulate distress" (emotion-focused coping) (p. 147).

Interventions for Coping Skills

Youth coping methods have been categorized in a number of overlapping ways (e.g., problem-solving versus emotion-focused; active versus

avoidance coping). The methods of coping used are often situation dependent and vary somewhat by age and gender. For example, individuals are
more likely to seek social support when a loved one's well-being is threatened than when personal esteem is at stake (Lazarus & Folkman, 1987).
Evidence suggests that problem solving and confrontive coping are used
more in situations seen as changeable and that distancing and avoidance-
focused coping are used more in situations deemed necessary to accept.
When self-esteem is threatened, confrontive or avoidance strategies are
more likely than planning or support seeking. Youth use different methods of coping, depending on their emotional states and the circumstances
(Gilbert & Morawski, 2005). Gilbert and Morawski found that rural adolescents overused avoidant coping when angry, for example. Boys rarely
used approach (engagement) coping strategies. Girls more often sought
guidance than boys. By middle childhood, ages 6 to 10, youth used emotion-focused (disengagement), problem-focused (engagement), and support-seeking coping methods. It is likely that children use combinations
of methods rather than individual methods to cope with specific evoked
emotions (Stallard, Velleman, Langsford & Baldwin, 2001). Youth may
use both withdrawal and distraction when feeling angry, for example.

Coping methods include behavioral responses (e.g., escape, avoidance, fight) and cognitive processing responses (e.g., problem solving,
attributions, anticipatory biases, denial, intellectualization) (Lazarus &
Folkman, 1987; Nader, 2008). When youth think of themselves as competent at coping, they are more likely to try known skills and to develop
new ones (Delaney, 2006). Folkman and colleagues assess eight coping
subscales: confrontational coping (e.g., stand one's ground, fight), distancing (e.g., act as if nothing happened), self-control (e.g., stop oneself
from expressing feelings), support seeking (e.g., talk to someone; accept
sympathy), accept responsibility (e.g., criticize or lecture oneself), avoidance (e.g., wish it would be over), problem solving (e.g., carry out a plan
of action), and positive appraisal or reappraisal (e.g., renewed faith, find
the positive in the situation, learn from it) (Lazarus and Folkman, 1987).

Some of the emotion-focused coping methods (i.e., methods of disengagement) that children may use are avoidance, attention shifting,
responding with a state of confusion, or distraction (Eisenberg, Spinard,
& Smith, 2004 cited in Delaney, 2006). Evidence suggests youth who
rely primarily on emotion-focused coping methods are at greater risk
for internalizing symptoms (e.g., anxiety, depression; Tolan, Gorman-
Smith, Henry, Chung, & Hunt, 2002). The nature and outcomes of different types of coping can be more complex than some studies suggest.
Eisenberg, Fabes, and Guthrie (1997) describe behavioral regulation coping as types of emotion-focused coping that may be engaging or disen-
gaging: venting emotions, crying, yelling, aggression, hostility, self-injury,

and confrontation. In these instances, the child may be attempting to deal with overwhelming emotions (to gain control) rather than trying to change aspects of the situation and rather than being out of control. Additionally, although inactive and emotion-focused coping have often been associated with negative outcomes such as severity of PTSD for trauma-exposed youth (Lengua, Long, & Meltzoff, 2006) or internalizing symptoms (Tolan et al., 2002), outcomes are influenced by a number of factors. For example, after 9/11, engaging in constructive activities such as patriotic gestures or volunteer efforts (active coping) was associated with increased child-reported symptoms for some youth (Phillips, Prince, & Schiebelhut, 2004). Moreover, methods such as distraction and attention shifting can be a part of effective behavioral self-regulation strategies to control, for example, aggressive impulses, appetite, and negative affect (see Ayduk, Mischel, & Downey, 2002 for a summary of findings).

Coping may vary with a child's nature or disorder. Some research has found a positive correlation between confrontive coping and psychological symptoms and a negative correlation between problem solving coping and psychological symptoms (Lazarus & Folkman, 1987). Some evidence suggests that depressed individuals use more confrontive, self-control, and avoidance coping. That is, they accepted more responsibility (or self-blame) and reacted with more anger/disgust and worry/fear. Avoidant coping has been associated with poor psychosocial adjustment (e.g., depression, distress, and PTSD; Min, Farkas, Minnes, & Singer, 2007) and with complicated grief (Boelen, van den Hout, & van den Bout, 2006; Melhem et al., in press).

There are many programs available to teach coping and social skills (Table 5.1). In the following section, one well-researched program to teach coping and social skills, The Incredible Years, is described. This and some of the programs that follow the discussion of social skills are designed to train teachers and parents to facilitate the development of children's coping and other skills in order to promote more positive overall adjustment.

THE INCREDIBLE YEARS

The Incredible Years (IY) Parent, Teacher and Child Training curricula (www.incredibleyears.com) are research-based programs proven effective for reducing children's aggression and behavior problems, and increasing social competence at home and at school (Abboud, 2005; Drugli, Larsson, & Clifford, 2007). The programs, designed to train parents and teachers to promote children's emotional, social, and academic competence, as well as to prevent, reduce, and treat aggression

TABLE 5.1   Programs for Coping and Social Skills Training

Topics Taught for Teachers	Programs That Teach the Topic[a]					
Classroom management	IY					
Dealing with misbehavior	IY					
Promoting emotional regulation	IY	StR				
Preventing negative reputations	IY					
Preventing bullying	IY	StR				
Promoting positive relationships with difficult students	IY	StR				
Coaching strategies to strengthen students social skills	IY	StR				
Collaborative problem-solving	IY	StR				
For students						
School rules	IY			SSI		
Academic achievement	IY			SSI		
Labeling feelings	IY		SkillS		SKids	2ndS
Problem-solving	IY	StR	SkillS		SKids	2ndS
Anger and/or emotion management	IY	StR	SkillS	SSI	SKids	2ndS
Stress and/or anxiety management	IY		SkillS	SSI	SKids	2ndS
Friendliness/friendship	IY	StR	SkillS	SSI		
Listening			SkillS	SSI		
Talking with friends	IY		SkillS	SSI		
Other social life		StR	SkillS			
Empathy		StR		SSI	SKids	2ndS
Planning		StR			SKids	2ndS

[a] 2ndS = Second Step; SKids = Strong Kids; SkillS = Skillstreaming; SSI = Social Skills Intervention; IY = Incredible Years (also includes a parent-training module). StR = *Steps to Respect*. See also Table 7.1 in Chapter 7. See Chapter 8 for a bullying prevention program that includes training for all school staff.

and emotional problems in young children, are available in versions for ages 0 to 11 months, 1 to 3, 3 to 6, 6 to 8, and 9 to 13. Although they are most effective when used in combination, the parent, teacher, and child versions can be used separately. The IY Training programs have been used in schools in the United States among diverse cultural groups and internationally (Baker-Henningham, Walker, Powell, & Gardner, 2009; Barrera et al., 2002; Webster-Stratton, 2009).

The IY programs have been widely endorsed for their prevention/ intervention efficacy by such review groups as the Office for Juvenile Justice and Delinquency Prevention (Webster-Stratton & Herman, 2009). The 12 to 20 sessions (2 hours each) for parent training have been associated with better parent–child interactions, reduced child-conduct problems at home and school, and reduced reliance on critical or violent forms of discipline (Webster-Stratton, 2009; Webster-Stratton & Reid, 2010). The IY teacher training includes modules on partnering with parents, developing positive relationships with children, preventing and reducing inappropriate behavior and teaching social and emotional skills (Baker-Henningham et al., 2009). The program uses videotape modeling, role-play, and discussions. Teachers are assigned tasks, such as developing individual behavior plans, using specific praise to promote a targeted behavior, and setting clear classroom rules and routines. Teachers are generally trained 1 day per month for 6 or 7 days of training. Training targets effective classroom management strategies for dealing with misbehavior, preventing negative reputations and bullying, promoting positive relationships with difficult students, as well as employing coaching strategies to strengthen students social skills, friendships, and emotional regulation in the classroom, playground, bus, and lunchroom (Webster-Stratton & Herman, 2009). It assists teachers' use of collaborative problem-solving processes and positive communication with parents (e.g., the importance of positive home communication, home visits, and successful parent conferences and coordinated behavior plans).

The IY Dina Dinosaur Classroom Curriculum (Webster-Stratton, 2000) consists of seven units to be delivered over a school year: (a) learning school rules; (b) learning how to do your best in school; (c) understanding and detecting feelings; (d) problem-solving skills; (e) anger and stress management; (f) learning how to be friendly; and (g) learning how to talk with friends. Lessons consist of a 15 to 20 minute circle discussion followed by a 20-minute group activity (Webster-Stratton & Reid, 2010). Video vignettes, stories, songs, art projects, group games, child-sized puppets, colorful cue cards, structured play sessions, Dinosaur homework activity books, and role-play of situations faced in young children's daily lives allow children to practice the skills learned. Children actively participate in identifying and solving problems and helping each other learn new skills. Training can be provided to small groups of children outside of the classroom or as a classroom training sequence.

Research

Parenting programs have proven effective in reducing early onset-conduct problems (Brestan & Eyberg, 1998; Taylor & Biglan, 1998) and reducing conduct and comorbid attention problems (Hartman, Stage,

& Webster-Stratton, 2003). Without the school-based interventions, evidence suggests that a number of children continue to have relationship, academic, and social problems at school (Webster-Stratton, 1990; Webster-Stratton & Reid, 2010). Research has demonstrated that trained teachers use fewer inappropriate and critical discipline strategies and are more nurturing than control teachers. After treatment, children in five intervention conditions (parent only, child only, parent + teacher, child + teacher, parent + child + teacher training) engaged in fewer aggressive and noncompliant behaviors in the classroom, and they demonstrated higher levels of school readiness (on-task, cooperative, attentive) than control children (Webster-Stratton, Hollinsworth & Kolpacoff, 1989; Webster-Stratton & Reid, 2010). By the 2-year follow up, evidence suggested that the addition of teacher training to either the parent or child treatment conditions or combining child and parent training enhanced school and long-term outcomes. Immediately after 20 to 22 weekly IY treatment programs and 1 and 2 years later, 4- to 7-year-old children had reductions in observed aggressive behaviors and increases in observed prosocial behavior, compared to a control group (Webster-Stratton & Hammond, 1997; Webster-Stratton, Reid & Hammond, 2004). For Head Start and elementary school children, findings suggest that the training has small-to-moderate effects on children with average-range baseline behavior, but large effects on youth with high pre-training levels of conduct problems (Webster-Stratton, Reid, & Stoolmiller, 2008).

Applied by counselors, therapists, or early childhood specialists and teachers experienced in treating children with conduct problems, the IY training programs have proven effective for individuals or groups of children with comorbid disorders (e.g., combinations of Oppositional Defiant Disorder, Attention Deficit Disorder, developmental delay, or autism with conduct or learning problems) or with language and reading problems (McIntyre, 2008; Webster-Stratton & Reid, 2008). Preliminary positive results have been found for children whose parents completed a hybrid model parent training offered via a computer- and web-based delivery system with professional intervention via phone, electronic messages, and home visits (Taylor et al., 2008). Baker-Henningham et al. (2009) applied the teacher training as well as 14 classroom sessions using four of the seven units in Jamaican schools. In contrast to matched schools that did not receive the training, whose classroom climate declined across the year, training recipients demonstrated increased positive and reduced negative teacher behaviors, increases in teacher warmth, and in their promotion of children's social and emotional skills. In addition, ratings of children showed increases in appropriate classroom behaviors and in interest and enthusiasm in class activities.

SOCIAL SKILLS

Social skills have been defined as socially acceptable learned behaviors that facilitate interactions with others in ways that elicit positive responses and avoid negative responses (Gresham & Elliott, 1984). Social skills begin to develop shortly after birth and continue to be a focus of early childhood development during preschool and early elementary school years. The teaching of social skills within the classroom setting is not something new; social skills development has long been an important outcome of schooling. Research has shown that children with social skills deficits are at risk for social–emotional difficulties and poor academic performance (Parker & Asher, 1987). Social skills development has also been an area of interest when looking at violence in schools and the social adjustment of the students (Vossekuil et al., 2002). Cohen (2006) notes that the fields of risk prevention, mental health, character education, and social emotional learning all suggest that there is a need to promote social skills in order to create safe caring and responsive schools. In addition to recognizing the importance of social skills development, changes in 21st century standards for education are emphasizing the role of schools in facilitating the development of critical thinking skills and problem-solving skills (Ross, Powell, & Elias, 2002).

Educational programs for social skills interventions emphasize (a) teaching children social skills in the classroom curriculum (Elliot & Gresham, 1991; McGinnis & Goldstein, 1997; Spence, 2003), (b) social emotional learning, including improving children's emotional intelligence (Merrell, 2010; Chapter 7), and (c) methods to decrease violence in our schools, improving children's prosocial behaviors (Beland, 1992). Some examples of programs that focus on each of these areas of social skills interventions are reviewed in the following sections.

Interventions for Social Skills

The first two programs discussed in this section are programs that were developed to address deficits in behaviors related to social skills. The programs are implemented in classrooms or small groups by teachers or other school professionals (e.g., school psychologists, counselors). Each program outlines a variety of skills to be taught using the techniques of modeling, practice (role-play or discussion), and a discussion of outcomes. The programs were influenced by Albert Bandura's social-learning theory and tenets of B. F. Skinner's operant learning methods. The third program described in this section, The Responsive Classroom, provides a framework for implementing social skills lessons in a school-wide intervention focused on improving academic achievement while working on improving social skills. Methods of teaching empathy and self-control are elaborated in Chapters 7 and 8.

Skillstreaming

One of the first social skills training programs was developed in the early 1970s by Dr. Arnold Goldstein and was initially designed for low-income adults deficient in social skills. Based on Goldstein's earlier work, *Skillstreaming* (Goldstein, 1999; McGinnis & Goldstein, 2003) has been adapted for preschool and elementary school children (McGinnis & Goldstein, 1997) and adolescents (Goldstein, McGinnis, Sprafkin, Gershaw, & Klein, 1997). *Skillstreaming* is also a skills deficits program. This model allows for teachers to focus on proactive instruction rather than reacting to problem behaviors. That is, it focuses on positive reinforcement of desired behaviors rather than providing negative reinforcement for problem behaviors. The students are encouraged to develop the skills rather than reprimanded for inappropriate behaviors. The *Skillstreaming* program uses the processes of modeling, behavioral rehearsal, and social reinforcement to teach specific social skills.

The *Skillstreaming* curriculum provides teachers with 40 prosocial skills divided into six skills groups. Some examples of the behaviors for elementary students in the *Skillstreaming* program include *classroom survival skills* (e.g., listening, asking for help, making corrections), *friendship-making skills* (e.g., introducing yourself, beginning a conversation, playing a game, sharing), *skills for dealing with feelings* (e.g., knowing your feelings, recognizing another's feelings, dealing with anger), *skill alternative to aggression* (e.g., using self-control, problem solving, accepting consequences), and *skills for dealing with stress* (e.g., making a complaint, dealing with losing, reacting to failure, relaxing) (McGinnis & Goldstein, 1997).

Skillstreaming actively engages children in learning through the use of role playing and practice. During the lessons, teachers facilitate discussion about a particular behavior, assist students with a scenario to model, and allow feedback from other students to help reinforce the behaviors being learned. Students are encouraged to compliment other students when they have done well. In addition, if a student is having difficulty with responding in a prosocial manner during a role-play, the teacher is allowed to prompt and encourage a response that everyone can learn from. The steps to follow for a *Skillstreaming* lessons are (a) *define the skill*, (b) *model the skills*, (c) *establish student skill need*, (d) *select the first role player*, (e) *set up the role play*, (f) *conduct the role play*, (g) *provide performance feedback*, (h) *assign skill homework*, and (i) *select the next role player* (McGinnis & Goldstein, 1997).

Research. Literature supports the use of *Skillstreaming* in small groups, classrooms and as part of a school-wide program to teach social skills (Evans & Stefanou, 2009; Leonardi, Roberts & Wasoka, 2001; McGinnis & Goldstein, 2003; Niehues, 2006). In a 6-week intervention with middle-school-aged youth, Evans & Stefanou (2009) found significant increases in teacher's ratings of student cooperation, but no achievement improvements. This study provides evidence that brief, targeted interventions may have positive effects on some aspects of social skills for at-risk students. Leonardi et al. (2001) found a substantial reduction in school disciplinary actions after implementing the *Skillstreaming* program with 12 elementary students diagnosed with emotional and/or behavior disorders. Niehues (2006) found improvement in 25 preschool children's level of mastery of social skills after a two-week intervention with *Skillstreaming*. In addition to providing direct instruction in prosocial skills the authors discuss how their program can be used in conjunction with school discipline policies to deal with bullying (McGinnis & Goldstein, 2003).

Social Skills Intervention Program

The *Social Skills Intervention* (SSI) program developed by Elliot & Gresham (1991) uses intervention techniques of modeling, role-playing, behavior rehearsal, and reinforcement in order to teach 43 social skills that parents and teachers have identified as important. Targeted social skills fall into five domains: *cooperation, assertion, responsibility, empathy,* and *self-control* (acronym: CARES). Some of the CARES behaviors are: cooperation skills—helping others, complying with rules and directions; assertion skills—asking others for information, responding to the actions of others; responsibility skills—demonstrating the ability to communicate with adults and to care for property; empathy skills—showing concern and respect for others' feelings and viewpoints; self-control skills—responding appropriately to teasing, and compromising (Elliot & Gresham, 1991). This program is designed to be used in small groups with a role-playing format that features five phases: *Tell, Show, Do, Follow Through and Practice,* and *Generalization.* The first three phases occur within the group lessons, while the follow-through and generalization are reinforced outside of the lesson in the classroom, on the playground, or at home (Elliot & Gresham, 1991). The *Social Skills Rating System* is available to assess skills (Gresham & Elliott, 1990).

Research. Research indicates that implementing social skills training improves children's social behavior (Elliot & Gresham, 1993).

Meta-analyses of studies of social skills interventions demonstrate improvement in social and academic skills, although the effect sizes are small (Evans, Axelrod, Sapia, 2000; Quinn, Kavale, Mathur, Rutherford, Forness, 1999). Programs that focus on specific skills have a greater impact on student outcomes than more global interventions (Quinn et al., 1999). Activities to increase generalization produce more significant results (Evans et al., 2000).

Responsive Classroom

The *Responsive Classroom* (Charney, 1993, 2002) is a school-wide prevention and intervention program that incorporates the constructs of social skills, academic enablers, and social support. The Responsive Classroom (Charney, 2002; Elliot, Malecki, Demaray, 2001) is an instructional approach that integrates the teaching of social and academic skills as part of everyday school life. There are six components: morning meeting, classroom organization, rules and logical consequences, guided discovery, academic choice time, and assessment and reporting. Charney (1993, 2002) outlines how to implement the program in a classroom setting, from setting up classroom rules to approaching problem solving and power struggles. The Responsive Classroom program uses the same components of the SSI program (CARES; Elliott & Gresham, 1991) to teach social skills within the context of the daily classroom environment (Horsch, Chen, & Nelson, 1999).

Research. Although this type of school-wide intervention is more difficult to implement than a discrete skill curriculum, positive educational outcomes have been reported (Elliott et al., 2001). Elliot (1995) found conclusive evidence of the positive effects of implementing the Responsive Classroom approach, including cooperation and assertion behaviors. In a study of teachers' beliefs and attitudes (Rimm-Kaufman & Sawyer, 2004), teachers using the Responsive Classroom program were more likely to report a positive attitude toward teaching. Rimm-Kaufman & Chiu (2007) found improvements in achievement (math and reading scores), greater closeness between children, better prosocial skills, more assertiveness, and less fearfulness in classes that used the Responsive Classroom approach.

Interventions for Social Emotional Learning and Violence Prevention

The programs that focus on social emotional learning have followed from the work of Salovey and Mayer (1990) and Daniel Goleman (1995) and the concept of emotional intelligence or EQ. Conceptually, EQ is comprised of five domains: knowing one's emotions, managing one's emotions, motivating oneself, recognizing emotions of others, and effectively using social skills when interacting with others (Goleman, 1995; Mayer & Salovey, 1997; Salovey & Mayer, 1990). Following events of violence in schools, the use of social emotional learning (SEL) and character education programs (Devine & Cohen, 2007) has been associated with academic performance (Zins et al., 2004) and with antibullying (Ragozzino & O'Brien, 2009).

As will be described in Chapter 8, the Collaborative for Academic, Social and Emotional Learning (CASEL) is an organization that was established to promote SEL as an essential part of the education system from preschool through high school (Payton et al., 2008; CASEL website: http://casel.org). The work of CASEL has identified five core categories of social and emotional skills: self-awareness, self-management, social awareness, relationship skills, and responsible decision-making. While CASEL does not promote any one SEL program, many programs are referenced on their website with intervention resources, research results, and testimonials regarding implementing programs.

Studies conducted during the past few decades indicate that SEL programming for elementary and middle school students is a very promising approach to improving skills, reducing problem behaviors, promoting positive adjustment, and enhancing academic performance (Zins et al., 2004). A meta-analysis of research (Payton, et. al. 2008) indicates that SEL programs that are most effective include four recommended practices for skill training: planned activities to develop skills sequentially, active learning such as role play or behavioral rehearsal with feedback, sufficient classroom time devoted to development of social and emotional skills, and explicit targeting of social emotional skills. Two of the many SEL programs are discussed here.

Strong Kids

The Strong Kids program was developed under the direction of Ken Merrell, PhD, and as a result of the work of the Oregon Resiliency Project (founded in 2001) (Merrell, Juskelis, Tran, & Buchanan, 2008). The Strong Kids programs are semiscripted SEL prevention and early intervention curricula (Merrell et al., 2008). The program is available in four parts, depending on the ages targeted: Strong Start is for use with kindergarten through second grade (Merrell, Parisi, & Whitcomb, 2007); the Strong Kids curricula are separated for grades 3 to 5 and grades 6 to 8 (Merrell, Carrizales, Feuerborn, Gueldner, & Tran, 2007a, 2007b);

and the Strong Teens curriculum is available for grades 9 to 12 (Merrell, Carrizales, Feuerborn, Gueldner, & Tran, 2007c). This program is designed to be used with a wide range of students, from high-functioning to at-risk or emotionally behaviorally disordered youth, and can be applied in a variety of settings, including small groups or classrooms.

The Strong Kids website (http://strongkids.uoregon.edu) describes the 12 lessons that are part of each curriculum. The lessons take 45 to 55 minutes each to teach, and may be taught by a teacher or other school professional (i.e., school psychologist or counselor). The lessons of this program are similar to those in the Skillstreaming and SSI programs, including lessons that focus on identifying, understanding, and expressing feelings, developing empathy for others, and improving problem solving skills. In addition to these skills, the Strong Kids program has lessons that focus on improving adaptive behaviors and setting goals for increasing activities as well as cognitive restructuring (to change faulty beliefs) and improving positive thinking. (Merrell et al., 2008; Strong Kids website).The lessons of the program are designed to teach social and emotional skills, promote resilience, strengthen assets, and increase coping skills of children. Each of the Strong Kids lessons provides for review of prior concepts, instruction in the new concept, corrective feedback, generalization activities, and student handouts/worksheets (Merrell et al., 2008).

Research. Studies have demonstrated the positive impact of the *Strong Kids* program across a variety of populations (Merrell et al., 2008; Merrell, 2010). A pilot study with elementary and middle school students showed increases in student's knowledge of social-emotional concepts and effective coping strategies after receiving 1-hour lessons over a 12-week period (Merrell et al., 2008). The Strong Start program demonstrated gains in prosocial behavior and decreases in internalizing behaviors based on parent and teacher ratings with 67 kindergarten students (Kramer, Caldarella, Christensen, & Shatzer, 2010), and with 26 second graders (Caldarella, Christensen, Kramer, & Kronmiller, 2009). A comprehensive review of studies (Merrell, 2010) indicates that the Strong Kids program has resulted in positive outcomes for children, including gains in social–emotional competence and decreases in problem behaviors.

SECOND STEP PROGRAM

The Second Step program (Beland, 1992) is a violence prevention curriculum that is focused on teaching social emotional skills to increase children's levels of social competence and to reduce impulsive and aggressive behavior. This is a classroom-based curriculum for preschool through junior high students. Like other social skills lessons, Second Step uses modeling, rehearsal, role-play, and verbal mediation to assist students with gaining new skills.

There are three units in the curriculum: empathy, social problem solving, and anger management. Lessons on empathy and perspective taking necessarily precede subsequent lessons on impulse control, social problem solving, and anger management (Duffell, Beland, & Frey, 2006). In the empathy lessons, students learn to identify emotional cues by viewing photographs of children displaying specific facial cues indicating different emotional states. The children then practice detecting and displaying emotions through role-play activities. In the problem-solving lessons, students are taught a five-step process to identify the problem, brainstorm solutions, evaluate solutions, select a plan, and try it. They then evaluate the solution. In the anger management lessons, students learn to identify and recognize physical anger cues, use positive self-statements, and practice strategies to calm down (Beland, 1992).

Research. Studies of the Second Step program support the efficacy of the program in improving social skills and reducing aggression (Duffell et al., 2006; Frey, Hirschstein, & Guzzo, 2000). After participating in the Second Step program, students were more likely to resolve conflicts without adult intervention (Duffell et al., 2006). After implementation of the Second Step curriculum, Edwards, Hunt, Meyers, Grogg, and Jarrett (2005) reported students' improved problem-solving and respectful and cooperative behaviors. Grossman et al., 1997 found reduced aggression and increased friendly, prosocial behavior. In a longitudinal study in a rural elementary school (grades 3–6), over the course of a year, Taub (2001) also found the Second Step program effectively improved prosocial behaviors and increased social competence.

CONCLUSIONS

Research has demonstrated that coping and social skills are important factors in child development and social–emotional adjustment (Lazarus & Folkman, 1987; Elliott & Gresham, 1993). New mandates in schools are requiring that curricula include instruction in social skills, character education, or antibullying curriculum. We have highlighted some of the programs developed to teach coping and social skills that may be utilized by schools to address some of these new mandates. Research suggests that the best results for programs that teach these skills are sustained when programs are implemented school-wide and include components that involve families. This poses a challenge in implementing programs for long periods as gains may not be seen in the short-term.

DuPaul (2003) suggests in the interest of gaining administrative support that, in addition to social skills, schools look at academic measures as another indicator of positive gains in order to keep schools vested in implementing these programs.

There is a great deal of overlap in the programs that focus on coping skill and social skill learning. The two sets of skills are interrelated. For example, coping skills such as problem solving, self-regulation (behavioral, emotional, and stress management), and thought management are important to social interactions as well as to dealing with situations of stress. Friendliness, empathy, and other interpersonal skills may make it more likely that one will receive social support. Social support has been associated with better outcomes for stressful experiences, such as traumatic stress and grief. Conflict resolution may be considered a way of coping with a stressful situation and/or a social skill.

Both coping and social skills have been issues of concern for school violence and other youth problems (Vossekuil et al., 2002; Leary, Kowalski, Smith, Phillips, 2003). The importance of both sets of skills was demonstrated dramatically in two of the most notable instances of school violence. Cho Seung-Hui exhibited behavioral inhibition in elementary school and continued to display severe shyness, poor social skills, and perceptions of rejection in college before opening fire at Virginia Tech and killing 33 (including himself) in 2007. Reportedly, Klebold and Harris failed to cope successfully with repeated bullying before planting bombs and opening fire on students at Columbine High School in 1999. Teaching coping and social skills is vital among preventive interventions.

REFERENCES

Abboud, L. (November 1, 2005). Researchers push counseling that teaches skills to curb antisocial, violent behavior, *The Wall Street Journal*, D1.

Ayduk, O., Mischel, W., & Downey, G. (2002). Attentional mechanisms linking rejection to hostile-reactivity: The role of "hot" versus "cool" focus. *Psychological Science, 13*(5), 443–448.

Baker-Henningham, H., Walker, S., Powell, C., & Gardner, J. (2009). A pilot study of the Incredible Years Teacher Training programme and a curriculum unit on social and emotional skills in community pre-schools in Jamaica. *Child: Care, Health, and Development,* 1365–2214.

Barrera, M., Biglan, A., Taylor, T., Gunn, B., Smolkowski, K., Black, C., Ary, D., & Fowler, R. (2002). Early elementary school intervention to reduce conduct problems: A randomized trial with Hispanic and non-Hispanic children. *Prevention Science, 3*(2), 83–94.

Beland, K. (1992). *Second step: A violence prevention curriculum for grades 1–5*. Revised edition. Seattle, WA: Committee for Children.

Birch, S., & Ladd, G. (1997). The teacher-child relationship and children's early school adjustment. *Journal of School Psychology, 35*, 61–79.

Boelen, P., van den Hout, M., & van den Bout, J. (2006). A cognitive-behavioral conceptualization of complicated grief. *Clinical Psychology Science and Practice, 44*, 109–128.

Brestan, E., & Eyberg, S. (1998). Effective psychosocial treatments of conduct-disordered children and adolescents: 29 years, 82 studies, and 5,272 kids. *Journal of Clinical Child Psychology, 27*, 180–189.

Caldarella, P., Christensen, L., Kramer, T. J., & Kronmiller, K. (2009). The effects of Strong Start on second grades students' emotional and social competence. *Early Childhood Education Journal, 37*(1), 51–56.

Charney, R. S. (1993). *Teaching children to care: Management in the responsive classroom*. Greenfield, MA: Northeast Foundation for Children.

Charney, R. S. (2002). *Teaching children to care: Classroom management for ethical and academic Growth, K-8*. Revised edition. Greenfield, MA: Northeast Foundation for Children.

Cohen, J. (2006) Social, emotional ethical, and academic education: Creating a climate for learning, participation in democracy, and well-being. *Harvard Educational Review, 76*(2), 201–237.

Collaborative for Academic, Social, and Emotional Learning [CASEL] (2009). What is SEL? Skills and competencies. Retrieved March 27, 2010, from http://www.casel.org/basic/skills.php.

Compas, B. E. (1998). An agenda for coping research and theory: Basic and applied developmental issues. *International Journal of Behavioral Development, 22*(2), 231–237.

Conoley, J. C., & Goldstein, A. P. (Eds.). (2004). *School violence intervention: A practical handbook,* second edition. New York: Guilford Press.

Delaney, K. R. (2006). Learning to observe relationships and coping. *Journal of Child & Adolescent Psychiatric Nursing, 19*(4), 194–202.

Devine, J., & Cohen, J. (2007) *Making your school safe: Strategies to protect children and promote learning.* New York: Teachers College Press.

Dodge, K. A., & Price, J. M. (1994). On the relation between social information processing and socially competent behavior in early school-aged children. *Child Development, 65*, 1385–1397.

Dodge, K., Coie, J., Pettit, G., & Price, J. (1990). Peer status and aggression in boys' groups: Developmental and contextual analyses. *Child Development, 61*(5), 1289–1309.

Drugli, M., Larsson, B., & Clifford, G. (2007). Changes in social competence in young children treated because of conduct problems as viewed by multiple informants. *European Child & Adolescent Psychiatry, 16*(6): 370–378.

Duffell, J. C., Beland, K., & Frey, K. (2006). The Second Step program: Social-emotional skills for violence prevention. In M. J. Elias & H. Arnold (Eds.), *The Educator's guide to emotional intelligence and academic achievement* (pp. 161–174). Thousand Oaks, CA: Corwin Press.

DuPaul, G. J. (2003). Commentary: Bridging the gap between research and practice. *School Psychology Review*, *32*(2), 178–180.

Edwards, D., Hunt, M. H., Meyers, J., Grogg, K. R., & Jarrett, O. (2005). Acceptability and student outcomes of a violence prevention curriculum. *The Journal of Primary Prevention*, 26 (5), 401–418.

Eisenberg, N., Fabes, R., & Guthrie, I. (1997). Coping with stress: The roles of regulation and development. In S. A. Wolchik & I. N. Sandler (Eds.), *Handbook of children's coping: Linking theory and intervention* (pp. 277–306). Mahwah, NJ: Erlbaum.

Elliott, S. N. (1995). The Responsive Classroom approach: Its effectiveness and acceptability. Final evaluation report prepared for the center for systematic educational change, Washington, DC.

Elliott, S. N., & Gresham, F. M. (1991). *Social skills intervention guide.* Circle Pines, MN: American Guidance Service.

Elliott, S. N., & Gresham, F. M. (1993). Social skills interventions for children. *Behavior Modifications*, 17, 2287–313.

Elliott, S. N., Malecki, C. K., & Demaray, M. K. (2001). New directions in social skills assessment and intervention for elementary and middle school students. *Exceptionality*, 9, 19–32.

Evans, S. W., Axelrod, J. L., & Sapia, J. L. (2000). Effective school-based interventions: The development of a social skills training paradigm. *Journal of School Health*, 70, 191–194.

Evans, A., & Stefanou, C. (2009). Behavioral and academic effects of Skillstreaming the adolescent for at-risk middle school students. Presented at the Northeastern Educational Research (NERA) Annual Conference, University of Connecticut.

Frey, K. S., Hirschstein, M. K., & Guzzo, B. A. (2000). Preventing aggression by promoting social competence. *Journal of Emotional and Behavioral Disorders*, 8 (2), 102–112.

Galen, B. R., & Underwood, M. K. (1997). A developmental investigation of social aggression among children. *Developmental Psychology*, *33*, 589–600.

Gilbert, J., & Morawski, C. (2005). Stress coping for elementary school children: A case for including lifestyle. *The Journal of Individual Psychology, 61*(4), 314–328.

Goldstein, A. P. (1999). Teaching prosocial behavior to antisocial youth. In D. J. Flannery & C. R. Huff (Eds.), *Youth violence: Prevention, intervention, and social policy* (pp. 253–271). Washington DC.: American Psychiatric Press.

Goldstein, A. P., McGinnis, E., Sprafkin, R. P., Gershaw, N. J., & Klein, P. (1997). *Skillstreaming the adolescent: New strategies and perspectives for teaching prosocial skills* (Revised edition). Champaign, IL: Research Press.

Goleman, D. (1995). *Emotional intelligence: Why it can matter more than IQ*. New York: Bantam Books.

Gresham, F. M., & Elliott, S. N. (1984). Assessment and classification of children's social skills: A review of methods and issues. *School Psychology Review, 13*(3), 292–301.

Gresham, F. M., & Elliott, S. N. (1990). *Social skills rating system*. Circle Pines, MN: American Guidance Service

Grossman, D. C., Neckerman, H. J., Koepsell, T. D., Liu, P., Asher, K. N., Beland, K., Frey, K., & Rivara, F. P. (1997). Effectiveness of a violence prevention curriculum among children in elementary school. *The Journal of the American Medical Association, 277*(20), 1650–1611.

Hartman, R., Stage, S., & Webster-Stratton, C. (2003). A growth curve analysis of parent training outcomes: Examining the influence of child factors (inattention, impulsivity, and hyperactivity problems), parental and family risk factors. *The Child Psychology and Psychiatry Journal, 44*(3), 388–398.

Hawkins, J., Catalano, R., & Miller, Y. (1992). Risk and protective factors for alcohol and other drug problems in adolescence and early adulthood: Implications for substance abuse prevention. *Psychological Bulletin, 112,* 64–105.

Horsch, P., Chen, J., & Nelson, D. (1999). Rules and rituals: Tools for creating a respectful, caring learning community. *Phi Delta Kappan, 81,* 223–227.

Kramer, T. J., Caldarella, P., Christensen, L., & Shatzer, R. H. (2010). Social-emotional learning in kindergarten classrooms: Evaluation of the Strong Start curriculum. *Early Childhood Education Journal, 37*(4), 303–398.

Kolbe, L., Collins, J., & Cortese, P. (1997). Building the capacity of schools to improve the health of the nation: A call for assistance from psychologists. *American Psychologist, 52*(3), 256–265.

Lazarus, R., & Folkman, S. (1987). Transactional theory and research on emotions and coping. *European Journal of Personality, 1,* 141–169.

Leary, M. R., Kowalski, R. M., Smith, L., Phillips, S. (2003). Teasing, rejection, and violence: Case studies of the school shootings. *Aggressive Behavior, 29*(3), 202–214.

Lengua, L., Long, A., & Meltzoff, A. (2006). Pre-attack stress load, appraisals, and coping in children's responses to the 9/11 terrorist attacks. *Journal of Child Psychology and Psychiatry, 47*(12), 1219–1227.

Leonardi, R., Roberts, J. Wasoka, D. (2001). Skillstreaming: A report to the Vermont State Department of Education.

Mayer, J. D., & Salovey, P. (1997). What is emotional intelligence? In J. D. Mayer & P. Salovey (Eds.*), Emotional development and emotional intelligence* (pp. 3–31) New York: Basic Books.

McGinnis, E., & Goldstein, A. P. (1997) *Skillstreaming the elementary school child: Revised edition: New strategies and perspectives for teaching prosocial skills.* Champaign, IL: Research Press.

McGinnis, E., & Goldstein, A. P. (2003). *Skillstreaming in early childhood: Revised edition: New strategies and perspectives for teaching prosocial skills.* Champaign, IL: Research Press.

McIntyre, L. (2008). Adapting Webster-Stratton's incredible years parent training for children with developmental delay: findings from a treatment group only study. *Journal of Intellectual Disability Research, 52*(12), 1176–1192.

Melhem, N., Moritz, G., Walker, M., & Shear, K. (2007). Phenomenology and correlates of complicated grief in children and adolescents. *Journal of the American Academy of Child and Adolescent Psychiatry, 46*, 493–499.

Merrell, K. W. (2010). Linking prevention science and social and emotional learning: the Oregon Resiliency Project. *Psychology in the Schools, 47*(1), 55–70.

Merrell, K. W., Carrizales, D. C., Feuerborn, L., Gueldner, G. A., & Tran, O. K. (2007a). *Strong Kids-grades 3–5: A social–emotional learning curriculum.* Baltimore, MD: Paul H. Brookes Publishing.

Merrell, K. W., Carrizales, D. C., Feuerborn, L., Gueldner, G. A., & Tran, O. K. (2007b). *Strong Kids-grades 6–8: A social–emotional learning curriculum.* Baltimore, MD: Paul H. Brookes Publishing.

Merrell, K. W., Carrizales, D. C., Feuerborn, L., Gueldner, G. A., & Tran, O. K. (2007c). *Strong teens-grades 9–12: A social–emotional learning curriculum.* Baltimore, MD: Paul H. Brookes Publishing.

Merrell, K. W., Juskelis, M. P., Tran, O. K., & Buchanan, R. (2008). Social and emotional learning in the classroom: Evaluation of *Strong Kids* and *Strong Teens* on students' social-emotional knowledge and symptoms. *Journal of applied school psychology, 24* (2), 209–224. Available on-line at http://japps.haworthpress.com

Merrell, K. W., Parisi, D., & Whitcomb, S. A. (2007). *Strong Start-grades K-2: A social emotional learning curriculum*. Baltimore, MD: Paul H. Brookes Publishing.

Miller, S., & Coll, E. (2007). From social withdrawal to social confidence: Evidence for possible pathways. *Current psychology, 26*, 86–101.

Min, M., Farkas, K., Minnes, S., & Singer, L. (2007). Impact of childhood abuse and neglect on substance abuse and psychological distress in adulthood. *Journal of Traumatic Stress, 20*(5), 833–44.

Nader, K. (2008). *Understanding and assessing trauma in children and adolescents: Measures, methods, and youth in context*. New York: Routledge.

Niehues, S. A. (2006). The effectiveness of Skillstreaming when used as a short-term intervention for preschool children. Retrieved from http://gradworks.umi.com/14/41/1441786.html.

Parker, J. G., & Asher, S. R. (1987). Peer relations and later personal adjustment: Are low-accepted children at risk? *Psychological Bulletin, 102*(3), 357–389.

Patterson, G. R., Capaldi, D., & Bank, L. (1991). An early starter model for predicting delinquency. In D. J. Pepler & K. H. Rubin (Eds.), *The development and treatment of childhood aggression* (pp. 139–168). Hillsdale, NJ: Erlbaum.

Patterson, G., Reid, J., & Dishion, T. (1992). *Antisocial boys: A social interactional approach* (Vol. 4). Eugene, OR: Castalia Publishing.

Payton, J., Weissberg, R. P., Durlak, J. A., Dymnicki, A. B., Taylor, R. D., Schellinger, K. B., & Pachan, M. (2008). *The positive impact of social and emotional learning for kindergarten to eighth-grade students: Findings from three scientific reviews*. Chicago, IL: Collaborative for Academic, Social, and Emotional Learning.

Phillips, D., Prince, S., & Schiebelhut, L. (2004). Elementary school children's responses 3 months after the September 11 terrorist attacks: A study in Washington, DC. *American Journal of Orthopsychiatry, 74(4)*, 509–528.

Quinn, M. M., Kavale, K. A., Mathur, S. R., Rutherford, R. B., Forness, S. R. (1999). A meta-analysis of social skill interventions for students with emotional and behavioral disorders, *Journal of Emotional and Behavioral Disorders, 7*(1), 54–64.

Ragozzino, K., & O'Brien, M. U. (2009) *Social emotional learning and bullying prevention*. Chicago, IL: Collaborative for Academic, Social, and Emotional Learning.

Rimm-Kaufman, S. E., & Chiu, Y. (2007). Promoting social and academic competence in the classroom: An intervention study examining contribution of the Responsive Classroom approach. *Psychology in the Schools, 44*(4), 397–413.

Rimm-Kaufman, S. E., & Sawyer, B. E. (2004). Primary-grade teachers' self-efficacy beliefs, attitudes toward teaching, and discipline and teaching practice priorities in relation to the Responsive Classroom approach. *The Elementary School Journal, 104*(4), 321–341.

Ross, M. R., Powell, S. R., & Elias, M. J. (2002). New roles for school psychologists: Addressing the social and emotional learning needs of students. *School Psychology Review, 31*(1), 45–52.

Salovey, P., & Mayer, J. D. (1990). Emotional intelligence. *Imagination, Cognition and Personality, 9*, 185–211.

Schore, A. N. (2003). Early relational trauma, disorganized attachment, and the development of a predisposition to violence. In M. Soloman & D. J. Siegel (Eds.), *Healing trauma* (pp. 107–167). New York: W. W. Norton.

Siegel, D. J. (1999). *The developing mind: How relationships and the brain interact to shape who we are.* New York: Guilford Press.

Snyder, H. (2001). Child delinquents. In R. Loeber & D. P. Farrington (Eds.), *Riskfactors and successful interventions.* Thousand Oaks, CA: Sage.

Snyder, J., Schrepferman, L., & St. Peter, C. (1997). Origins of antisocial behavior: Negative reinforcement and affect dysregulation of behavior as socialization mechanisms in family interaction. *Behavior modification, 21*(2), 187–215.

Spence, S. H. (2003). Social skills training with children and young people: Theory, evidence and practice. *Child and Adolescent Mental Health, 8*(2), 84–96.

Stallard, P., Velleman, R., Langsford, J., & Baldwin, S. (2001). Coping and psychological distress in children involved in road traffic accidents. *British Journal of Clinical Psychology, 40*, 197–208.

Taub, J. (2001). Evaluation of the Second Step violence prevention program at a rural elementary school. *School Psychology Review, 31*(2) 186–200.

Taylor, T., & Biglan, A. (1998). Behavioral family interventions for improving child-rearing: A review for clinicians and policy makers. *Clinical Child and Family Psychology Review, 1*(1), 41–60.

Taylor, T., Webster-Stratton, C., Feil, E., Broadbent, B., Widdop, C., & Severson, H. (2008). Computer-based intervention with coaching: An example using the Incredible Years Program. *Cognitive Behaviour Therapy, 37*(4), 233–246.

Tolan, P., Gorman-Smith, D., Henry, D., Chung, K., & Hunt, M. (2002). The relation of patterns of coping of inner-city youth to psychopathology symptoms. *Journal of Research on Adolescence, 12*, 423–449.

Vossekuil, B., Fein, R.A, Reddy, M., Borum, R., & Modzeleski, W. L. (2002). *The final report and findings of the Safe School Initiative: Implications for the prevention of school attacks in the United States.* US Secret Service & US Department of Education.

Webster-Stratton, C. (1990). Long-term follow-up of families with young conduct problem children: From preschool to grade school. *Journal of Clinical Child Psychology, 19*(2), 144–149.

Webster-Stratton, C. (2000). The Incredible Years training series. Office of Juvenile Justice and Delinquency Prevention, *Juvenile Justice Bulletin*, Washington, DC.

Webster-Stratton, C. (2009). Affirming diversity: Multi-cultural collaboration to deliver the incredible years parent programs. *International Journal of Child Health and Human Development, 2*(1), 17–32.

Webster-Stratton, C., & Hammond, M. (1997). Treating children with early-onset conduct problems: A comparison of child and parent training interventions. *Journal of Consulting and Clinical Psychology, 65*(1), 93–109.

Webster-Stratton, C., & Herman, K. (2009). Disseminating Incredible Years series early-intervention programs: Integrating and sustaining services between school and home. *Psychology in the Schools, 47*(1), 36–54.

Webster-Stratton, C., Hollinsworth, T., & Kolpacoff, M. (1989). The long-term effectiveness and clinical significance of three cost-effective training programs for families with conduct-problem children. *Journal of Consulting and Clinical Psychology, 57*(4), 550–553.

Webster-Stratton, C., & Reid, J. (2010). A school-family partnership: Addressing multiple risk factors to improve school readiness and prevent conduct problems in young children. In S. L. Christenson & A. L. Reschly (Eds.), *Handbook on school-family partnerships* (pp. 204–227). New York: Routledge/Taylor & Francis.

Webster-Stratton, C., Reid, M. , & Hammond, M. (2004). Treating children with early-onset conduct problems: Intervention outcomes for parent, child, and teacher training. *Journal of Clinical Child and Adolescent Psychology, 33*(1), 105–124.

Webster-Stratton, C., & Reid, M. (2008). Adapting the Incredible Years child dinosaur social, emotional, and problem- solving intervention to address comorbid diagnoses. *Journal of Children's Services, 3*(3), 17–30.

Webster-Stratton, C., Reid, M. J., & Stoolmiller, M. (2008). Preventing conduct problems and improving school readiness: Evaluation of the Incredible Years teacher and child training programs in high-risk schools. *Journal of Child Psychology and Psychiatry, 49*(5), 471–488.

Zins, J. E., Bloodworth, M. R., Weissberg, R. P., & Walberg, H. J. (2004). Scientific base linking social and emotional learning to school success. In J. E. Zins, R. P. Weissberg, M. C. Wang, & H. J. Walberg, (Eds.), *Building academic success on social and emotional learning: What does the research say?* (pp. 3–21). New York: Teachers College Press.

Zins, J. E., Weissberg, R. P., Wang, M. C., & Walberg, H. J. (Eds.) (2004). *Building academic success on social and emotional learning: What does the research say?* New York: Teachers College Press.

Zins, J. E., & Wagner, D. I. (1997). Educating children and youth for psychological competence. In R. J. Illback, C. T. Cobb, & H. M. Joseph, Jr. (Eds.), *Integrated services for children and families: Opportunities for psychological practice.* APA: Washington, DC.

CHAPTER 6

Treating Insecure and Disorganized Attachments in School-Aged Children

Ellen Moss, Katherine Pascuzzo, and Valerie Simard

A class of 7-year-old children arrives for their first day of school.* The teacher assigns seats to the students who, for the most part, accept this without questioning and sit down. One child becomes angry, goes over to another child and says in a commanding voice, "Get up from that chair! I want it. Go sit over there." The surprised child turns to the teacher for assistance, who promptly directs the first child to sit in his assigned seat without further disruptive behavior. He looks her directly in the eye and says, "That's the seat I want, and you keep out of my business!" The child is sent to the principal's office. After a "discussion" with the principal about the value of respect for others, the child returns to the classroom. Several weeks go by during which the teacher notices that the child is having difficulty organizing his work, focusing on tasks, and completing assignments. On the playground, the child is frequently involved in fights and is isolated socially. The teacher requests a meeting with the child's parents who listen to the teacher recount these events. The father then says, "He needs to know who's boss here. You need to manage these kids!" Mom sits sheepishly, saying nothing, looking quite detached.

---
* This research was supported by grants received from the Social Sciences and Humanities Research Council of Canada, the Canadian Institutes for Health Research, the FQRSC Quebec funding agencies and the Public Safety Canada's National Crime Prevention Centre (NCPC) in collaboration with the Quebec Minister of Public Security. We thank our collaborators, les Centres Jeunesses de Lanaudière and their clinical workers, as well as Chantal Cyr, Karine Comtois-Dubois, George Tarabulsy, Annie Bernier and Diane St-Laurent for their invaluable support and contributions to this work.

This scene, repeated in classrooms all over the country, is familiar to most educational professionals. Educators often identify children who distinguish themselves from their peers by showing high levels of disruptive behavior in the classroom and playground, often accompanied by difficulty with executive functions in the class setting such as planning school-related tasks, monitoring their performance, and evaluating the attainment of goals. In the vignette presented here, it is notable that the attempt to solicit parental cooperation in some kind of treatment plan is met by defiance, with attribution of blame away from the child to the school. The profile of school difficulties is compounded with a difficult family situation, suggesting that relational dysfunction is a common theme in both home and school contexts. A variety of solutions can be proposed. Some of these children are transferred to classes for children with aggressive behavior problems. Some receive tutoring for academic subjects, but often this is not oriented to development of metacognitive skills, that is, planning, monitoring, and evaluation. Parents of these children are often uncooperative with school authorities. In some cases, vulnerable, young teachers are accused by these parents of being unable to manage their classrooms. In general, the aggressive problems of the child become worse, and if the child is evaluated professionally, psychologists will also often note increasing signs of comorbid depressive symptoms, anxiety and social isolation from the normative peer group. Academically, there is also increasing difficulty.

In this chapter, our objective is to bring a perspective from attachment theory in understanding and identifying aggressive behavior and related socio-emotional and cognitive difficulties often seen in the school setting. We begin by discussing theoretical links between the quality of the child–parent attachment relationship and school-related functioning. We present guidelines for identifying children with secure, insecure, and disorganized attachment patterns at school-age. We review the current empirical literature documenting associations between attachment at school-age and developmental risk. Finally, we discuss intervention methods that have demonstrated efficacy in treating attachment-related school difficulties.

INDIVIDUAL DIFFERENCES IN ATTACHMENT: SECURE, ORGANIZED-INSECURE, AND DISORGANIZED PATTERNS

According to Bowlby (1969/1982), the infant's attachments with the primary caregiver develop in the course of the first year with identifiable individual patterns appearing by 7 to 9 months of age. By this age, secure infants can be distinguished from their insecure peers by their ability to balance dependency on the caregiver with autonomous exploration (Bowlby, 1969/1982). According to attachment theory, the quality of the infants' exploration of novel environments is dependent on the degree to which the baby has internalized a model of a caregiver who will meet the child's need for protection and physiological regulation (Ainsworth, Bell, & Stayton, 1971; Bowlby, 1969/1982). The *secure* infant is able to maintain a balance between the attachment and exploratory systems. When the infant feels himself to be in a comfortable, nonthreatening situation, exploration is increased, but when the attachment system is activated through feelings of distress, play and exploration diminish and proximity-seeking is increased. Infant insecure patterns, *avoidance* and *ambivalence*, are adaptive strategies for maintaining proximity to attachment figures who are unresponsive to some aspect of infant emotional behavior. Infants who develop avoidant attachment patterns learn to inhibit the expression of distress and to distance themselves from the caregiver in stressful situations (Ainsworth, Blehar, Waters, & Wall, 1978; Main, 1981). Avoidance is believed to develop from repeated experiences of rejection by the caregiver. These parents prefer children who show precocious autonomy, self-reliance, and are undemanding. Conversely, infants who develop the ambivalent category exaggerate distress and helplessness and are often in close proximity to the caregiver. The ambivalent pattern is an adaptive response to parental inconsistency in responding to child distress. Put simply, by exaggerating emotional displays of sadness and anger, ambivalent children keep the parent involved with them, even though the attention is activated by negative emotion (Cassidy & Berlin, 1994; Moss, Bureau, Cyr, Mongeau, & St-Laurent, 2004).

Secure, ambivalent, and avoidant infants are considered to show organized attachment strategies in the sense that they have developed a consistent, coherent, behavioral strategy that is adaptive for relationship continuity with their parental figure. However, a fourth group of infants have been identified who show *disorganized* attachment, that is, they fail to show an organized strategy for seeking proximity to the attachment figure in times of distress (Main & Solomon, 1990). These infants display bouts or sequences of behaviors that seemingly lack a goal and often appear contextually bizarre and incoherent. For example, certain infants will show extensive crying during separation from the mother, and then, on her return, will at first approach and then suddenly sharply avoid the mother. Other disorganized infants show fear at the moment of mother's return following a separation, or freeze and fall to the ground when in close proximity to the parent. These behaviors are interpreted as indicators of stress and anxiety generated by the irresolvable paradox of the attachment figure's being at the same time the source of fright and the only possible safe haven (Main & Hesse, 1990). Subsequent empirical work supported this hypothesis in showing that disorganized infants experience the most dysfunctional parenting when compared with other attachment groups (Carlson, 1998; Lyons-Ruth, Bronfman, & Parsons, 1999; Moss et al., 2004; van IJzendoorn, Schuengel, & Bakermans-Kranenburg, 1999). Maternal frightening behavior such as speaking in eerie voices, emotional detachment, or helplessness at moments of high infant distress, and hostile intrusiveness, which ignores infant individuality are some of the behaviors that were observed in mothers of disorganized infants (Lyons-Ruth, Repacholi, McLeod, & Silva, 1991; Main & Hesse, 1990). These behaviors may frighten the infant, leave them feeling abandoned and unprotected, and thus interfere with infant processing of affective, social, and cognitive information (Main & Hesse, 1990; Solomon & George, 1996).

Beyond Infancy: Identification of Preschool/ School-Age Attachment Patterns

When Bowlby wrote his definitive works on attachment theory (Bowlby, 1969/1982, 1973, 1980), he conceptualized attachment relationships as serving a broad-based adaptive function relevant to the life span rather than to only restricted periods of development.

One of the strengths of research in the attachment field is that efforts have been made to validate systems for measuring the four attachment patterns across the lifespan. Although the bulk of early research efforts were concentrated on infant research, the last 25 years have witnessed intense efforts to understand and evaluate attachment and its correlates beyond infancy.

During the preschool/school-age years, attachment patterns are distinguished using both behavioral measures based on separation–reunion episodes between child and caregiver, as well as representational measures based on narratives that children create during doll-play. A core concept in attachment theory is the internalization of attachment-related experiences in internal working models (IWMs), which influence attitudes and expectations concerning the self and others (Bowlby (1969/1982). IWMs also function as a control system vital to behavioral and emotional regulation, becoming a structure for self-regulation within the person during middle childhood (Zimmermann, 1999). Thus, at school-age, even in the absence of parental figures, children's ability to represent parental availability in stressful contexts allows them to regulate negative arousal when feelings of insecurity arise (Kerns, Klepac, & Cole, 1996; Kerns, Tomich, Aspelmeier, & Contreras, 2000).

The preschool and school-age attachment patterns of secure, avoidant, and ambivalent children are conceptually similar to those displayed by such children in infancy, although conversational patterns assume increasing importance as a function of child age. The *secure* (B) child shows relaxed, mutually enjoyable parent–child interaction. Owing to an internalized sense of confidence in the responsiveness of others, the secure child uses the caregiver and other close adults (e.g., teachers) as a base that facilitates exploration of the environment. With the growth of language and perspective-taking skills during the preschool and school-age periods, the child becomes able to communicate his or her own intentions and plans to both adults and peers, understand those of others, and engage in negotiations aimed at jointly achieving a common goal (Marvin, 1977). These new modes of interaction that are acquired by secure children replace the aggressive exchanges which are normative in toddlerhood, but continue to persist in the behavior of insecure, particularly disorganized children. Using family doll-play figurines, secure children create stories which depict parental figures as sensitive to the child's needs and as a secure haven in times of distress.

By contrast, at preschool and school-age, insecure avoidant children show neutral coolness toward the parent, as well as a minimization of physical and verbal contact and displays of intimacy. These children display excessive self-reliance, rarely seeking assistance even when facing difficult tasks. This interactive style may also characterize behavior with teachers and peers in the school setting, where conversations are focused on the child's play activities rather than personal references. In doll-play, avoidant children are less likely to represent themselves as submissive to parents and in need of parental guidance in comparison with secure peers (Bureau & Moss, 2010). These findings support the idea that repeated experiences of rejection from parents are internalized in representations of caregivers as unavailable and less involved in emotional regulation (Cassidy & Kobak, 1988). Children classified *insecure–ambivalent* give excessive emphasis to the relationship with the caregiver to the detriment of exploration. This pattern is often characterized by immature and dependent behaviors with adults and peers, which are attention-seeking strategies presumably linked to the child's representation of the caregiver as being inconsistently available. Correspondingly, in doll-play, ambivalently-attached children are more likely to create stories in which parents are less efficient at soothing the character's distress, and where the child protagonist's emotional expression is exaggerated.

Concerning children with disorganized attachment, a remarkable change occurs in their behavior with the caregiver. By the end of the preschool period, the majority of disorganized children come to take charge of the relationship with the parent, in a caregiving or punitive fashion

(Main & Cassidy, 1988; Moss, Cyr, Bureau, Tarabulsy, & Dubois-Comtois, 2005). The onset of controlling behavior in disorganized children may be linked to attempts by the child to regulate distressing negative emotional states which cannot be expressed in the presence of the caregiver. Disorganized children have already learned that they cannot rely on their attachment figure for comfort and that dependent behavior is likely to evoke subtle or overt hostile or helpless parental behavior, thereby increasing child distress. As noted by Mason (1968), one of the psychological determinants of stress response is an individual's feeling of not having control over a situation. In this perspective, the development of parentified behavior over the preschool period may be the disorganized child's adaptive attempt to reduce stress levels, which cannot be regulated through child dependency on the caregiver.

This behavioral pattern may be extended to the school setting where such children may have problems with authority figures, as in the vignette presented in the introduction. Despite the organized behavioral pattern inherent in such role-reversal, several studies (Bureau & Moss, in press; Moss et al., 2005; Solomon, George, & De Jong, 1995) have shown that representational disorganization (e.g., chaotic and frightening story content) still characterizes the internal working models of disorganized/controlling children. In their doll-play narratives, parents may be represented as unable to help the child who finds himself in dangerous situations. For example, a child is on top of a huge rock and is about to fall off, while mother is passively watching. Parental figures may also be the source of fear, as in one story created by a boy who reported being visited by witches in his bed, one of whom was transformed into his mother. This unintegrated mental content has been seen in the communications of children involved in rampage shootings. Because it is so characteristic of disorganized children, it may serve to identify certain children with violent potential.

Individual Differences in Child Attachment and School-Related Outcomes

According to attachment theory, the child's internal working model, or internalized representation, of caregiver responsiveness should influence interactive exchanges with both caregivers and other adults or peers in both home and extrafamilial settings. Recent empirical studies have supported this idea in demonstrating associations between children's attachment patterns and school-related functioning. Decades of research have supported Bowlby's idea (1969/1982) that security in the child–parent attachment relationship is associated with later socio-emotional competence, emotion regulation skills, and more positive attitudes toward self and other (De Klyen & Greenberg, 2008). A significant body of research has broadened Bowlby's developmental ideas by establishing links between insecurity, and disorganization in particular, and the development of later cognitive abilities, executive functioning, and academic achievement (Jacobsen, Edelstein, & Hoffmann, 1994; Moss & St-Laurent, 2001).

The idea that the quality of attachment behavior in childhood has lasting implications for later socio-emotional development has sparked decades of research on the links between attachment and development of peer relations and behavior problems of an externalizing (aggressive, disruptive, conduct disordered) and internalizing (depressive, anxious, socially withdrawn) nature. Recent review articles and meta-analyses of the association between insecurity and these domains of socio-emotional development, based on more than 10,000 children has confirmed the long-held assumption that insecurity (versus security) is predictive of externalizing (Fearon, Bakermans-Kranenburg, van IJzendoorn, Lapsley, & Roisman, 2010), as well as internalizing problems (Brumariu & Kerns, 2010). Notable among reviewed studies are several which showed that early mother–child security measured in infancy predicted greater social competence 5 to 20 years later (Carlson, Sroufe, & Egeland, 2004; Englund, Levy, Hyson, & Sroufe, 2000; Freitag, Belsky, Grossman, Grossman, & Scheurer-Englisch, 1996; NICHD, 2005; Sroufe, Egeland, & Carlson, 1999). Significant associations, both longitudinal and concurrent, between attachment and aggressive behavior problems are also found in studies using preschool and school-age attachment measures (Anan & Barnett, 1999; Booth, Rubin, & Rose-Krasnor, 1998; Bureau & Moss, 2010; Easterbrooks, Davidson, & Chazan, 1993; Moss, Bureau, Béliveau, & Lépine, 2009; Moss, Rousseau, Parent, St-Laurent, & Saintonge, 1998; Moss et al., 2004; NICHD, 2001; 2005; Solomon et al., 1995; Teti & Ablard, 1990). These findings support the idea that early promotion of secure attachment patterns may interrupt risk trajectories for children with socio-emotional difficulties.

Concerning the predictive role of types of insecure attachment, reviews and meta-analyses (Fearon et al., 2010; van IJzendoorn et al., 1999) have shown that disorganization is a more significant predictor of both aggressive and depressive behavior problems than the organized-insecure patterns (avoidance and ambivalence). Although at preschool and early school age, it is primarily an aggressive, disruptive behavior pattern that is associated with disorganization (e.g., Lyons-Ruth & Jacobvitz, 2008; Moss et al., 2004), depression, anxieties and fears related to performance, abilities, and self-worth become more pronounced in middle childhood and adolescence (Carlson, 1998; Moss, Smolla, Cyr, Dubois-Comtois, Mazzarello, & Berthiaume, 2006).

Studies that have examined children's narratives in middle childhood have found that children with disorganized patterns of attachment to the caregiver are more likely than their peers to represent conflict themes and to depict chaotic and violent interpersonal relationships in their narratives (Bureau & Moss, 2010). Children's attachment scripts elicited by doll-play story stems are thought to reveal children's internal working models, as expressed in the relational themes evoked, resolution/nonresolution of distress, as well as the defences and coping mechanisms used by the child (Bretherton & Oppenheim, 2003). Given the important role of internal working models as mechanisms of continuity in attachment theory, the content of children's narratives may be indicators of children's future behavior with peers and adults in school settings. This suggests that stories that children create in the school setting and messages they send on the Internet to friends and teachers should be taken as serious indictors of their mental state and potential for violent acts.

These motivational and self-dimensions are important predictors, not only of behavior problems, but also of a wide range of competences related to school performance. Children who focus attention on coping with parental figures who induce fear or feelings of abandonment in them, have fewer cognitive and attentional resources available for learning and exploration (Main, 1991; Moss, St-Laurent, & Parent, 1999). Extensive child exposure to a disorganized or frightening parent, who does not assist the child in dealing with negative feelings, may also lead to problems in cognitive self-regulation, which influences both the processing of social–emotional information and tasks of an academic nature (Moss & St-Laurent, 2001; Solomon & George, 1996). In order for children to develop executive functions, particularly those metacognitive skills involved in planning, monitoring, and evaluating school-related tasks, parental involvement in scaffolding children's emerging competences is necessary. Appropriate parental guidance is later internalized in the development of child self-regulation in learning tasks (Moss, 1992; Moss, Gosselin, Parent, Rousseau, & Dumont, 1997; Zimmerman, 2002).

In support of these theoretical ideas, we found a number of important results related to the school performance of insecure children, and the disorganized/controlling group in particular at early school-age and middle childhood in two studies that we conducted (Moss & St-Laurent, 2001; Moss et al., 1999). Secure children had significantly higher scores than insecure children on two school-performance-related measures, cognitive engagement in problem-solving tasks and mastery motivation. However, disorganized/controlling children showed the poorest school performance of all attachment groups. Despite their similarity in IQ to other attachment groups, these children had the lowest perceived competence, showed the greatest deficits in planning, monitoring and evaluating school-related tasks, and had the poorest academic performance in middle childhood. In addition, as discussed above, teachers reported disrupted and aggressive behavior with peers. As hypothesized, disorganized children and their mothers were also least likely of all attachment groups to display a collaborative pattern facilitative of joint problem solving at early school-age. These results show continuity with studies indicating that mothers of disorganized infants and preschoolers were lowest on involvement, teaching skill, positive parent–infant mutuality, and conversational skill (Lyons-Ruth, Easterbrooks, & Cibelli, 1997; Main, Kaplan, & Cassidy, 1985; Moss et al., 2004; Solomon & George, 1999a; Stevenson-Hinde & Shouldice, 1995). Our analyses also indicated that both the negative self-evaluations of children with a disorganized classification and their dysfunctional mother–child interactive patterns played an important role in explaining the demonstrated relation between disorganized attachment and poor academic performance. These findings are also supported by those of Jacobsen and her colleagues (Jacobsen et al., 1994; Jacobsen & Hoffmann, 1997) indicating that disorganization at 7 years of age predicted deficits in cognitive and metacognitive functioning during middle childhood and adolescence that were explained by low self-confidence (Jacobsen et al., 1994). Together, these findings indicate a multiple school risk profile for disorganized children and adolescents not limited to the processing of socio-emotional information but extending to tasks of an academic nature.

INTERVENTION METHODS FOR TREATING INSECURE AND DISORGANIZED ATTACHMENT

Attachment theory provides a solid foundation for both understanding the risk and resiliency factors involved in the development of aggressive children, and guiding the development and evaluation of intervention programs for this multiple-risk population. As discussed above, one type of child attachment insecurity, disorganization, has been consistently shown to be quite stable in the absence of intervention, to be a significant risk factor for psychopathology, and to longitudinally predict maladaptation between early childhood and young adulthood (Lyons-Ruth & Jacobvitz, 2008; Moss et al., 2005). The negative effects of insecurity, and particularly disorganization, on child development, and the enormous human, social and health-related costs associated with these problems, have inspired researchers to develop and test intervention programs aimed at increasing maternal sensitivity and child attachment security and reducing child attachment disorganization and related behavior problems. The majority of studies to date have targeted infants and preschoolers and prioritize the early mother–child relationship. The idea is that given the substantial developmental plasticity in early childhood, early intervention efforts are likely to be the most productive.

Experimental studies with both animal and human populations have shown that early parental sensitivity to child needs and signals, and the parent's capacity to respond to them appropriately, is a key mechanism in shaping brain development and the substrate of mental processes involved in different aspects of cognitive functioning related to emotion regulation and communication (see Schore, 2001 for a review). Longitudinal studies with human populations have demonstrated that both sensitive caregiving behavior and secure attachment relationships at infancy and preschool are associated with significantly lower risk for development of psychopathology and school underachievement (Carlson, 1998; Moss & St-Laurent, 2001; NICHD, 2005). Given the central role of maternal sensitivity in the development of secure and insecure forms of attachment, a number of prevention and intervention trials, conducted with clinical and nonclinical samples aimed at improving the quality of early parent–child interaction and child attachment have been tested.

Long-Term Intervention Methods

Long-Term Intervention Programs Targeting the Parent–Child Relationship

Several studies (Cicchetti, Rogosch, & Toth, 2006; Lieberman, Gosh Ippen, & Van Horn, 2006; Lieberman, Van Horn, & Gosh Ippen, 2005; Lyons-Ruth, Connell, Grunebaum, & Botein, 1990; Osofsky et al., 2007; Toth, Maughan, Manly, Spagnola, & Cichetti, 2002) have tested the efficacy of long-term ($M = 46$ weeks) attachment-based preventive interventions with mother–child dyads from families where children were at high risk for school-related cognitive and socio-emotional deficiencies. The intervention models in all these studies use the child–parent relationship as the primary vehicle for improving child outcomes with additional elements of maternal and child psychotherapy and social support. The focus in many of these programs is on mothers' reinterpretation of their own childhood experiences in relation to their current caregiving. Some of the most important studies in this group, particularly those relevant to samples of children at-risk for aggressive behavior problems, are reviewed below.

Longer-Term Intervention Programs Targeting High-Risk Infants

Olds and colleagues, in numerous randomized trials, have tested a long-term home-visiting intervention strategy, conducted by nurses, targeting multiple outcomes for mothers and children, including the reduction of aggressive behavior problems (Olds et al., 1997; 1998; Olds, Sadler, & Kitzman, 2007). More recent trials have integrated attachment theory in emphasizing both the promotion of sensitive and responsive caregiving in parent–child interactions, discussion concerning mothers' own childrearing history, and development of an empathic nurse–client relationship. Results have shown improvements in maternal sensitivity and responsiveness and in infant responsiveness and mental development. Long-term follow-up effects of nurse home visitation have shown reductions in children's aggressive behavior problems, serious antisocial behavior, and emergent substance abuse (Olds et al., 1998). Given the diversity of services embedded in the home visiting program, it is not clear what component of the program is responsible for different effects. In addition, it is not clear that child attachment security or disorganization was influenced, as these constructs were not measured directly.

Cichetti et al. (2006) worked with 1-year-old infants at high-risk for aggressive behavior problems owing to the fact that their mothers had been identified as maltreating. Results of the Cicchetti et al. study, notable for its use of random assignment and outcome measures of the quality of the caregiver–child relationship and of child functioning, showed a substantial reduction in infant disorganized attachment and increase in secure attachment for the intervention group. Osofsky et al. (2007) conducted a similar long-term intervention with mothers who were maltreating or at high-risk for maltreatment with a wider age range of children (0–48 months). In the Osofsky et al. study, results indicated improvements in parental sensitivity and child communication, gross and fine motor skills, problem-solving, and personal–social functioning. A weakness of the study is that it did not involve random assignment to treatment and control groups, which is the gold standard in this type of research.

Longer-Term Intervention Programs Targeting High-Risk Preschool and School-Aged Children

Several studies have tested the effects of longer-term attachment-based models primarily with post-infancy high-risk children and their parents. Hoffman, Marvin, Cooper, & Powell (2006) developed a program called Circle of Security, which is a group-based intervention targeting child emotion regulation, interactive synchrony, and parental states of mind regarding attachment and intimate relationships. The intervention method involves video-feedback, a technique, which encourages the caregiver to share attachment-related reflections, emotions, and perspectives with the intervener and also plays a key role in short-term attachment-based approaches (to be discussed below). Studies evaluating the efficacy of this approach have reported positive treatment effects on child attachment, caregiver sensitivity, and parent–child communication, although, to date, studies have not included random assignment.

Toth et al. (2002) and Lieberman et al. (2005; 2006) did use randomized designs with preschool-aged samples. Toth et al. worked with a sample of 4- to 5-year-old maltreated children and specifically targeted mothers' and children's internal working models related to attachment experiences. Their program, preschooler-parent psychotherapy (PPP), involves therapists in assisting mothers in changing their negative representations of themselves and their children into more positive relationship models. The therapist helps the mother recognize how her representations are enacted during her interactions with her own child, through use of observation and empathic comments. In addition, the therapist may help the parent understand how her present perceptions, attitudes and behavior are linked to the mothers' difficult childhood history. This allows the mother to clarify distorted perceptions and modify how she perceives and experiences her child and herself. More positive perceptions lead to greater maternal sensitivity, which, in turn, should facilitate the development of positive representational models in the child. Following preschooler–parent psychotherapy, Toth et al. found that children of families in the treatment group evidenced a greater decline in both maladaptive maternal representations and negative self-representations than those whose families participated either in a psychoeducational home visitation program or standard community care. In addition, they found that the preschoolers in the intervention group experienced increases in their positive mother–child relationship expectations. Although no direct measures of children's aggressive behavior problems were included in this study, this is one of the few that have used narrative measures at pre- and post-test to directly evaluate children's representational models. Results of the Lieberman et al. (2005) study, conducted with children aged 3 to 5 at high risk for aggressive behavior problems owing to the presence of marital violence in the family, showed improvements in children's behavior problems, traumatic stress symptoms, and diagnostic status, as well as mothers' avoidance and distress symptoms at posttest. A 6-month follow-up of this sample revealed durability of improvement in child behavior problems and maternal distress, although both these latter measures were based on maternal reports, and therefore subject to maternal bias. In several studies, positive outcomes for mothers have been found to be uncorrelated with positive child changes. For example, studies that have found decrease in maternal depression or stress following treatment have not found concomitant changes in parental interaction or improved developmental outcomes for children.

Parental child interaction therapy (PCIT) is a long-term mother–child intervention program based on social learning theory, which has also demonstrated efficacy in changing outcomes for children of 4 to 12 years of age with aggressive behavior problems (Chaffin et al., 2004). PCIT resembles the attachment-based approaches described above in focusing on improving the quality of parent–child interactions (e.g., reducing coercive cycles, increasing praise) through involvement in 25 to 28 week sessions, the majority of which include the parent–child dyad. PCIT has been demonstrated to reduce aggressive behavior problems and dysfunctional parent–child interaction patterns in a variety of populations (e.g., Eisenstadt, Eyberg, McNeil, Newcomb, & Funderburk, 1993; Hembree-Kigin & McNeil, 1995). Treatment benefits for children have been documented to generalize to children's behavior at school, to other nontarget children in the home, and to be durable over time (Chaffin et al., 2004).

In summary, studies have suggested that long-term interventions targeting improvement in the quality of the parent–child relationship may modify the early developmental trajectory of children at risk for aggressive behavior problems and other school-related maladaptation. However, given limitations in available funding for intervention, it is important to test whether improvements in both maternal and child behavior can occur following short-term attachment-based intervention. In the following section, we describe a short-term intervention program recently tested in Quebec with children (12 to 71 months) at high risk for cognitive and socio-emotional maladaptation.

Short-Term Intervention Methods

Short-Term Intervention Programs Targeting the Parent–Child Relationship

Given the important role of maternal sensitivity in attachment theory, a number of researchers have developed and tested short-term attachment-based intervention programs oriented directly at improving the predictability, consistency, and warmth of parental behavior towards the child. Similar to more long-term approaches, these programs have generally involved mother–infant dyads in weekly visits in the home setting. However, the duration of these programs is shorter (5 to 16 weeks) than that of the more long-term approaches reviewed above (20 weeks to a year). In the shorter-term model, interveners focus primarily on modifying the caregiver's interactive behavior with the child towards greater sensitivity, often by providing video-feedback (e.g., Bakermans-Kranenburg, Juffer, & Van IJzendoorn, 1998; Dozier et al., 2006; Moran, Pederson,

& Krupka, 2005). An important meta-analysis of attachment-based intervention programs comparing the efficacy of shorter and longer-term programs demonstrated that the former were more effective than the longer-term, representational approaches (Bakermans-Kranenburg, Van IJzendoorn, & Juffer, 2003) in improving attachment security. A subsequent meta-analysis (Bakermans-Kranenburg, Van IJzendoorn, & Juffer, 2005) also showed that "less is more" in that brief, sensitivity-based intervention programs were also more effective in changing disorganized attachment.

Short-Term Intervention Programs Targeting High-Risk Infants and Toddlers

The success of short-term attachment-based intervention has been demonstrated for high-risk populations including mothers and children at risk for aggressive problems (Van Zeijl et al., 2006), highly reactive infants (Velderman et al., 2006), and depressed mothers and their infants (Van Doesum, Riksen-Walraven, Hosman, & Hoefnagels, 2008). In the majority of these studies, mothers and their infants under a year of age have been targeted. Although aggressive behavior problems were not yet evident in such young children, those growing up with maternal, environmental, and child temperament factors indicating high developmental risk are likely to benefit. For example, maternal depression (Van Doesum et al., 2008) is associated with impaired socio-emotional and cognitive functioning, lower frustration tolerance, temper tantrums, and child insecurity. In the Velderman et al. (2006) study, highly-reactive infants who already showed low soothability, high activity level, and distress were included. In both studies, which used randomized control designs, following short-term (8 to 10 weeks) intervention aimed at improving caregiver sensitivity, significant improvement in quality of mother–child interaction was noted. Van Doesum et al. also noted significant improvement in child security, although this was not the case in the Velderman et al. study. In the latter study, highly reactive infants and their mothers were found to be more susceptible to the influence of treatment. The theory that children may vary in their susceptibility to both adverse and beneficial effects of rearing influences (Belsky, Bakermans-Kranenburg, & van IJzendoorn, 2007), and to attempts to alter rearing conditions, has important implications for intervention with aggressive children. Children at risk for aggressive behavior problems may have genetic vulnerabilities, which, in interaction with rearing conditions, influence levels of maladaptation. For example, Bakermans-Kranenburg, Van IJzendoorn, Pijlman, Mesman, & Juffer (2008), showed that toddlers with the dopamine receptor 4, 7-repeat allele (DRD4-7) were more likely to show decreases in externalizing behavior problems following short-term intervention to promote positive parenting than children without the allele. Their mothers also showed larger increases in positive discipline. However, this also suggests that weak intervention attempts with this vulnerable population are insufficient to prevent them from embarking on the negative developmental trajectory associated with maltreatment, involving increasing levels of aggressive and delinquent behavior problems.

The Van Zeijl et al. study (2006) is highly relevant to our discussion here owing to the fact that this study specifically targeted children (aged 1 to 3) already showing aggressive behavior problems. Using a randomized control design, these researchers tested a short-term six-session program, which included both sensitivity and discipline training. Results showed that the intervention was effective in improving maternal attitudes toward sensitivity, in promoting sensitive discipline interactions, and reducing child overactive problem behavior, but not in changing maternal sensitivity or child aggressive and oppositional behavior.

A New Short-Term Intervention Program for High-Risk Preschool Children

Building on these short-term attachment-based programs, in collaboration with the Lanaudiere youth protection agency in Quebec, we conducted the first study that evaluates the effectiveness of a short-term, attachment-based intervention with 67 maltreating parents and their children age 12 to 71 months, using a randomized control design (Moss, Dubois-Comtois, Cyr, Tarabulsy, St-Laurent, & Bernier, 2011). Since the majority of children referred to the program were preschoolers, we adapted principles of attachment theory relevant to preschool children, focusing equally on verbal as well as nonverbal interactions representative of the secure, insecure–organized and disorganized/controlling attachment patterns, and on containing parent–child role-reversed behavior. However, interveners familiar with attachment behavior at various age levels (e.g., infancy, early school-age) should be able to adapt the program for use with parents and children of these ages. Although the target group was maltreated children, the program is appropriate for other children at-risk for aggressive behavior problems. Maltreated children are at high risk for the development of aggressive behavior delinquency and substance abuse, in addition to academic underachievement and school drop-out (Salzinger, Feldman, Hammer, & Rosario, 1993; Shonk & Cicchetti, 2001; Toth, Cicchetti, Macfie, Rogosch, & Maughan, 2000). Maltreatment has also been associated with the adoption of negligent parental conduct and violence in adulthood, therefore contributing to the establishment of an intergenerational cycle of violence (Egeland, Jacobvitz, & Sroufe, 1988). In fact, in our sample, the mean pretest score for child aggressive behavior problems exceeded the clinical cut-off level. In addition, 70% of the families in our sample had incomes below the Canadian poverty line, and 65% did not finish high school.

Intervention goals. Our objectives for the study were as follows: We expected that parents (63 mothers, 5 fathers, all of which were their child's principal attachment figure) in the intervention group would show an increase in sensitivity following the 8-week intervention program. Concerning child outcomes, we expected an increase in the proportion of children showing secure attachment and a decrease in the proportion showing disorganized attachment and behavior problems of an externalizing and internalizing nature. In designing the study, we also wished to widen the age range of children that could potentially benefit, as well as adhere to the highest standards of research design. The sample included children aged 12 to 71 months with the average age of 3.35 years. Although previous attachment-based intervention studies had shown efficacy in modifying maternal sensitivity, and insecure and disorganized attachment in diverse samples, few short-term studies had included children beyond infancy. Although maternal responsiveness to child needs, and child security can be assumed to be essential intervention targets for older children as well as infants, it is important to modify the intervention program according to the needs of older children. In particular, it is important that caregivers are sensitive to the child's increasing need to be autonomous and self-regulating at preschool and school-age. At the same time, patterns of child controlling behavior need to be stopped before a pattern of parentification develops. Parentification refers to a role-reversed situation, in which children gradually assume the role of a parent in the family context and the parent takes on the role of a child. Interveners can help parents recognize and interrupt role-reversed, insecure-controlling patterns of parent–child interaction, which are highly predictive of development of externalizing and internalizing problems in middle childhood (Lyons-Ruth & Jacobvitz, 2008; Moss et al., 2005; 2006). In addition, professionals should be familiar with the peer behavior patterns and representational models that characterize children with different attachment patterns at preschool and early school-age.

Intervention methods and evaluation. As mentioned above, we sought to evaluate outcomes of the study according to the most rigorous standards. Participants were randomly assigned to intervention and control groups and we used a multi-informant approach to assess key developmental child outcomes. Different sets of observers rated child attachment based on pre and post-test separation-reunion behavior, and maternal sensitivity, in addition to maternal reports of child behavior problems. Following pretest assessments, families were randomly assigned to the intervention or control group. Both the intervention and control groups received the standard agency services, consisting of a monthly visit by a child welfare caseworker. Agency standards for these meetings are not uniform and usually consist of monitoring family conditions with respect to neglect and abuse (e.g., nutrition and hygiene, use of noncoercive discipline, crisis intervention) by agency caseworkers. The two post-test assessment meetings were identical to the pretest assessments and took place approximately 10 weeks following pre-test.

The intervention program, similar to other short-term attachment-based programs (e.g., Bakermans-Kranenburg et al., 2003), targets the improvement of maternal sensitivity to child emotional and behavioral signals, to promote greater security. Sensitivity involves (a) responding to child distress signals in a comforting and structuring way and (b) supporting child exploration when the child is not distressed. All intervention sessions were focused on reinforcing parental sensitive behavior by means of personalized parent–child interaction, video feedback, and discussion of attachment/emotion regulation-related themes (e.g., child negative emotion, discipline, separation anxieties).

The program consisted of eight home visits of approximately 90 minutes composed of the four following elements: (a) a 20-minute discussion on a theme chosen by the parent, with the parents relating recent events, asking child-related questions, and developing responses to problematic parent–child interactions; (b) a 15-minute videotaped interactive session with toys provided by the intervener and an activity chosen by the intervener based on child age and dyadic needs (e.g., building reciprocity, child proximity-seeking, encouraging parent to follow child's lead); and (c) a 20-minute video feedback session during which the intervener played back the just-completed filmed sequence and discussed the parent's feelings and observations of self and child during the interaction. The intervener's probes focused on positive sequences and provided feedback that reinforced parental sensitive behavior and its impact on child behavior; (d) a 15-minute wrap-up during which progress was highlighted and the parent was encouraged to continue similar activities with the child until the next meeting.

Intervention results. Our data analyses showed significant improvements in the targeted parental and child outcomes. Results indicated that the intervention was effective in enhancing parental sensitivity, improving child attachment security, and reducing disorganization and child behavior problems. Specifically, parents in the intervention group raised their level of sensitivity to a normative level following the intervention program, whereas parents in the control group remained at a low level, similar to that of other high-risk samples. Children in the intervention group were more likely to develop a secure attachment pattern than those in the control group. Although both the control and intervention groups had low proportions of secure children at pre-test (22% and 26%, respectively, consistent with statistics for maltreating samples), by post-test, 66%t of children in the intervention group were classified as secure (similar to low-risk groups), whereas little change was found in the control group (28% secure). There were 43% of intervention children who moved to security in comparison to only 16% of the control group (one secure child at pre-test in the intervention group (3% of the sample) became insecure at post-test which explains why 26% plus 43% does not equal 66%).

Before intervention, a high proportion of children in both the intervention (54%) and control groups (50%) were in disorganized attachment relationships, similar to findings in other maltreatment samples. These high levels are particularly troubling, given that disorganized attachment is associated with long-term risk for psychopathology (Lyons-Ruth & Jacobvitz, 2008; Moss et al., 2005). Following intervention, the percentage of children with disorganized attachments was reduced to 20% in the intervention group, while 56% of children in the control group remained in this category.

In addition, the intervention led to reductions in behavior problems for preschool-aged children in the sample. Longitudinal studies have shown that the maladaptive trajectories of maltreated children diverge from those of their non maltreated peers during the preschool period, during which the latter develop more socially and verbally competent modes of interaction, while the former maintain dysfunctional patterns of aggression and social withdrawal (Cicchetti & Valentino, 2006). Our results suggest that intervention may serve to interrupt this trajectory for maltreated children.

Discussion and Implications for Treating Insecure and Disorganized Attachment at School

This is the first study to demonstrate that a short-term intervention designed to enhance parental sensitivity and child attachment can be effective with maltreating parents. In addition, this is one of the first studies to demonstrate the effectiveness of an attachment-based intervention program that included preschoolers using a rigorous experimental design. The gold standard involves use of pretests, post-tests, and randomized assignment of participants to intervention and control groups. The intervention was effective in enhancing parental sensitivity, improving child security of attachment, and reducing disorganization for exposed children and reducing aggressive and depressive, anxious child behavior problems. These changes in critical developmental areas are of considerable theoretical and practical importance. On a clinical level, these findings indicate that targeted, well-timed programs oriented directly at increasing the predictability, coherence, and warmth of parental behavior towards the child can be effective even with extremely high-risk populations. On a social policy level, it is important to call attention to the potential consequences of not conducting such intervention. The children in the control group received standard services consisting of a monthly visit by a child welfare caseworker to monitor family conditions, and to respond to crises (e.g., separation or abandonment, episode of violence perpetrated by parent or other). However, these practices were clearly insufficient to effect change towards security and reduction in aggressive behavior problems.

Although it will be important in future research to test longer-term outcomes of the intervention program, the attachment-based model tested in this study may be an effective intervention tool for maltreated children and others at risk of aggressive behavior problems. Our own results and those of researchers who have successfully applied similar programs to infants and children beyond preschool age (e.g., Chaffin et al.), further suggest that the approach described here may also be effective with children in these developmental periods. Although we did not have enough infants to complete final analyses with this group, data on the infants who participated showed improvements in certain domains of the Bayley Scales of Infant Development, suggesting positive neurological changes, which could have wide-ranging effects on child development. Concerning use of the program with early school-age children, the program was more effective for older children in our sample compared with younger ones with respect to changing behavior problem outcomes. This is not surprising given that maladaptive trajectories of at-risk children diverge from those of their non at-risk peers over time, becoming more severe as children get older (Cicchetti & Valentino, 2006). However, it s also important to remember that, in general, there is decreasing developmental plasticity as children age, and identification and intervention with at-risk children should proceed as early as possible. One of the advantages of an attachment-based approach is that years of empirical research has enabled us to reliably identify disorganized children by 12 months of age. Given that studies have shown that disorganization in infancy is a predictor of aggressive disorders in childhood and adolescence (Carlson, 1998), early intervention efforts may prevent children from embarking on the negative developmental trajectories associated with school maladaptation.

Implications for Classroom Intervention

Although attachment-based approaches generally target the family as the primary intervention milieu, we believe that there are a number of implications of attachment theory for intervention in the classroom as well (see Table 6.1). Disorganized/controlling children are likely to show role-reversed behavior with the teacher, other school authority figures and peers as well as the parent. It is important to convey the message to these children that failure to respect rules, and language or actions that humiliate others will not be tolerated. At the same time, teachers need to find domains of competence in order to build self-esteem in these children. One of the surprising results in our study of the academic correlates of disorganization was the fact that disorganized/controlling children, unlike other insecure children, scored high on mastery motivation tests. Thus, the desire to assume mastery of others in social situations may have a positive corollary. A skillful teacher may be able to channel this desire in a positive direction which is also in keeping with the normative school age developmental goal of feeling superior to others in some domain (e.g., academic, sports, artistic) (Erikson, 1950). In addition, it is important that disorganized children receive tutoring in learning meta-cognitive skills. Although their aggressive behavior problems will elicit the attention of school personnel and may result in placement in a class for behaviorally-challenged children, this will not remediate their problems of an academic nature. If difficulties in organizing school-related tasks and executing cognitive strategies toward performance goals are left without remediation, problems of an academic nature will increase, as these abilities become increasingly important to academic success. In addition, problems of low self-esteem will become exacerbated, leading to further acting out of an aggressive nature. Finally, owing to the fact that the controlling behavior of the disorganized child serves a function in the family setting, such as assuming neglected parental functions, meetings with parents of disorganized children are likely to be difficult. Parents may have difficulty accepting the view of the teacher and school authorities and accepting an intervention plan. It is important for teachers to be assertive in such situations. In general, teacher assessments of children's behavior problems are better long-term predictors of developmental risk than are parental reports.

With respect to other insecure children showing either avoidant or ambivalent attachment patterns, behavior problems in the classroom may become more severe in times of family stress. This is in keeping with the idea that attachment strategies may help or hinder children's ability to deal with stressful family circumstances. Children with secure strategies are better able to use the parent–child relationship to deal with the

TABLE 6.1   Teacher Interventions to Deal With Problematic Behaviors
Associated with Attachment Styles

Attachment Styles	Problematic Behaviors	Teacher Interventions in the Classroom Setting
Avoidant	Aggressive behaviors towards peers Displays of anxious/ depressive behaviors Low emotional competency (can't use emotion language)	Develop emotional competency: Assist the child in communicating anger, sadness, fears or other distressing emotions Encourage good problem-solving skills in times of conflict Encourage children's positive behaviors
Ambivalent	Preoccupation with negative emotional states to the detriment of performance goals Displays of exaggerated dependency Reluctance to undertake difficult tasks	Help the child refocus attention on given tasks Encourage and reward autonomy Reassure the child that they are capable of behaving autonomously These children have learned that adults will generally yield to displays of anger and distress; therefore, teachers must ignore these displays and show consistency
Disorganized	Role-reversal behaviors with teachers, school authorities, peers, and parents Desire to assume mastery of others Low impulse control (don't think before they act) Difficulty organizing school-related tasks Academic difficulties	Communicate to the child that failure to respect rules is not tolerated Find domains of competence on which to build the child's self-esteem Tutor the child in learning meta-cognitive skills

distress activated by family crises such as parental separation or financial problems. However, as discussed above avoidant children are unlikely to communicate their difficulties to parents and may try to deny, or internalize distressing emotions. These efforts may result in increased anxiety or depression or alternatively aggressive acts, particularly with peers, when efforts to contain negative emotions prove unsuccessful and uncontrolled explosions occur. Insecure–ambivalent children, who use exaggerated anger or helplessness to gain attention, may increase these tactics when family stress is high and parents are even more inconsistently available. Thus, insecure–ambivalent children may also increase levels of aggressive or depressive/anxious behavior problems at these times.

Teachers play an important role in signalling the need for assistance, since they are often more likely to notice behavioral changes in children in the classroom setting that parents may be unaware of. This is particularly true for avoidant children who will make efforts to appear unperturbed at home, but may act out in school. When teachers notice abrupt, unexpected negative changes in children's behavior, it is often a good idea to ask parents if difficult family events have occurred. Parents may have been unaware of the impact of these events on the child. Together, parents and teachers can work together to assist the child through the difficult period.

In the case of children who act out with aggressive behavior, whether only in times of family stress or as a more habitual behavioral profile, attachment theory suggests certain interventions, which may prove useful in the classroom or home setting. Assisting children in interpersonally communicating anger, sadness, frustration or other distressing emotions in words is likely to reduce aggressive acts, which result from efforts to either unsuccessfully contain or exaggerate distress. Empirical studies have shown that children who participate in adult–child exchanges that involve sharing of emotional states, interpretations, and cognitive reflection about personal experience show increased social competence and security (Cyr, Dubois-Comtois, & Moss, 2008; Ontai & Thompson, 2008). While it is important to increase children's ability to verbalize and reflect on emotions, it is also vital that children who tend to become preoccupied with negative emotional states to the detriment of performance goals learn to refocus attention on tasks. In the case of insecure–ambivalent children who may show exaggerated dependency in the classroom, reluctance to undertake difficult tasks, and helplessness, it is important for teachers to encourage and reward child autonomy. These children often require reassurance from adults that they are capable of performing in an autonomous manner. If self-regulation is rewarded and dependency discouraged, ambivalent children can learn to place greater value on their own efforts and develop greater self-regulatory competence.

It may be helpful to repeat overall performance, rules and routines in order to help ambivalent children focus less on negative emotions (e.g., frustration), which may detract from moving ahead in social and cognitive tasks. Since these children have learned that adults will generally capitulate to displays of anger and distress, it is important for teachers to ignore these displays and show consistency. It is important for teachers to remember that it will be extremely difficult to change dysfunctional child patterns in the classroom that continue to function well in the home setting. Thus, if child attempts to use exaggerated distress to manipulate rules and routines at home (e.g., bedtime), are successful, then similar strategies are likely to be used in the classroom. School social workers or psychologists can assist in developing a plan that targets child consistency in self-regulation in both the family and school settings.

CONCLUSION

In summary, in this chapter we have discussed how early expectations concerning the accessibility and responsiveness of attachment figures develop into broader representations concerning the self and other, interpretations of socio-emotional experiences, and emotion regulation abilities. The idea that the quality of attachment behavior in childhood has lasting implications for later socio-emotional development has sparked decades of research on the links between attachment and development of peer relations and behavior problems as well as systematic intervention programs aimed at changing insecure and disorganized patterns. Increasingly, preschool and early school-age children are being referred for intervention for attachment-related problems and caregivers for improvements in parenting skills (Hoffman et al., 2006). Thus, intervention programs, such as those described here have important implications for the health of children and families, as well as for improvements in classroom functioning.

REFERENCES

Ainsworth, M. D. S., Bell, S. M., & Stayton, D. (1971). Individual differences in Strange Situation behavior of one-year-olds. In H. R. Schaffer (Ed.), *The origins of human social relations* (pp. 17–57). London: Academic Press.

Ainsworth, M. D. S., Blehar, M. C., Waters, E., & Wall, S. (1978). *Patterns of attachment: A psychological study of the strange situation.* Hillsdale, NJ: Erlbaum.

Anan, R. M., & Barnett, D. (1999). Perceived social support mediates between prior attachment and subsequent adjustment: A study of urban African American children. *Developmental Psychology, 35,* 1210–1222.

Bakermans-Kranenburg, M. J., Juffer, F., & Van IJzendoorn, M. H. (1998). Interventions with video feedback and attachment discussions: Does type of maternal insecurity make a difference? *Infant Mental Health Journal, 19,* 202–219.

Bakermans-Kranenburg, M. J., Van IJzendoorn, M. H., & Juffer, F. (2003). Less is more: Meta-analyses of sensitivity and attachment interventions in early childhood. *Psychological Bulletin, 129,* 195–215.

Bakermans-Kranenburg, M. J., Van IJzendoorn, M. H., Pijlman, F. T., Mesman, J., & Juffer, F. (2008). Experimental evidence for differential susceptibility: Dopamine D4 receptor polymorphism (DRD4 VNTR) moderates intervention effects on toddlers' externalizing behavior in a randomized controlled trial. *Developmental Psychology, 44,* 293–300.

Bakermans-Kranenburg, M. J., Van IJzendoorn, M. H., & Juffer, F. (2005). Disorganized infant attachment and preventive interventions: A review and meta-analysis. *Infant Mental Health Journal, 26,* 191–216.

Belsky, J., Bakermans-Kranenburg, M. J., & Van IJzendoorn, M. H. (2007). For better and for worse: Differential susceptibility to environmental influences, *Science, 16,* 300–304.

Booth, C. L., Rubin, K. H., & Rose-Krasnor, L. (1998). Perceptions of emotional support from mother and friend in middle childhood: Links with social-emotional adaptation and pre-school attachment security. *Child Development, 69,* 427–442.

Bowlby, J. (1969/1982). *Attachment and loss: Vol. 1. Attachment* (2nd ed). New York: Basic Books.

Bowlby, J. (1973). *Attachment and loss: Vol. 2. Separation.* New York: Basic Books.

Bowlby, J. (1980). *Attachment and loss: Vol. 3. Loss.* New York: Basic Books.

Bretherton, I., & Oppenheim, D. (2003). The MacArthur Story Stem Battery: Development, directions for administration, reliability, validity and reflections about meaning. In R. N. Emde, D. P. Wolf, & D. Oppenheim (Eds.), *Revealing the inner worlds of young children: The MacArthur story stem battery and parent-child narratives* (pp. 55–80). New York: Oxford University Press.

Brumariu, L. E., & Kerns, K. K. (2010). Parent-child attachment and internalizing symptoms in childhood and adolescence: A review of empirical findings and future directions. *Development and Psychopathology, 22,* 177–203.

Bureau, J.-F., & Moss, E. (2010). Behavioral precursors of attachment representations in middle childhood and links with child social adaptation. *British Journal of Developmental Psychology, 28,* 657–677.

Carlson, E. A. (1998). A prospective longitudinal study of disorganized/disoriented attachment. *Child Development, 69,* 1970–1979.

Carlson, E. A., Sroufe, L. A., & Egeland, B. (2004). The construction of experience: A longitudinal study of representation and behavior. *Child Development, 75,* 66–83.

Cassidy, J., & Berlin, L. J. (1994). The insecure/ambivalent pattern of attachment: Theory and research. *Child Development, 65,* 971–991.

Cassidy, J., & Kobak, R. R. (1988). Avoidance and its relation to other defensive processes. In J. Belsky & T. Nezworski (Eds.), *Clinical implications of attachment: Child psychology* (pp. 300–323). Hillsdale, NJ: Erlbaum.

Chaffin, M., Silovsky, J., Funderbunk, B., Valle, L., Brestan, E., Balachova, T. et al. (2004). Parent-child interaction therapy with physically abusive parents. Efficacy for reducing future abuse reports. *Journal of Consulting and Clinical Psychology, 72,* 500–510.

Cicchetti, D., Rogosch, F. A., & Toth, S. L. (2006). Fostering secure attachment in infants in maltreating families through preventive interventions. *Development and Psychopathology, 18,* 623–649.

Cicchetti, D., & Valentino, K. (2006). An ecological-transactional perspective on child maltreatment: Failure of the average expectable environment and its influence on child development. In D. Cicchetti & D. J. Cohen (Eds.), *Developmental psychopathology, Vol 3: Risk, disorder, and adaptation* (2nd ed., pp. 129–201). Hoboken, NJ: John Wiley & Sons.

Cyr, C., Dubois-Comtois, K., & Moss, E. (2008). Les conversations mère-enfant et l'attachement des enfants à la période préscolaire. *Canadian Journal of Behavioural Science, 40,* 140–152.

De Klyen, M., & Greenberg, M. T. (2008). Attachment and psychopathology in childhood. In J. Cassidy & P. R. Shaver (Eds.), *Handbook of attachment: Theory, research, and clinical applications* (pp. 637–665). New York: Guilford Press.

Dozier, M., Peloso, E., Lindhiem, O., Gordon, M. K., Manni, M., Sepulveda, S. et al. (2006). Developing evidence-based interventions for foster children: An example of a randomized clinical trial with infants and toddlers. *Journal of Social Issues, 62,* 767–785.

Easterbrooks, M. A., Davidson, C. E., & Chazan, R. (1993). Psychosocial risk, attachment, and behaviour problems among school-aged children. *Development & Psychopathology, 5,* 389–402.

Egeland, B., Jacobvitz, D., & Sroufe, A. (1988). Breaking the cycle of child abuse. *Child Development, 59,* 1080–1088.

Eisenstadt, T. H., Eyberg, S., McNeil, C. B., Newcomb, K., & Funderburk, B. (1993). Parent-child interaction therapy with behaviour problem: relative effectiveness of two stages and overall treatment outcome. *Journal of Clinical Child Psychology, 22,* 42–51.

Englund, M. M., Levy, A. K., Hyson, D. M., & Sroufe, L. A. (2000). Adolescent social competence: Effectiveness in a group setting. *Child Development, 71,* 1049–1060.

Erikson, E. H. (1950). *Childhood and society.* New York: Norton.

Fearon, R. P., Bakermans-Kranenburg, M. J., van Ijzendoorn, M. H., Lapsley, A. M., & Roisman, G. I. (2010). The significance of insecure attachment and disorganization in the development of children's externalizing behavior: A meta-analytic study. *Child Development, 81,* 435–456.

Freitag, M. K., Belsky, J., Grossman, K., Grossman, K. E., & Scheurer-Englisch, H. (1996). Continuity in parent–child relationships from infancy to middle-childhood and relations with friendship competence. *Child Development, 67,* 1437–1454.

Hembree-Kigin, T. L., & McNeil, C. (1995). *Parent child interaction therapy.* New York: Plenum Press.

Hoffman, K. T., Marvin, R. S., Cooper, G., & Powell, B. (2006). Changing toddlers' and preschoolers' attachment classifications: The circle of security intervention. *Journal of Consulting and Clinical Psychology, 74,* 1017–1026.

Jacobsen, T., Edelstein, W., & Hoffmann, V. (1994). A longitudinal study of the relation between representations of attachment in childhood and cognitive functioning in childhood and adolescence. *Developmental Psychology, 30,* 112–124.

Jacobsen, T., & Hoffmann, V. (1997). Children's attachment representations: Longitudinal relations to school behavior and academic competency in middle childhood and adolescence. *Developmental Psychology, 33,* 703–710.

Kerns, K. A., Klepac, L., & Cole, A. (1996). Peer relationships and pre-adolescents' perceptions of security in the child-mother relationship. *Developmental Psychology, 32,* 457–466.

Kerns, K. A., Tomich, P. L., Aspelmeier, J. E., & Contreras, J. M. (2000). Attachment based assessments of parent-child relationships in middle childhood. *Developmental Psychology, 36,* 614–626.

Lieberman, A. F., Ghosh Ippen, C., & Van Horn, P. (2006). Child-parent psychotherapy: 6-month follow-up of a randomized control trial. *Journal of the American Academy of Child and Adolescent Psychiatry, 45,* 913–918.

Lieberman, A. F., Van Horn, P., & Ghosh Ippen, C. (2005). Towards evidence-based treatment: Child-parent psychotherapy with preschoolers exposed to marital violence. *Journal of the American Academy of Child and Adolescent Psychiatry, 44,* 1241–1248.

Lyons-Ruth, K., Bronfman, E., & Parsons, E. (1999). Maternal frightened, frightening, or atypical behavior and disorganized infant attachment patterns. *Monographs of the Society for Research in Child Development, 64,* 67–96.

Lyons-Ruth, K., Connell, D. B., Grunebaum, H. U., & Botein, S. (1990). Infants at social risk: Maternal depression and family support services as mediators of infant development and security of attachment. *Child Development, 61,* 85–98.

Lyons-Ruth, K., Easterbrooks, M. A., & Cibelli, C. D. (1997). Infant attachment strategies, infant mental lag, and maternal depressive symptoms: Predictors of internalizing and externalizing problems at age 7. *Developmental Psychology, 33,* 681–692.

Lyons-Ruth, K., & Jacobvitz, D. (2008). Attachment disorganization: Genetic factors, parenting contexts, and developmental transformation from infancy to adulthood. In J. Cassidy & P. R. Shaver (Eds.), *Handbook of attachment second edition: Theory, research, and clinical applications* (pp. 666–697). New York: Guilford Press.

Lyons-Ruth, K., Repacholi, B., McLeod, S., & Silva, E. (1991). Disorganized attachment behavior in infancy: Short-term stability, maternal and infant correlates, and risk-related subtypes. *Development and Psychopathology, 3,* 377–396.

Main, M. (1981). Avoidance in the service of attachment: A working paper. In K. Immelman, G. Barlow, M. Main & L. Petrinovitch (Eds.), *Behavioral development: The bielefeld interdisciplinary project*. New York: Cambridge University Press.

Main, M. (1991). Metacognitive knowledge, metacognitive monitoring and singular (coherent) vs. multiple (incoherent) models of attachment: Findings and directions for future research. In C. Parkes, J. Stevenson-Hinde, & P. Marris (Eds.), *Attachment across the life cycle* (pp. 127–157). London: Routledge.

Main, M., & Cassidy, J. (1988). Categories of response to reunion with the parent at age six: Predictable from infant attachment classifications and stable over a 1-month period. *Developmental Psychology, 24,* 415–526.

Main, M., & Hesse, E. (1990). Parents' unresolved traumatic experiences are related to infant disorganized attachment status: Is frightened and/or frightening parental behavior the linking mechanism? In M. T. Greenberg, D. Cichetti, & M. Cummings (Eds.), *Attachment in the preschool years* (pp. 161–182). Chicago: University of Chicago Press.

Main, M., Kaplan, N., & Cassidy, J. (1985). Security of attachment in infancy, childhood, and adulthood: A move to the level of representation. In I. Bretherton & E. Waters (Eds.), *Growing points in attachment theory and research. Monographs of the Society for Research in Child Development, 50*(1–2), Serial No. 209, 66–104.

Main, M., & Solomon, J. (1990). Procedure for identifying infants as disorganized/disoriented during the Ainsworth Strange Situation. In M. Greenberg, D. Cicchetti, & M. Cummings (Eds.), *Attachment in the preschool years: Theory, research, and intervention* (pp. 121–160). Chicago: University of Chicago Press.

Marvin, R. S. (1977). An ethological-cognitive model for the attenuation of mother-child attachment behavior. In T. M. Alloway, L. Krames, & P. Pliner (Eds.), *Advances in the study of communication and affect: Vol. 3. Attachment behaviors* (pp. 25–60). New York: Plenum Press.

Mason, J. W. (1968). A review of psychoendocrine research on the pituitary-adrenal cortical system. *Psychosomatic Medicine, 30,* 576–607.

Moss, E. (1992). The socioaffective context of joint cognitive activity. In L. T. Winegar & J. Valsiner (Eds.), *Children's development within social context: Vol. 2. Research and methodology* (pp. 117–154). Hillsdale, NJ: Erlbaum.

Moss, E., Bureau, J.-F., Béliveau, M.-J., & Lépine, S. (2009). Links between children's attachment behavior at early school-age, their attachment-related representations, and behavior problems in middle childhood. *International Journal of Behavioral Development, 1,* 1–12.

Moss, E., Bureau, J-F., Cyr, C., Mongeau, C., & St-Laurent, D. (2004). Correlates of attachment at age 3: Construct validity of the preschool attachment classification system. *Developmental Psychology, 40,* 323–334.

Moss, E., Cyr, C., Bureau, J-F., Tarabulsy, G., & Dubois-Comtois, K. (2005). Stability of attachment between preschool and early school-age and factors contributing to continuity/discontinuity. *Developmental Psychology, 41,* 773–783.

Moss, E., Dubois-Comtois, K., Cyr, C., Tarabulsy, G. M., St-Laurent, D., & Bernier, A. (2011). Efficacy of a home-visiting intervention aimed at improving maternal sensitivity, child attachment, and behavioral outcomes for maltreated children: A randomized control trial. *Development and Psychopathology, 23,* 195–210.

Moss, E., Gosselin, C., Parent, S., Rousseau, D., & Dumont, M. (1997). Attachment and joint problem-solving experiences during the preschool period. *Social Development, 6,* 1–17.

Moss, E., Rousseau, D., Parent, S., St-Laurent, D., & Saintonge, J. (1998). Correlates of attachment at school-age: Maternal-reported stress, mother–child interaction and behavior problems. *Child Development, 69,* 1390–1405.

Moss, E., Smolla, N., Cyr, C., Dubois-Comtois, K., Mazzarello, T., & Berthiaume, C. (2006). Attachment and behavior problems in middle childhood as reported by adult and child informants. *Development and Psychopathology, 18,* 425–444.

Moss, E., & St-Laurent, D. (2001). Attachment at school age and academic performance. *Developmental Psychology, 37,* 863–874.

Moss, E., St-Laurent, D., & Parent, S. (1999). Disorganized attachment and developmental risk at school age. In J. Solomon & C. George (Eds.), *Attachment disoganization* (pp. 160–187). New York: Guilford Press.

Moran, G., Pederson, D. R., & Krupka, A. (2005). Maternal unresolved attachment status impedes the effectiveness of interventions with adolescent mothers. *Infant Mental Health Journal, 26,* 231–249.

NICHD Early Child Care Research Network (2001). Child-care and family predictors of preschool attachment and stability from infancy. *Developmental Psychology, 37,* 847–862.

NICHD Early Child Care Research Network (2005). Predicting individual differences in attention, memory, and planning in first graders from experiences at home, child care, and school. *Developmental Psychology, 41,* 99–114.

Olds, D., Henderson, C., Cole, R., Eckenrode, J., Kitzman, H., Luckey, D. et al. (1998). Long-terms effects of home visitation on children's criminal and antisocial behaviour. *Journal of the American Medical Association, 280,* 1238–1244.

Olds, D., Eckenrode, J., Henderson, C., Kitzman, H., Powers, J., Cole, R. et al. (1997). Long-terms effects of home visitation on maternal life course and child abuse and neglect. *Journal of the American Medical Association, 278,* 637–643.

Olds, D., Sadler, L., & Kitzman, H. (2007). Programs for parents of infants and toddlers: Recent evidence from randomized trials. *Journal of Child Psychiatry and Psychology, 48,* 355–391.

Ontai, L. L., & Thompson, R. A. (2008). Attachment, parent-child discourse, and theory of mind development. *Social Development, 17,* 47–60.

Osofsky, J. D., Kronenberg, M., Hammer, J. H., Lederman, J. C., Katz, L., Adams, S. et al. (2007). The development and evaluation of the intervention model for the Florida Infant Mental Health Pilot Program. *Infant Mental Health Journal, 28,* 259–280.

Salzinger, S., Feldman, R. S., Hammer, M., & Rosario, M. (1993). The effects of physical abuse on children's social relationships. *Child Development*, 64, 169–187.

Schore, A. N. (2001). Effects of a secure attachment relationship on right brain development, affect regulation, and infant mental health. *Infant Mental Health Journal. Special Issue: Contributions from the Decade of the Brain to Infant Mental Health*, 22, 7–66.

Shonk, S. M., & Cicchetti, D. (2001). Maltreatment, competency deficits, and risk for academic and behavioral maladjustment. *Developmental Psychology*, 37, 3–17.

Solomon, J., & George, C. (1996). Defining the caregiving system: Toward a theory of caregiving. *Infant Mental Health Journal*, 17, 183–197.

Solomon, J., & George, C. (1999a). The measurement of attachment security in infancy and childhood. In J. Cassidy & P. R. Shaver (Eds), *Handbook of attachment: Theory, research, and clinical applications* (pp. 287–316). New York: Guilford Press.

Solomon, J., George, C., & De Jong, A. (1995). Children classified as controlling at age six: Evidence of disorganized representational strategies and aggression at home and at school. *Development and Psychopathology*, 7, 447–464.

Sroufe, L. A., Egeland, B., & Carlson, E. (1999). One social world: The integrated development of parent-child and peer relationships. In W. A. Collins & B. Laursen (Eds.), *Relationships as developmental context: The 30th Minnesota symposium on child psychology* (pp. 241–262). Hillsdale, NJ: Erlbaum.

Stevenson-Hinde, J., & Shouldice, A. (1995). Maternal interactions and self-reports related to attachment classifications at 4.5 years. *Child Development*, 66, 583–596.

Teti, D. M., & Ablard, K. E. (1990). Security of attachment and infant-sibling relationships: A laboratory study. *Child Development*, 60, 1519–1528.

Toth, S. L., Cicchetti, D., Macfie, J., Rogosch, F. A., & Maughan, A. (2000). Narrative representations of moral-affiliative and conflictual themes and behavioral problems in maltreated preschoolers. *Journal of Clinical Child Psychology*, 29, 307–318.

Toth, S. L., Maughan, A., Manly, J. T., Spagnola, M., & Cichetti, D. (2002). The relative efficacy of two interventions in altering maltreated preschool children's representational models: Implications for attachment theory. *Development & Psychopathology*, 14, 877–908.

Van Doesum, K. T. M., Riksen-Walraven, J. M., Hosman, C. M. H., & Hoefnagels, C. (2008). A randomized controlled trial of a home-visiting intervention aimed at preventing relationship problems in depressed mothers and their infants. *Child Development*, 79, 547–561.

van IJzendoorn, M. H., Schuengel, C., & Bakermans-Kranenburg, M. J. (1999). Disorganized attachment in early childhood: Meta-analysis of precursors, concomitants, and sequelae. *Development and Psychopathology, 11,* 225–250.

Van Zeijl, J., Koot, H., Mesman, J., Van IJzendoorn, M. H., Bakermans-Kranenburg, M. J., Juffer et al. (2006). Attachment-based intervention for enhancing sensitive discipline in mothers of 1- to 3-year-old children at risk for externalizing behavior problems: A randomized controlled trial. *Journal of Consulting Psychology, 74,* 994–1005.

Velderman, M. K., Bakermans-Kranenburg, M. J., Juffer, F., Van IJzendoorn, M. H., Mangelsdorf, S. C., & Zevalking, J. (2006). Preventing preschool externalizing behavior problems through video-feedback intervention in infancy. *Infant Mental Health Journal, 27,* 466–493.

Zimmermann, P. (1999). Structure and functioning of internal working models of attachment and their role for emotion regulation. *Attachment and Human Development, 1,* 55–71.

Zimmerman, G. J. (2002). Achieving academic excellence: A self-regulatory perspective. In M. Ferrari (Ed.), *The pursuit of excellence through education* (pp. 85–110). The educational psychology series. Hillsdale, NJ: Erlbaum.

CHAPTER 7

Promoting Empathy in School-Aged Children
Current State of the Field and Implications for Research and Practice

Kimberly Schonert-Reichl

Yet, taught by time, my heart has learned to glow for other's good, and melt at other's woe.

— **Homer (8th Century BC)**

Empathy may be uniquely well suited for bridging the gap between egoism and altruism, since it has the property of transforming another person's misfortune into one's own feeling of distress.

— **Martin Hoffman (1981, p. 133)**

INTRODUCTION

For hundreds of years, empathy has garnered much scholarly attention and discussion.* Across many disciplines from philosophy and psychology to theology and education, scholars as well as teachers, clinicians,

* I would like to thank Jenna Whitehead for her assistance with preparing references, and Jennifer Hanson for her help with preparing tables and information on school-based prevention and intervention programs that promote empathy that are included in the CD. I am also grateful to two anonymous reviewers for their thoughtful and helpful comments on an earlier version of this chapter.

and the general public have critically debated the topic of empathy, posing such questions as: Are humans innately good or bad? What is the relationship between empathy and behavior? Do young children have the capacity for empathy? Can empathy be taught? Questions such as these spark heated debate and some controversy because the answers have both theoretical and practical implications for human nature and functioning.

In this chapter, issues relevant to the understanding and teaching of empathy in childhood are examined. First, extant definitions of empathy and related processes such as sympathy, personal distress, and compassion are described. Following, current theoretical and empirical work regarding the development of empathy and concern for others in childhood is put forth. Also included in this section is a review of some of the empirical work examining sex differences in empathy and prosocial behavior, as well as socialization practices inside and outside the family that can hinder or promote empathy and concern for others. Next, research that examines the relation of empathy to positive (prosocial) and negative (aggressive) behavior is reviewed. In this section, consideration of the relation of empathy to psychopathic tendencies in children is also discussed. Finally, implications of this work for prevention and intervention are delineated in relation to the promotion of social and emotional learning (SEL) in school. Also included in this section is a description of several high-quality, evidence-based classroom programs that include lessons and activities that foster the development of empathy-related processes, including the development of perspective-taking and prosocial behaviors. The chapter ends with some conclusions, implications, and directions for future work in this area.

EMPATHY 101

During the past few decades, the empathy construct has received considerable attention by psychologists and educators alike because of its association with positive behavior and psychological adjustment. Indeed, empathy has been identified by some as one of the most essential of all personality traits because it motivates helping and other prosocial behaviors (e.g., sharing, cooperation) and inhibits aggressive behaviors (Batson, 1991; Hoffman, 2000; Eisenberg & Miller, 1987; Miller & Eisenberg, 1988; Schonert-Reichl & Oberle, 2011a). However, it is important to note that while research findings are generally in accord in demonstrating a significant and positive association between empathy and prosocial behaviors (for a review, see Eisenberg, Fabes, & Spinrad, 2006), this does not necessarily imply that empathy *always* results in prosocial behavior, or even the desire to respond in prosocial ways. Nonetheless, empathy and its related characteristics play a key role in social understanding (Schonert-Reichl, 1999; Schultz, Selman, & LaRusso, 2003), and serves as the foundation for positive social relationships (Schonert-Reichl, 1993) and academic achievement (Caprara, Barbanelli, Pastorelli, Bandura, & Zimbardo, 2000; Wentzel, 1993). Although debates arise when trying to come to agreement regarding the primary function of empathy in both human and nonhuman species, recent theoretical, methodological, and empirical advances seem to point to the importance of empathy in helping individuals form and maintain lasting social bonds (Anderson & Keltner, 2002; deWaal, 2008; Thompson, in press). Thus, empathy is an aspect of human development that is critical for overall social functioning.

The past decade has witnessed a burgeoning interest in the empirical investigation of empathy. There are at least three reasons for this growing attention to the empathy construct. First, this increased focus on empathy may be due, in part, to recent historical events surrounding one of the topics of this book—lethal school shootings—as well as increased theoretical and empirical attention to school bullying—both topics that point to an empathy deficit in today's children and youth. Second, the emerging fields of positive psychology (Seligman & Csikszentmihalyi, 2000) and positive youth development (Damon, 2004) may also be responsible for more attention being paid to the development of children's positive human qualities, including the development of empathy. Finally, recent advances in neuroscience and brain imaging techniques, such as functional magnetic resonance imaging (fMRI) and physiology, are undoubtedly also responsible for the increased empirical attention to empathy. Although a discussion of this topic is beyond the scope of this chapter, interested readers are directed to some excellent reviews of this research (Carter, Harris, & Porges, 2009; Decety & Jackson, 2004; Decety & Lamm, 2006; Fogassi et al., 2005; Gallese & Goldman, 1998; Hastings, Zahn-Waxler, & McShane, 2006; Pfeifer, Iacoboni, Mazziotta, & Dapretto, 2008; Preston & deWaal, 2002; Shirtcliff et al., 2009).

Empathy Defined

Although empathy has been studied for hundreds of years spanning disciplines from philosophy, theology, ethology, and neuroscience to developmental psychology, and social and personality psychology, at present there exist disparate definitions for empathy and as a consequence, there is much heterogeneity in the ways in which researchers and theoreticians describe and study empathy. Some have used the word "empathy" to describe different phenomenon while others have used different words such as "sympathy" and "compassion" to describe the same phenomenon. This definitional ambiguity in describing and defining empathy has led to a conceptual quagmire regarding the precise nature of the term and the processes and mechanisms that underlie it, resulting in gaps and inconsistencies in our understanding of the concept (Davis, 2002).

In his book *Theory of Moral Sentiments* written over two centuries ago, Adam Smith (1790) described empathy as "the ability to understand another's perspective and to have a visceral or emotional reaction" (as cited in Hastings et al., 2006). Contemporary definitions of empathy hold the essence of Smith's definition, as illustrated by the following descriptions of empathy from some of the preeminent researchers and theorists in the field:

- *One particular set of congruent vicarious emotions, those that are more other focused than self-focused, including feelings of sympathy, compassion, tenderness, and the like....empathy is distinct from feelings of personal distress* (Batson, 1991, p. 86).
- *An affective response that stems from the apprehension or comprehension of another's emotional state or condition, and that is similar to what the other person is feeling or would be expected to feel* (Eisenberg, Fabes, & Spinrad, 2006, p. 647).
- *An affective response more appropriate to another's situation than one's own* (Hoffman, 2000, p. 4).
- *[R]efers ... to the experiencing of another's affective or psychological state and has both affective and cognitive components* (Zahn-Waxler & Radke-Yarrow, 1990).

Common to most of the extant definitions of empathy is the notion that empathy includes (a) an affective response ("feeling with another"), and (b) a distinction between self and other. With regard to this latter dimension, however, there is a general lack of consensus among theorists about the self-other facet of empathy. While some theorists believe that there be at least a minimal differentiation between self and other for empathy to ensue (e.g., Feshbach, 1975), others assume that this differentiation is not necessary for early phases of empathy (Hoffman, 1982).

Many researchers have spent considerable time trying to distinguish empathy from other related constructs, including sympathy, compassion, and personal distress (Batson, Fultz, & Schoenrade, 1987; Eisenberg, 1986; Feshbach, 1975; Hoffman, 2000; Wispé, 1986). Eisenberg, Spinrad, and Sadovsky (2006), for instance, have posited a clear distinction between empathy and sympathy. In their view, *empathy* is considered a mirroring or vicarious experience of another's emotions whereas *sympathy* "is an affective response that frequently stems from empathy, but can derive directly from perspective taking or other cognitive processing, including retrieval of information from memory. It consists of feeling sorrow or concern for the distressed or needy other (rather than feeling the same emotion as the other person is experiencing or is expected to experience)" (p. 647). In other words, empathy reflects *feeling as* the other feels whereas sympathy reflects *feeling for* the other. In contrast, *personal distress*, which also emerges from exposure to another person's distress, refers to a self-focused and aversive reaction (e.g., anxiety, discomfort) to the vicarious experiencing of another's emotion (Batson, 1991; Eisenberg, Shea, Carlo, & Knight, 1991). Personal distress—an aversive, self-focused emotional reaction to the apprehension or comprehension of another's emotional state or condition—is believed to undermine other-oriented prosocial behavior.

Compassion, which is much like sympathy because it is instigated from the suffering of another, is considered to be both a dimension of morality and an important aspect of both ethical behavior and interpersonal responsibility (Knafo, Zahn-Waxler, Van Hulle, Robinson, & Rhee, 2008). Compassion, however is distinguished from sympathy in that it moves beyond the sole focus on a *concern* for the well-being of someone in distress and includes a need or desire to *alleviate* that person's suffering (Eisenberg, 2002). Both empathy and prosociality are considered to be essential components of compassion.

EMPATHY AND ITS DEVELOPMENT IN CHILDREN AND ADOLESCENTS

For centuries, there has been a belief held by parents, educators, professionals, and others in the general public that children are inherently selfish and egocentric and characterized by a lack of caring for others' needs. A couple decades of research, however, has debunked this perspective, and we know now that already at the age of 2, children "show (a) the cognitive capacity to interpret the physical and psychological states of others, (b) the emotional capacity to experience affectively the states of others, and (c) the behavioral repertoire that permits the possibility of trying to alleviate discomforts in others to alleviate discomfort in others" (Zahn-Waxler & Radke-Yarrow, 1990, pgs. 113–114). Indeed, there is a plethora of data that have been accumulated over the past few decades illustrating that even very young children are capable of acting in ways that demonstrate empathy. Zahn-Waxler and colleagues (e.g., Hastings, Zahn-Waxler, Robinson, Usher, & Bridges, 2000; Zahn-Waxler, Robinson, & Emde, 1992; Zahn-Waxler,

Radke-Yarrow, Wagner, & Chapman, 1992) use the term "concern for others" to describe a compilation of qualities reflecting empathy and related processes (including affective and cognitive components of empathy), hypothesis-testing or inquisitiveness about the nature of the other's distress, and prosocial behaviors, including helping and comforting others. Research by Zahn-Waxler and colleagues on the development of concern for others generally has found that even very young children are responsive to the distress of others. One longitudinal study examining the development of concern for others conducted by Zahn-Waxler, Radke-Yarrow, Wagner, and Chapman (1992), for instance, found that children's reparative behaviors after they had caused harm to another increased with age. Additionally, children's behavioral expressions of concern for others occurred in concert with their development of self-awareness and the cognitive dimension of empathy. Zahn-Waxler et al. (1992) found sex differences as well, with girls expressing more empathy than boys, but only for witnessed and not for caused distresses.

In the following section, I begin with a brief overview of a theory of empathy development put forth by Martin Hoffman, followed by a description of some of the research on sex differences in empathy and prosocial behavior. This section ends with a discussion of some of the socialization practices that have been identified as promoting the development of empathy children.

Hoffman's Theory of Empathy Development

Hoffman (1982, 2000) has been acknowledged as being one of the first in the field to propose a theoretical model that describes the development of empathic distress from infancy to childhood. In his four-level model, he delineates a developmental shift that occurs across childhood that moves from an egocentric self-concern in response to others' distress to empathic concern for others that results in prosocial behavior that is other-oriented. In his first stage, Global Empathy, which occurs between the ages of 0 and 12 months, Hoffman (2000) posits that witnessing another person in distress may result in a global empathic distress response that is elicited from distress cues from a dimly perceived "other." At this stage, because infants cannot yet distinguish themselves from the other, they may act as though what they witnessed happened to the other, happened to themselves. One example of this may be when a child, upon seeing another child fall and cry, responds by crying himself/herself and seeks comfort from his/her mother—behaviors that he/she does when hurt. At this stage, however, it is not clear whether the infant can distinguish who is in distress.

The second stage in Hoffman's theory is identified as Egocentric Empathy. Hoffman (1984) identifies the acquisition of "object permanence" at this stage in development as the mechanism responsible for leading children to have a sense of the other as a physical entity distinct from themselves. In other words, the child can now be aware that it is the other person and not oneself who is in distress. Nonetheless, the internal states of others are unknown, and the child still confuses others' inner state with his/her own. For example, upon hearing the cry of another, a toddler will provide help that he himself would find comforting, such as offering his own favorite toy or getting his/her own mother.

Hoffman's third stage of empathy, Empathy for Another's Feeling, occurs between the ages of 3 and 8 years. The child becomes increasingly aware of other people's feelings and that other people's perspectives may be different from his/her own. Hence, the child becomes more responsive to emotional cues from others. Increases in language skills enable the child to derive meaning from symbolic cues. He/she is able to empathize with a wide range of complex emotions, including disappointment, feelings of betrayal, and, later in this stage, distress (Hoffman, 1984). Moreover, it is at this stage when a child can begin to exhibit the ability to experience empathic responses even when the distressed person is not physically present—as is the case when the child hears or reads about another person's distress.

Finally, during late childhood and early adolescence, the fourth stage emerges, Empathy for Another's Condition. It is during this fourth stage of development in which the child is now able to have feelings of empathic distress for an entire group or class of people (e.g., homeless, poor, or oppressed). Owing to increased cognitive maturity and sophistication in conceptions of self and other as continuous persons with separate identities and histories, the child realizes that she/he and others are independent persons whose emotions may be tied to not only the current situation but also to a unique history of past events and large life experience.

Although Hoffman's theory is not data-based, empirical research generally supports Hoffman's (2000) view that empathy shifts from a less mature and surface level understanding of another's distress to a more complex and sophisticated understanding of distress that is not transitory but chronic from the early years and into adolescence. This development shift in empathic understanding is partly due to increased competence in children's ability for detecting and understanding emotions in themselves and others (Eisenberg, Murphy, & Shepard, 1997) and advances in perspective-taking (Selman, 1980). Hoffman (1982) proposed that improvement in young children's perspective taking is critical to their abilities to differentiate between their own and others' distress and to accurately understand others' emotional reactions. These skills are believed to foster empathy and sympathy and, consequently, more and higher quality prosocial behavior.

Sex Differences in Empathy and Prosocial Behaviors

Gender stereotypes typically depict females as more empathic and prosocial than males, who are often expected to be relatively independent and achievement-oriented (Eisenberg, Fabes, & Spinrad, 2006). In an early meta-analytic review of sex differences in empathy and related processes, Eisenberg and Lennon (1983) found large differences favoring females, especially when data were collected via self-report questionnaires. Eisenberg and Lennon concluded that the general pattern of results was often due, in part, to differences among measures when demand characteristics were high (the intent of the measure was obvious), and people could control their responses (e.g., when self-report measures were used). Sex differences in empathy favoring females have often been found when the sample sizes were large and the samples were comprised of older versus younger children (Eisenberg et al., 2006). In other research, sex differences in facial reactions to empathic stimuli, generally favoring females, have been found (see Eisenberg, Martin, & Fabes, 1996).

Findings about sex differences in prosocial behaviors, like empathy and sympathy, have been found to vary across studies, depending on the type of prosocial behavior examined and the age of the actor. For instance, Eagly and Crowley (1986) conducted a meta-analysis of older adolescents' and adults' helping behaviors and found that men helped *more* than women, particularly in situations involving either instrumental or chivalrous helping. In contrast, Eisenberg and Fabes (1998) in their meta-analysis of 259 studies with children and adolescents, found a significant effect indicating higher levels of prosocial behaviors in girls versus boys. Similar to the findings regarding sex differences in empathy, effect sizes favoring girls were generally larger when the prosocial behaviors were measured via self or other reports than with observational measures. Additionally, sex differences in prosocial behaviors favoring females were also stronger with increasing age, and when aggregated indices or indices reflecting behaviors such as and kindness and consideration were taken into account, in contrast to indices reflecting instrumental help, comforting, or sharing.

More recent research has continued to find sex differences in reports of children's prosocial behaviors, with girls being identified as more prosocial than boys (e.g., Caprara, Barbaranelli, & Pastorelli, 2001; Oberle, Schonert-Reichl, & Thomson, 2010; Schonert-Reichl, 1999).

For example, when peers are asked to assess their peers' behaviors, girls are more likely to nominate girls as being prosocial and to nominate boys as being bullies (Warden & Mackinnon, 2003; Warden, Cheyne, Christie, Fitzpatrick, & Reid, 2003). Fewer sex differences have been found in some observational studies (Fabes, Martin, & Hanish, 2002). As noted by Eisenberg, Fabes, and Spinrad (2006), " ... although girls appear to be more prosocial than boys, the issue of sex differences in prosocial responding and their origins is far from resolved" (p. 698).

Socialization of Empathy: Discipline and Induction

In a search for the processes and mechanisms that lead to problems in empathy often seen in children with disruptive behavior disorders (Tremblay, Masse, Vitaro, & Dobkin, 1995), there are some suggestions that poor parenting practices may be responsible, in part, for some of the empathy deficits found in these youth. For instance, the family environments of early-starting antisocial adolescents are often characterized by harsh, inconsistent parenting (e.g., Patterson, 1982, 1995; Patterson, DeBaryshe, & Ramsey, 1989) and abuse (Luntz & Widom, 1994), poor environments in which children are inadvertently trained to make angry, coercive responses rather than empathic, prosocial ones.

According to Hoffman (2000) and others (e.g., Eisenberg, Spinrad et al., 2006; Staub, 2003), empathy can be nurtured and promoted through socialization experiences in which adults in the child's environment practice and model inductive approaches to discipline—socialization practices in which the parent, caregiver, or teacher highlight the other's perspectives, point out the another's distress, and make clear to the child that his/her actions caused it. This would include situations in which children are confronted with having to resolve conflicts in which their own interests are contrasted with the needs of others. These social situations—in which children harm or about to harm others whose interests conflict with their own—can occur at home, in child care settings, and in schools, and offer an opportunity for adults to intervene and guide children on a positive path toward higher levels of empathy. Hoffman (1984) outlines five ways in which parents and/or caregivers can promote empathy in young children:

1. *Permit children to experience a wide range of emotions.* Because it is generally considered to be easier to empathize with someone's emotions when you have experienced that emotion yourself, children need to develop a wide repertoire of emotion experiences to make them more empathically responsive.

2. *Direct children to the internal states of others.* Empathy is typically considered to be an involuntary response if one actively witnesses a victim's distress; therefore, it is critical that parents and caregivers provide experiences in which a child has the opportunity to witness the other's emotional distress. Inductive discipline approaches discussed earlier in which the parent or caregivers calls attention to the pain or injury caused by the child's action or encourages the child to imagine how he/she would feel to be in the victim's place are examples of this approach.

3. *Provide role-taking/perspective-taking opportunities across contexts.* In order to hone children's competencies in "standing in the shoes of another," they need repeated opportunities to take the perspectives of others. These activities can be promoted through a variety of mediums, including books and television.

4. *Give children lots of affection.* Hoffman argues that providing children with affection will make them less absorbed in their own needs and more open to the needs of others.

5. *Be a role model by behaving in a prosocial manner and verbalizing your empathic feelings.* Children learn from what they observe, and they need to be in contexts in which adults are helpful and kind to one another and to the children with whom they interact. It is also critical that children are in contexts in which the discussion of empathy and empathic feelings is part of everyday conversations. This will result not only in children learning a large corpus of emotion words, but will also lead to higher levels of empathic responsiveness in children.

THE RELATION OF EMPATHY TO PROSOCIAL AND AGGRESSIVE BEHAVIOR

Self-absorption in all its forms kills empathy, let alone compassion. When we focus on ourselves, our world contracts as our problems and preoccupations loom large. But when we focus on others, our world expands. Our own problems drift to the periphery of the mind and so seem smaller, and we increase our capacity for connection—or compassionate action.

—**Daniel Goleman**
Social Intelligence: The New Science of
Human Relationships (2006)

Numerous theorists have suggested that empathy is an important factor in motivating positive, helpful behavior (Batson, 1991; Hoffman, 2000;

Staub, 1979) and for inhibiting hurtful and aggressive behavior (Joliffe & Farrington, 2006). In examining the major theoretical and empirical approaches to understanding the determinants of prosocial and aggressive behaviors, most efforts have been directed at identifying the situational, social, and individual factors that affect the degree to which prosocial and aggressive behavior is learned and enhanced. Throughout most of these discussions, empathy and sympathy have been implicated in prosocial development and action (Eisenberg, Spinrad et al., 2006).

In the following section, some of the research examining the relation of empathy to prosocial behavior is summarized. Following, some of the extant research on the association between empathy and aggression in general, and bullying in particular, are put forth. The section ends with a discussion on the relation between empathy and psychopathy in children.

Empathy and Prosocial Behavior

The study of prosocial behavior is both relevant and important to the understanding of empathy because it is often assumed that empathy is the catalyst for the enactment of caring and helpful behavior (Batson, 1991). Prosocial behavior has been defined as "voluntary behavior intended to benefit another" (Eisenberg, Fabes, & Spinrad, 2006, p. 646). This type of behavior, including helpful or caring behaviors and related cognitions, are valued in most cultures, probably because of their contributions to harmonious human relationships. It is important to note that prosocial behaviors can occur for a number of reasons, ranging from egoistic and practical concerns (e.g., a child shares with another child in order to obtain a reward) to altruistic and other-oriented concerns. Although this latter type of motivation is the one assumed to be truly representative of prosocial behavior, one must also be cognizant that prosocial behaviors can be enacted for a variety of reasons.

Decades of research have expected and found a significant and positive relationship between empathy and prosocial behavior across childhood and adolescence, although the degree of this relation appears to vary as a function of the measure of empathy utilized (Catherine & Schonert-Reichl, 2011; see Zhou, Valiente, & Eisenberg, 2003 for a review). In addition to empathy, cognitive development, perspective-taking, and emotion understanding (e.g., emotion identification) have also been identified as factors that underlie children's prosocial responding. For example, toddlers who display evidence of self-recognition (signifying that they have the ability to distinguish self from others) tend to be relatively empathic and are likely to display prosocial behaviors (Zahn-Waxler, Schiro, Robinson, Emde, & Schmitz, 2001). Young children's perspective-taking, in the form of being able to label and/or understand why another person is distressed, also has been found to be positively related to their prosocial responding (Kiang, Moreno, & Robinson, 2004). Furthermore, young children's emotion knowledge has been found to be positively associated with prosocial behavior toward younger siblings (Garner, Jones, & Palmer, 1994), and adults expressing negative emotions (Denham & Couchouad, 1991).

A number of researchers and theorists have also argued that empathy is central to the engagement in other-oriented moral responding (e.g., Batson, 1991; Eisenberg, 1986). Support for this supposition has been found in some studies conducted by Eisenberg and her colleagues. For example, in a study of Brazilian adolescents, Eisenberg, Zhou, and Koller (2001) examined the relation of empathy-related responding to prosocial moral reasoning (i.e., reasoning about moral dilemmas in which one person's needs or wants conflict with those of others in a context where authorities, laws, rules, punishment, and formal obligations play a minimal role). Results revealed that composite and internalized reasoning scores from a prosocial moral reasoning measure (Carlo, Eisenberg, & Knight, 1992) were significantly and positively related to both sympathy and empathy. Moreover, empathy and perspective taking were found to be positively associated with adolescents' self-reports of prosocial behaviors.

There is some evidence that displays of empathic and prosocial behaviors in the form of comforting responses to other's distress begin to appear in early childhood and increase throughout development. Several researchers (Robinson, Zahn-Waxler, & Emde, 2001; Zahn-Waxler, Schiro et al., 2001), for instance, have studied toddlers' empathic responses to an experimenter and a mother feigning distress from an injury in young children, and found age-related increases in both empathy and prosocial behavior. Similarly, Lamb and Zakhireh (1997) found a significant and positive relation between toddlers' prosocial behavior toward peers. Around ages 2 and 3, the increase in empathic and prosocial responding to others' distress is accompanied with a corresponding decrease in nonempathic, self-oriented distress reactions (Zahn-Waxler, Radke-Yarrow et al., 1992; Zahn-Waxler et al., 2001). Overall, with increasing age, preschoolers are more likely to respond to others' distress with empathy and prosocial behaviors (Hastings et al., 2000; Lennon & Eisenberg, 1987).

Research on children has found a significant and positive relation between age and empathy and prosocial responding. In a 1998 meta-analysis of studies on prosocial behavior across childhood and adolescence conducted by Eisenberg and Fabes (1990), for instance, significant increases between age and prosocial behavior were found when comparing preschoolers and the child and adolescent age groups, indicating a general increase in prosocial behaviors across preschool and the school years. Nonetheless, Eisenberg and Fabes note that the studies they reviewed in their meta-analyses were largely cross-sectional in nature and varied greatly in quality and methodological rigor. Hence, further research is needed to explore age-related trajectories of prosocial behavior across childhood using well-designed longitudinal studies to offer any firm conclusions on the continuity and discontinuity of prosocial behavior across childhood and adolescence.

Of particular relevance to the understanding of prosocial responding in children is the identification of those mechanisms and processes that underlie altruism, which is defined as "intrinsically motivated voluntary behavior intended to benefit another—acts motivated by concern for others or by internalized values, goals, and self-rewards rather than by the expectation of concrete or social rewards or the avoidance of punishment" (Eisenberg, Fabes et al., 2006, p. 647). During the past few years there has been a surge in research exploring the early antecedents and manifestations of altruism in very young children (see Keltner, 2009 for a review). At the forefront of some of this work are Felix Warneken and Michael Tomasello, researchers who have conducted a series of studies exploring the cognitive and motivational components of prosocial behavior and altruism in infancy. In one of these studies (Warneken & Tomasello, 2006), they presented 18-month-old infants with 10 different situations in which an adult experimenter was having trouble achieving his goal. The variety of situations probed the children's ability to discern a variety of goals and intervene in a variety of ways. For instance, the experimenter used clothespins to hang towels on a line, and, when he accidentally dropped a clothespin on the floor and unsuccessfully reached for it, the toddler helped by walking over to the experimenter, picking up the clothespin, and handing it to the experimenter. In another situation identified as the "cabinet task," the experimenter tried to put a large stack of magazines into a cabinet, but he was unable to open the cabinet doors because his hands were full of the large stack of magazine. In this experiment, the child walked over to the cabinet doors and opened them for the experimenter. For each of the 10 tasks there were control conditions to rule out the possibility that children would perform the target behavior (offering the clothespin; opening the door) irrespective of the other's need (e.g., because they like to hand things to adults or like to open cabinet doors when their attention is drawn to it). In these control conditions, the same basic physical situation was established, but with no indication that the experimenter needed help. The finding of this study was that children displayed spontaneous, unrewarded helping, "altruistic" behaviors when another person was unable to achieve his goal (but performed these behaviors significantly less often in control conditions where no help is necessary).* This research described above and other research conducted by Warneken and Tomasello (2006, 2007, 2008, 2009) and Vaish, Carpenter, and Tomasello (2010) suggests that further research is necessary to explore the underlying mechanisms and processes by which young children behave altruistically and/or prosocially in order to determine the role of empathy in motivating their behavior.

Empathy, Aggression, and Bullying

Among developmental psychologists, there is a long interest in when and why children act aggressively. Indeed, research on the relation between empathy and aggressive behavior among children and youth has received considerable attention (Cohen & Strayer, 1996; Miller & Eisenberg, 1988), with studies demonstrating that empathy provides a buffer against aggressive tendencies and behaviors, in part due to the notion that highly empathic individuals can emotionally anticipate the harmful effects that their behavior might have on another (Hoffman, 2000). Moreover, both cognitive and emotional components of empathy have been found to play a mitigating role in interpersonal aggression and violence (Joliffe & Farrington, 2004, 2006; Kaukiainen et al., 1999).

In exploring the antecedent conditions and correlates of antisocial and aggressive behaviors, many researchers have become particularly sensitive to the potentially potent role that empathy may play in different forms of children's aggression. Nesdale, Milliner, Duffy, and Griffiths (2009), for example, found that empathy was a significant negative predictor of direct (e.g., name-calling, taking things from another, hitting, pushing, or teasing another) but not indirect (e.g., ignoring, gossiping about, deceiving, rejecting, or excluding another) aggression intentions.

Another way in which researchers have explored the role of empathy in aggression has been to examine empathy in relation to bullying behaviors in children and adolescents. Surprisingly however, despite the popular contention that bullies lack empathy, to date there are few studies that have empirically examined the empathy–bullying link. Endresen and Olweus (2001), in a large sample of Norwegian adolescents (13–16 years of age), found relatively weak correlations between self-reported empathic responsiveness and bullying, although their measure of empathy did not

---

* To see video examples of these experiments, see Dr. Warneken's Research Lab website in the Department of Psychology at Harvard University: http://email.eva.mpg.de/~warneken/video.

take into account the multidimensional nature of the construct. Espelage, Mebane, and Adams (2004) examined the relation between empathy and bullying in a sample of 565 American middle school students (grades 6–8) using a well established measure of empathy, the *Interpersonal Reactivity Index* (IRI; Davis, 1983), a measure that taps both empathic concern (i.e., the emotional dimension of empathy) and perspective-taking (i.e., the cognitive component of empathy). These researchers reported significant negative relations overall between self-reported bullying and both perspective-taking and empathic concern, although the relations for empathic concern were stronger for boys than for girls. Gini, Albiero, Benelli, and Altoe (2007) in a sample of 318 Italian adolescents (grades 7 and 8) found significant negative relations between peer-assessed bullying and both empathic concern and perspective-taking, but only for boys. Research linking empathy and aggression has also shown stronger relations for boys (see Miller & Eisenberg, 1988).

Taken together, studies to date generally support the notion that children who bully, especially boys, report lower levels of both cognitive and affective empathy. Interestingly, both Endresen and Olweus (2001) and Espelage et al. (2004) found evidence that students' attitudes toward bullying mediated the relationship between empathy and bullying. That is, students high in empathy reported negative attitudes toward bullying and therefore were less likely to engage in such behavior. Future research is needed to determine whether the low to modest correlations observed between empathy and bullying differ depending on the social intelligence and status of the bully (Sutton, Smith, & Swettenham, 1999). As skilled manipulators, some bullies may be able to cognitively understand the perspective of others, but are deficient with regard to the emotional components of empathy, lacking the ability to anticipate the *emotional consequences* of their actions.

Empathy and Psychopathic Tendencies

The classification of psychopathy was first introduced by Hare (1980, 1991) to identify a relatively homogeneous pathology involving a pervasive pattern of both emotional (e.g., considerably reduced empathy and lack of remorse, callousness) and behavioral (criminal activity and, frequently, violent) symptoms. Blair, Peschardt, Budhani, Mitchell, and Pine (2006), in a review of the development of psychopathy, argue that the emotional component of psychopathy in the form of reduced empathy and guilt is the most crucial one in the development of psychopathy because it is emotional dysfunction that puts an individual at risk for learning antisocial behaviors.

Psychopathy is considered to be a developmental disorder in that it can be identified in both childhood and adulthood (Frick, O'Brien, Wootton, & McBurnett, 1994; Hare, 1980, 1991). Although there is a lack of longitudinal research showing that those identified as psycho-pathic in childhood are also identified as psychopathic in adulthood, the neuro-cognitive impairments seen in children with psychopathic tenden-cies are, for the most part, also seen in adults with psychopathic tenden-cies (see Blair et al., 2006 for a review).

Research on children with psychopathic tendencies has generally shown that these children are low in empathy (Dadds et al., 2009; Mullins-Nelson, Salekin, & Leistico, 2006) and lack some of the fun-damental emotional skills necessary for empathic responding, includ-ing reduced sensitivity to distress cues of others (Blair, 1999) and reduced moral reasoning (Blair, 1997). Blair, Colledge, Murray, and Mitchell (2001) investigated the sensitivity to facial expressions in a sample of children with psychopathic tendencies and a comparison group ($n = 30$), as defined by the Psychopathy Screening Device (PSD; Frick & Hare, 2000). Children were shown cinematic displays of a standardized set of facial expressions that depicted six basic emotional expressions—sadness, happiness, anger, disgust, fear, and surprise. Findings revealed significant differences in the understanding of the facial expressions between the two groups of children, with significant impairments in those children with psychopathic tendencies relative to controls. Children with psychopathic tendencies needed significantly more time to process the facial expressions and made significantly more errors when processing fearful expressions than the comparison group—often misclassifying fear as one of the five other basic emo-tions. Moreover, children with psychopathic tendencies were signifi-cantly less sensitive to the facial expression depicting sadness than the comparison children.

More recent research on the relation between psychopathic traits and reduced sensitivity to signs of distress in others was conducted by van Baardewijk, Stegge, Bushman, and Vermeirien (2009) with a community sample of 224 children (53% boys). These researchers were interested in testing the hypothesis that aggression in children with psychopathic traits can be attenuated when the emotional distress cues of others are made more salient. Using a computer-based competitive reaction-time game with a simulated opponent who, for half of the participants (ran-domly selected), expressed his or her fear via a written message, the find-ings revealed a significant relationship between psychopathic traits and aggression, but only in the no-distress condition. Hence, the research demonstrated that the relation between psychopathic traits and aggres-sion could be attenuated when making another's distress cues more obvious. The authors conclude by countering the relatively pervasive and pessimistic view held by researchers and clinicians on the malleability of psychopathy and its behavioral concomitants, and argue that empathy-based treatment approaches may reduce aggression in children with psychopathic tendencies. As van Baardewijk et al. posit "The finding that aggression in children with high psychopathic traits can, at least temporarily, be inhibited by intensifying the display of the victim's distress may provide a small but essential piece of the puzzle of future intervention strategies aimed at reducing the risk for a deviant and societally harmful development in this important group" (p. 723).

CAN EMPATHY AND PROSOCIAL RESPONDING BE TAUGHT?

The School-Based Promotion of Empathy and Prosocial Responding

The past few years have seen a convergence of evidence supporting the need for early prevention via school-based programs designed both to stave off an upward trajectory of aggressive and maladaptive behaviors and to promote students' positive and prosocial behaviors and social and emotional health (Wilson, Lipsey, & Derzon, 2003). Bolstered by evidence indicating that empirically based curricula can deter the onset of problem behaviors and emotional difficulties (see Durlak, Weissberg, Dymnicki, Taylor, & Schellinger, 2011), many school districts throughout North America have strengthened their efforts to include programs that promote students' social and emotional competence because such factors have been identified as those that reduce or ameliorate risk, promote positive child development, and prevent problems. Schools have been identified as contexts that can play a crucial role in fostering children's mental health and deterring aggression (Elias et al., 1997). Indeed, according to the Consortium on the School-Based Promotion of Social Competence (1994): "Schools are widely acknowledged as the major setting in which activities should be undertaken to promote students' competence and prevent the development of unhealthy behaviors. In contrast to other potential sites for intervention, schools provide access to all children on a regular and consistent basis over the majority of their formative years of personality development" (p. 278). Given that maladaptive behaviors during the early school years can be potent warning signs for later more serious forms of problems including criminality, mental illness, and underachievement (Tremblay et al., 1995), elementary schools in particular are considered to be the locus for *primary* prevention (Fonagy, Twemlow, Vernberg, Sacco, & Little, 2005) because early instantiations of problem behaviors may be more amenable to prevention efforts than their later manifestations. Additionally, because emotion-evoking interpersonal experiences (e.g., interpersonal conflict with peers) are a regular part of children's everyday lives, children in elementary school are continuously exposed to situations in which adults intervene in order to help them negotiate these experiences. And, thus are exposed to experiences in which their empathy can be promoted.

Social emotional learning, or SEL, is the process of acquiring the competencies to recognize and manage emotions, develop caring and concern for others, establish positive relationships, make responsible decisions, and handle challenging situations effectively (Greenberg et al., 2003).* In short, SEL competencies comprise the foundational skills for positive health practices, engaged citizenship, and school success. SEL is sometimes called "the missing piece," because it represents a part of education that is inextricably linked to school success, but has not been explicitly stated or given much attention until recently. The good news is that these skills can be taught through nurturing and caring learning environments and experiences (Elias et al., 1997; Greenberg, 2010). Some of the most compelling evidence for the assertion that SEL programs promote children's and adolescents' social-emotional wellbeing and academic achievement comes in the form of a recent meta-analysis conducted by Durlak et al. (2011) of 213 school-based universal SEL programs involving 270,034 students from kindergarten through high school. Their findings revealed significant and positive effects for students in SEL programs relative to controls. More specifically, in contrast to students not enrolled in SEL programs, SEL students demonstrated significantly improved social-emotional competencies, attitudes, and behavioral adjustment in the form of increased prosocial behavior and decreased conduct problems and internalizing problems. SEL students also out performed non-SEL students on indices of academic achievement by 11 percentile points. In addition to the positive effects of SEL programs for students, Durlak et al. found that classroom teachers and other school personnel effectively implemented SEL programs—a finding that suggests that SEL programs can be easily incorporated into routine school practices and do not require staff from outside the school to successfully deliver an SEL program.

---

* Note that a discussion of social and emotional learning is also presented in Chapter 5.

Selected SEL Programs Designed to Promote Empathy and Empathy-Related Behaviors

Following, I review six SEL programs that are aligned with theoretical principles for preventive interventions designed to promote children's social and emotional competence. There is a seventh program, Second Step, that incorporates specific lessons on empathy and this program is described in Chapter 5. All seven of the programs are summarized in Table 7.1. The programs selected for inclusion in this chapter were chosen based on the following criteria: (a) an explicit focus in the curriculum on the promotion of empathy and/or empathy-related processes associated with prosocial behavior, (b) the program is considered to be "universal"—in other words, the program is implemented to all children in the general classroom and not targeted to a special group of children, (c) the program has empirical evidence supporting its effectiveness via rigorous methodological design (i.e., experimental or quasi-experimental), and (d) the program is manualized, available commercially, and requires that teachers receive some training before implementing the program in their classrooms. Programs that were not included in this section are those in which the focus is on the development of skills and behaviors not explicitly associated with empathy and empathy-related responding, and programs that are targeted specifically at students who are already experiencing identified social and emotional problems (e.g., depression, anxiety, conduct problems) and are in need of more intensive treatment approaches. Because several extensive reviews of SEL prevention programs already exist (for example see CASEL's *Safe and Sound Guide: An Educator's Guide to Evidence-Based Social and Emotional Learning Programs* (2003), for a compendium of school- and classroom-based social and emotional learning programs, http://www.casel.org/pub/safeandsound.php), another such review is neither necessary nor within the scope of the present chapter. It is important to note that many of the SEL programs that target school-aged children draw mainly from cognitive and social cognitive theories of children's social and emotional competence. They generally do not involve a specific focus on the development of empathy per se, but they deal with a general focus on the promotion of social and emotional competence on a more global level, in terms of perspective-taking and the promotion of prosocial behavior. Although a few school-based programs have a specific focus on empathy, to my knowledge there is only one evidence-based program that has integrated the concept of empathy into all aspects of its curriculum. This program is entitled the "Roots of Empathy," and will be discussed first in more detail in the following section. The other few programs that have specific empathy and/or emotion component focus it more on social

TABLE 7.1 Social and Emotional Learning (SEL) Programs That Promote Empathy and Empathy-Related Constructs

Program Name	Developer/Website	Target Age/Grade Group	Main Components of the Program	Research Findings (Examples)[a]
Caring School Community® (CSC) Project	Program developer: Developmental Studies Center, Oakland, CA Website: www.devstu.org	Kindergarten to sixth grade Some activities are age-specific and others can be implemented across grades	Class meetings Cross-age Buddies Program Homeside activities School-wide community building activities Optional read-aloud libraries	Greater sense of school as a caring community More frequent altruistic behavior More concern for others Better conflict resolution skills Stronger commitment to democratic values Higher achievement test scores
The Emotions Course (EC)	Program developer: Carroll Izard, PhD, University of Delaware Contact: Frances Haskins, MA Lab Coordinator, HumanEmotions Lab 181 McKinly Lab–Psychology University of Delaware Newark, DE 19716 302-831-2700	Preschool (Head Start programs)	Materials include two manuals for teachers: one that presents the conceptual framework and another that details 20 lessons Lessons focus mainly on joy/happiness, sadness, anger, and fear. Part 1 of each lesson begins with the teacher and assistant teacher doing a puppet show that illustrates the gist of the lesson. The rest of the lesson consists of interactive games relating to aspects of the emotions	Increased emotion knowledge and emotion regulation Increased positive emotion expression Increased social competence Decreased negative emotion expression, aggression, anxious/depressed behavior Decreased negative peer and adult interactions

Program	Program developer	Grade range	Description	Outcomes
The 4Rs Program (Reading, Writing, Respect, and Resolution)	Program developer: Morningside Center for Teaching Social Responsibility, New York, New York. Website: www.morningsidecenter.org	Kindergarten to fifth grade	Each unit is based on a children's book, carefully chosen for its high literary quality and relevance to the theme. All of the units have two parts; Book Talk suggests activities, promotes discussion, writing, and role play for deepening students' understanding of the book and connecting it to their lives. Applied Learning consists of conflict resolution lessons related to the theme	Lower levels of teacher-rated aggression; Less tendency to ascribe hostile motives to others in ambiguous social situations, Fewer symptoms of attention and hyperactivity problems, and Increases in social competence
PATHS® (Promoting Alternative Thinking Skills) Program	Program developers: Mark Greenberg, PhD & Carol Kusche, PhD. The curriculum is available for purchase at Channing Bete http://www.channing-bete.com/prevention-programs/paths/paths.html	Preschool to fourth grade	Teaches children skills for generating a variety of solutions to interpersonal problems, considering the consequences of situations. Recognizes thoughts, feelings, and motives that generate problem situations	

Continued

TABLE 7.1 (*Continued*) Social and Emotional Learning (SEL) Programs That Promote Empathy and Empathy-Related Constructs

Program Name	Developer/Website	Target Age/Grade Group	Main Components of the Program	Research Findings (Examples)[a]
The MindUP™ Program	Program developer: The Hawn Foundation, Santa Monica, California Website: www.thehawnfoundation.org Manuals for the program can be purchased at Scholastic (http://teacher.scholastic.com/products/mindup/.com)	Kindergarten to eighth grade (K–2, 3–5, 6–8)	The MindUP™ consists of 15 lessons in which a set of social, emotional, and self-regulatory strategies and skills developed for pre-kindergarten through eighth-grade students to cultivate well-being and emotional balance	Increased optimism and self-concept Improvements in social competence, attention and control, behavioral dysregulation, and aggression
The Roots of Empathy	Program developer: Mary Gordon Contact: Roots of Empathy, Toronto, Ontario, Canada Website: www.rootsofempathy.org	Pre-K (Seeds of Empathy) kindergarten to eighth grade (kindergarten, grades 1–3, 4–6, 7–8)	ROE is a 9-month program that has as its cornerstone a monthly classroom visit by an infant and his/her parent(s) whom the class "adopts" at the beginning of the school year Facilitated by a trained ROE instructor, each visit of the baby and his or her parent follows a lesson plan with nine different themes, helping children to understand and reflect on their own and others' feelings	Increased emotion understanding Increased prosocial behavior Greater sense of classroom as a community Decreased aggression Increased peer acceptance

| Second Step | Pre-kindergarten to middle school (Early Learning, K–1, 2–3, 4–5, middle school) | Each of the 27 lesson plans is designed to capitalize on shared observations from the family visit; Lesson plans and accompanying activities are scripted to match the age of the baby and are calibrated to the students' level of development | Increased prosocial behavior Decreased aggression and hostile attributions |
| | Program developer: Committee for Children, Seattle, Washington Website: www.cfchildren.org | The program is organized on three sections (i.e., empathy, anger management, and impulse control) and provides a multiyear coverage of violence prevention | |

[a] A more complete description of research findings accompanied by citations can be found in the main text descriptions of each of these programs.

understanding and perspective-taking and incorporate activities designed
to take advantage of the inherently adaptive functions of emotions.

The Roots of Empathy Program

> Darren was the oldest child I ever saw in a Roots of Empathy class.
> He was in Grade 8 and had been held back twice. He was two years
> older than everyone else and already starting to grow a beard. I knew
> his story. His mother had been murdered in front of his eyes when he
> was four years old, and he had lived in a succession of foster homes
> ever since. Darren looked menacing because he wanted us to know he
> was tough. His head was shaved except for a ponytail at the top, and
> he had a tattoo on the back of his head. The instructor of the Roots
> of Empathy program was explaining to the class about differences in
> temperament that day. She invited the young mother who was visiting
> the class with Evan, her six-month-old baby, to share her thoughts
> about her baby's temperament. Joining in the discussion, the mother
> told the class how Evan liked to face outwards when he was in the
> Snugli and didn't want to cuddle into her, and how she would have
> preferred to have a more cuddly baby. As the class ended, the mother
> asked if anyone wanted to try on the Snugli, which was green trimmed
> with pink brocade. To everyone's surprise, Darren offered to try it,
> and as the other students scrambled to get ready for lunch, he strapped
> it on. Then he asked if he could put Evan in. The mother was a little
> apprehensive, but she handed him the baby, and he put Evan in, facing
> towards his chest. That wise little baby snuggled right in, and Darren
> took him into a quiet corner and rocked back and forth with the baby
> in his arms for several minutes. Finally, he came back to where the
> mother and the Roots of Empathy instructor were waiting and he
> asked: "If nobody has ever loved you, do you think you could still be a
> good father?" (Gordon, 2005, p. 5–6)

Program Description The above real-life example is illustrative of the
emotional insights and empathic reactions that can be instigated when
children are exposed to school programs designed explicitly to educate
both their hearts and minds. The Roots of Empathy (ROE) program has
as its cornerstone monthly visits by an infant and his/her parent(s) that
serve as a springboard for lessons on emotion knowledge, perspective-
taking, and infant development. Through explicit classroom lessons
designed to recognize a baby's facial and nonverbal expression, children
are led through a discussion of how we might know how a baby feels
and why the baby might feel that way; this then leads to a discussion of
a time when they might have experienced a similar emotion (e.g., a time

that they were sad or excited). The discussion then culminates in a larger discussion of emotion identification and emotion expression, namely, why people feel the way they do and why (e.g., why a classmate might have looked sad that day). In SEL programs like ROE that are designed to promote children's empathy and prosocial behaviors, the recognition and discussion of emotions and emotion understanding—including how we feel, why we feel the way we do, how our actions make others feel— comes to the fore in the classroom context. This emotion knowledge provides a foundation for empathic responding and prosocial action.

The Roots of Empathy (ROE) program is a theoretically-derived, universal preventive intervention that facilitates the development of children's social-emotional understanding in an effort to reduce aggression and promote prosocial behavior. Facilitated by a trained ROE instructor, each visit of the baby and his/her parent follows a lesson plan with nine different themes (Meeting the Baby, Crying, Caring and Planning for the Baby, Emotions, Sleep, Safety, Communication, Who Am I?, Goodbye and Good Wishes), helping children to understand and reflect on their own and others' feelings. Over the course of the school year, children learn about the baby's growth and development via interactions and observations with the baby. Each month the ROE program instructor visits his/her participating classrooms three times, once for a pre-family visit, another time for the visit with the parent and infant, and finally, a post-family visit. The lessons for the visits from the instructor foster empathy, emotional understanding, and problem-solving skills through discussion and activities in which the parent–infant visit serves as a springboard for discussions about understanding feelings and infant development and effective parenting practices. Specifically, each lesson plan is designed to capitalize on shared observations from the family visit. Lesson plans and accompanying activities are scripted to match the age of the baby and are calibrated to the students' level of development. Each of the ROE lessons provides opportunities to discuss and learn about the different dimensions of empathy, namely emotion identification and explanation, perspective-taking, and emotional sensitivity. For example, across various lessons children are invited to identify the emotions of the baby and to provide explanations for those emotions. Following, children then become engaged in lessons either through stories, art activities, and general classroom discussion in which they reflect and discuss their own emotions and the emotions of others. For Theme 3 (Caring and Planning for the Baby), for instance, in the pre-family visit, the instructor reads the book *Sasha and the Wriggly Tooth* (Tregebov, 1993) to the children. After the story, the instructor leads a discussion with the children about the mixed feelings that can ensue when one loses a tooth (e.g., "happy to be getting a visit by the tooth fairy," "embarrassed because you may look funny with a missing tooth"). In the subsequent parent and infant visit, children are provided opportunities to perspective take through asking questions of the parents about their feelings about their infant's teething experience (e.g., "How does it feel to see your baby in pain," "What do you do to help your baby feel better?"). Also included in the ROE program are lessons that engage children *collectively* in a series of activities that benefit the baby—those activities identified by Staub (1988) as ones in which a prosocial value orientation can be fostered. From singing a welcoming song to the baby upon his/her arrival to the classroom, to creating a book of nursery rhymes, in every lesson children are brought together to form a unified "we." The ROE curriculum is aligned with the *functionalist* approach to emotions (Campos, Mumme, Kermoian, & Campos, 1994), wherein emotion understanding and expressivity are seen as playing central roles in the establishment and maintenance of children's interpersonal relationships (Mostow, Izard, Fine, & Trentacosta, 2002; Saarni, 1999; Shipman, Zeman, Penza, & Champion, 2000). As well, the ROE model's "roots" are founded on the belief that "emotions form the motivational bases for empathy and prosocial behavior" (Izard, Fine, Mostow, Trentacosta, & Campbell, 2002, p. 761).

Program evaluations. To date, there have been several outcome studies examining the efficacy of ROE (see Schonert-Reichl & Scott, 2009 for a review). These include an examination of ROE's effectiveness with primary grade children, a multisite evaluation (including children in Vancouver and Toronto), and two randomized controlled trials (RCT). Research on the effectiveness of ROE has yielded consistent and highly promising findings regarding the impact of the program across age and sex (Schonert-Reichl, Smith, Zaidman-Zait, & Hertzman, 2011a). Children who have participated in ROE, compared to those who have not, demonstrate advanced emotional and social understanding, as well as reduced aggressive behavior (specifically proactive aggression) and increased prosocial behavior. Consistent findings emerged across our research studies evaluating the effectiveness of ROE. Specifically, results revealed that children who had experienced the ROE program, compared to children who had not, were more advanced in their emotional and social understanding on almost all dimensions assessed. Developmental changes in children's social and emotional knowledge were associated with concomitant reductions in aggressive behaviors and increases in pro-social behaviors (helping, sharing, cooperating). Most notably, while ROE program children significantly decreased in aggression across the school year, comparison children demonstrated significant increases in aggression. Subsequent studies evaluating changes in experiences within the classroom found a significant increase in children's assessments of classroom supportiveness and their sense of belonging in the classroom.

The Caring School Community Project

Program description. The Caring School Community (CSC) program (formerly called the Child Development Project) was developed by researchers at the Developmental Studies Center (see www.devstu.org), a nonprofit organization with a focus on developing and disseminating programs that promote children's social–emotional development and academic success. CSC was developed for children in grades kindergarten through sixth grade and teaches teachers to employ participatory instructional practices such as cooperative learning groups, mastery teaching, and experiential activities that promote relevant, interactive classroom learning. The program aims to promote core values, prosocial behavior, and a school-wide feeling of community and consists of four program elements: (a) class meeting lessons to promote dialogue among students, (b) a cross-age "buddies" program that pairs students across grades to build relationships and trust, (c) "homeside" activities that promote family involvement and inform parents of school activities while providing them with opportunities to participate and, (d) school-wide community building activities that involve school, home, and community. Class lessons provide teachers and students with a forum to get to know one another, discuss classroom issues as they arise, identify and solve problems collaboratively, and make a range of decisions collaboratively that affect classroom life. The CSC is unique in that it involves both extensive classroom-wide and school-wide efforts to create a sense of common purpose and commitment to prosocial norms and values such as caring, justice, responsibility, and learning. These efforts are designed to promote a "caring community" of learners. The entire faculty and student body at CSC schools must commit to these values and to an extensive 3-year school development program. The ultimate goal is the development of students who are ethically sophisticated decision makers and caring human beings (Kohn, 1997). Adults act as role models and offer guidance that helps children understand the effects of their actions upon others. Students in the CSC are expected to demonstrate involvement in prosocial activities that benefit others through meaningful school and community service-learning experiences (e.g., School-Wide Buddies program).

Program evaluations. The CSC is one of the most researched of the SEL programs. There have been over 20 years of research indicating that students who have participated in the program demonstrate more prosocial and less aggressive behaviors, and a range of positive school and motivation outcomes compared to children who have not received CSC (e.g., Battistich, 2003; Battistich, Schaps, Watson, & Solomon, 1996; Battistich, Solomon, Watson, & Schaps, 1997; Battistich, Solomon,

Watson, Solomon, & Schaps, 1989). In the schools in which CSC has been implemented, increases in students' sense of the school as a caring community has been reflected in a positive orientation toward school and learning, mutual trust in and respect for teachers, and overall increases in prosocial behavior and social skills. These positive effects remained stable in high poverty schools with the highest sense of community, suggesting the effectiveness of this program for high-risk settings (Battistich et al., 1997). A follow-up study evaluated program effects on 525 students after they reached middle school. Findings at follow-up included higher grade point averages and achievement test scores, greater involvement in positive youth activities, and less frequent problem behavior at school and acts of violence (Battistich, Schaps, & Wilson, 2004).

The Emotions Course

Program description. The emotions course (EC) is comprised of 22 lessons, is a theoretically-coherent program based on differential emotions theory (DET), and is designed to be implemented by teachers in Head Start classrooms (see Izard, Trentacosta, King, & Mostow, 2004). In keeping with key tenets of DET, the central goal of the EC curriculum is to increase young children's ability to understand and regulate emotions, utilize modulated emotions, and reduce maladaptive and problem behavior. The EC course makes no use of the extrinsic rewards typical of many of the behavioral and cognitive–behavioral programs (Izard, 2002; Izard et al., 2008). The first part of each lesson begins with the teacher and assistant teacher doing a puppet show that illustrates the general focus of the lesson. Following this, each lesson consists of interactive games relating to aspects of the emotions. Throughout all of the lessons, opportunities are given to children to label or name emotion expressions depicted on EC posters. Children are urged to compare the expressions of different emotions, and they compare different intensities of each of the individual emotions. Throughout EC, the teachers give children opportunities and some coaching in drawing expressions of the emotions, and encoding the expressions for peers to see. The primary aim of these exercises is to increase children's skills in decoding emotion signals or recognizing emotion expressions.

Program evaluations. There have been two studies conducted to date evaluating the effectiveness of the EC curriculum (Izard et al., 2008). Both studies were conducted in the context of Head Start programs. In the first study, conducted in a rural community, findings showed that

EC children, compared to children in the control condition (Head Start, as usual), evidenced greater increases in emotion knowledge and emotion regulation and greater decreases in negative emotion expressions, aggression, anxious/depressed behavior, and negative peer and adult interactions. In the second study, conducted in an urban setting, results revealed that compared to the established prevention program, the EC program led to greater increases in emotion knowledge, emotion regulation, positive emotion expression, and social competence. In Study 2, emotion knowledge mediated the effects of EC on emotion regulation, and emotion competence (an aggregate of emotion knowledge and emotion regulation).

The 4Rs (Reading, Writing, Respect, and Resolution)

Program description. The 4Rs Program is a universal school-based intervention for children in kindergarten to fifth grade that was developed by the Morningside Center for Teaching Social Responsibility (http://www. morningsidecenter.org/) in response to several national and local policy shifts in the United States. More specifically, the 4Rs evolved in response to the tension between the movement to reform education between standards-based accountability with its focus on academic achievement, on the one hand (e.g., the policy and practice promoted by the No Child Left Behind Act of 2001), and SEL, on the other (e.g., the growing recognition of social–emotional skills as critical to school success) and provides a pedagogical link between the teaching of social–emotional competencies and fundamental academic skills. The 4Rs Program has two primary components: (a) a comprehensive seven-unit, 21–35 lesson, literacy-based curriculum in conflict resolution and SEL (provided to teachers in a standardized, grade-specific teaching guide); and (b) 25 hours of training followed by ongoing coaching of teachers to support them in teaching the 4Rs curriculum with a minimum of 12 contacts in one school year. The theory of change underlying the 4Rs program emphasizes the importance of introducing teachers to a set of SEL skills and concepts, and then supporting them in the use of these skills and concepts in their everyday interactions in the school with one another, with school administrators, and with the children in their classrooms. Moreover, emphasis is given to attending to the social–cognitive and social–emotional processes that previous research has shown link individual, family, school, and community risk factors to the development of aggressive behavior, and that place children at higher risk for future violence. By highlighting universal themes of conflict, feelings, relationships, and community, the 4Rs curriculum adds meaning and depth to literacy instruction. Because reading and writing are excellent tools for exploring conflict, feelings, and problem-solving, the 4Rs program also provides opportunities for conflict resolution instruction as well.

Program evaluations. Although the 4Rs is a relatively new SEL program, there have already been two rigorous evaluation studies conducted. In the first study, Brown, Jones, LaRusso, and Aber (2010) employed a cluster randomized controlled trial design to examine whether teaching social–emotional functioning predicts differences in the quality of third-grade classrooms, and to test the effectiveness of the 4Rs program on the quality of classroom processes controlling for teacher social–emotional functioning. Participants included 82 third-grade teachers and 82 classrooms in 18 public urban elementary schools in a large metropolitan city in the eastern United States. Their findings yielded positive effects of teachers' perceived emotional ability on classroom quality. More specifically, teachers' perceptions of their own emotion abilities at the beginning of the year, significantly and positively predicted their ability to create high-quality social processes in their classroom by the end of the year, as evidenced via classroom observations. Moreover, positive and significant effects of the 4Rs Program on overall classroom quality were demonstrated after taking into account differences in these teacher factors.

More recently, Jones, Brown, and Aber (2011) conducted a 2-year experimental study of the 4Rs program on children's social–emotional, behavioral, and academic functioning. Their study employed a school-randomized, experimental design with 1,184 children in 18 elementary schools. Findings revealed that children in the intervention schools showed significant improvements across several domains of functioning, including self-reports of hostile attributional bias, aggressive interpersonal negotiation strategies, and depression. Teacher reports of attention skills, aggression, and socially competent behavior also improved. In addition to the program's positive effects on children's behaviors, the results showed effects of the intervention on children's math and reading achievement for those children identified by teachers as having the highest behavioral risk at baseline.

The MindUP™ Program

The MindUP™ Program is a comprehensive classroom-based program for children from pre-kindergarten to eighth grade aimed at fostering children's social and emotional competence, psychological well-being, and self-regulation while decreasing acting-out behaviors and aggression. The MindUP program was designed to enhance children's self-awareness, social awareness, focused attention, self-regulation, problem solving, prosocial behaviors, and positive human qualities, such as happiness, optimism, and altruism. The curriculum is theoretically-derived and informed by the latest scientific research in the fields of cognitive neuroscience, mindfulness-based stress reduction, social and emotional learning (SEL), and positive psychology (Seligman & Csikszentimihalyi, 2000). Further, the MindUP™ Program was developed as an approach to teaching, as opposed to a curriculum that is separate from other subject areas. There are daily activities (three times a day) that consist of deep belly breathing and attentive listening to a single sound (i.e., a resonating instrument), which are central to the program with the intention of enhancing children's self awareness, focused attention, self-regulation, and stress reduction.

Program evaluations. To date, there are two experimental studies examining the effectiveness of the MindUP program (Schonert-Reichl & Stewart Lawlor, 2010; Schonert-Reichl et al., 2011b). For the first one, a quasi-experimental, pretest/posttest, control group design was used to evaluate the MindUP program (formerly called the Mindfulness Education program) among 246 fourth to seventh grade children drawn from 12 classrooms. Six MindUP program classes were matched with six comparison classes where the average age, gender, and race/ethnicity of the class was equivalent. Overall, both teachers and students reported satisfaction with the program. In addition, results revealed that children who participated in the MindUP Program, compared to children who did not, showed significant improvements on teacher-rated attention and social competence, and decreases in aggressive/dysregulated behavior in the classroom. In addition, children in the ME program self-reported greater optimism and mindful attention than those not in the program. Student and teacher reports indicate that MindUP promotes enhanced feelings of empathy, more frequent prosocial behaviors, focused attention, emotional regulation, and greater appreciation for "school and learning in general." The skills and strategies of MindUP help children become more optimistic and willing to face the challenges they encounter in school and elsewhere. The second study (Schonert-Reichl et al., 2011b) both replicated and extended the findings of the previous study showing significant improvements in children's optimism, empathy, emotional control, attention, self-concept, and prosocial behaviors in the classroom.

PATHS (Promoting Alternative Thinking Strategies) Program

Program description. The PATHS (Promoting Alternative Thinking Strategies) curriculum is a comprehensive program for promoting emotional and social competencies and reducing aggression and behavior problems in elementary school-aged children. The PATHS curriculum is designed to be used by educators and counselors in a multiyear, universal prevention model. The PATHS Curriculum, taught three times per week for a minimum of 20–30 minutes per day, provides teachers with systematic, developmentally-based lessons, materials, and instructions for teaching their students emotional literacy, self-control, social competence, positive peer relations, and interpersonal problem-solving skills. Students have many opportunities to practice identifying a wide range of feelings and their associated bodily sensations, calming themselves through breathing techniques, and taking others' perspectives while solving interpersonal problems using an 11-step model. Consistent opportunities are provided for students to apply many of these competencies beyond the lesson. PATHS lessons include instruction in identifying and labeling feelings, expressing feelings, assessing the intensity of feelings, managing feelings, understanding the difference between feelings and behaviors, delaying gratification, controlling impulses, reducing stress, self-talk, reading and interpreting social cues, understanding the perspectives of others, using steps for problem solving and decision making, having a positive attitude toward life, self-awareness, nonverbal communication skills, and verbal communication skills. Creative instructional strategies include meetings to resolve conflicts that arise during class. Although primarily focused on the school and classroom settings, information and activities are also included for use with parents.

Program evaluations. PATHS has been field-tested and researched with children in regular education classroom settings, as well as with a variety of special needs students (deaf, hearing-impaired, learning disabled, emotionally disturbed, mildly mentally delayed, and gifted).

The PATHS program has robust evidence from well-designed and methodological rigorous studies showing its effectiveness in reducing children's aggression and hyperactive-disruptive behavior and in increasing their positive and prosocial behaviors (e.g., Conduct Problems Prevention Research Group, 1999, 2010; Domitrovich, Cortes, & Greenberg, 2007; Greenberg, Kusche, Cook, & Quamma, 1995). Specific positive outcomes found across a range of studies inclusive of a range of populations have included better understanding of emotional and social situations, greater toleration of frustration, improved problem-solving and conflict resolution, and decreased sadness and disruptive behaviors. PATHS has been rated as a "select program' by CASEL and as a "model program" by SAMSHA's National Registry of Evidence-Based Programs and Practices, and has received many accolades including awards from the Office of Safe and Drug-Free Schools and Center for Disease Control.

CONCLUSIONS AND DIRECTIONS
FOR FUTURE RESEARCH

Certain conditions in children's lives—such as warmth and affection from adults and peers, and effective guidance, especially when this guidance is not punitive—have been found to contribute to caring for and helping others (Staub, 2003).

As is evident in this review, there is considerable research examining both the antecedents and correlates of children's empathy and prosocial responding. This work has provided a beginning for understanding the factors that may promote children's prosocial behaviors and lead children to desist from aggression toward others. Nonetheless, in many cases, it is premature to confidently assume causation. Although much has been learned in the past few decades about the development of empathy and its behavioral concomitants, the field has much further to go. Moreover, many questions still remain regarding the ways in which programs designed to promote children's empathy and prosocial behaviors influence children's development both in the short and long terms. For example, what are the processes and mechanisms that lead to successful improvements in children's behaviors across programs? What role does context play? Which programs work best for which children? And under what conditions is empathy and prosocial responding best fostered?

In order to advance the science and practice of the school-based promotion of empathy, prosocial responding, and other related processes, a direction for future research is to examine how basic and applied can be better integrated into the development and implementation of universal classroom-based programs that promote empathy and prosocial responding in school-aged children. Advances in brain research hold some promise for shedding light on some of the neurological mechanisms responsible for empathy. For example, there has been increased attention to exploring the relation between empathy and the mirror neuron system (MNS), a system of the brain thought to constitute a neural substrate for understanding other's actions and intentions (Fogassi et al., 2005) through a "stimulation" mechanism whereby seeing the actions of others elicits the same kind of neural activity in the same cells that are activated as when we perform the same actions ourselves (Gallese & Goldman, 1998). In a recent investigation of the relation among the MNS, cognitive and affective dimensions of empathy, and interpersonal competence in 10-year-old children, Pfeifer, Iacoboni, Mazziotta, and Dapretto (2008) found that (a) the observation and imitation of emotional expressions bring about significant activity in the MNS, and (b) the activity in the MNS is significantly related to empathy and interpersonal competence. The findings of Pfeiffer et al.'s research are of particular importance because they suggest that the neural mirroring of the emotions of others may play a significant role in allowing individuals not only to *understand* other's emotional states, but that this neural mechanism is also linked with *feeling with* another—the affective component of empathy. Interestingly, whereas their findings found positive relations between the MNS and the more affect-laden dimensions of empathy, no relations between MNS and the cognitive component of empathy—perspective-taking—emerged. Such insights can inform preventive and intervention efforts designed to promote empathy in children and suggest that interventions may need to be tailored differently depending on the empathy outcome targeted.

Recent research conducted by Knafo, Israel, and Ebstein (2011) exploring the heritability of children's prosocial behavior points to the importance of taking into account gene-environment interactions when determining which children may benefit most from which intervention. Specifically, they found that although parenting did not directly relate to prosociality, heritability of children's prosocial behavior and differential susceptibility to parenting varied by the dopamine receptor D4 gene. Knafo et al.'s results indicate that, depending on their genetic predisposition, some children may be more or less susceptible/receptive to different kinds of parenting in ways that can be detrimental or beneficial to their prosocial responding. Such findings may be extrapolated to the classroom context and suggest that interventions may need to be tailored differently, depending on the outcome targeted.

Taken together, this research suggests that future studies must consider the interrelations among the biological, psychological, and contextual mechanisms that underlie the development of empathy and prosocial responding. Generating an applicable biopsychosocial-contextual model of empathy development to children in school settings will be a meaningful step in developing comprehensive interventions to promote empathy and alleviate aggressive and antisocial behavior in both girls and boys in school setting as well as the other important influential contexts (families, communities) in children's lives. Additionally, to advance the theoretical and applied fields of empathy and prosociality, it is critical to systematically evaluate the ways in which theory and research can inform practice and, in turn, how practice can inform theory and research. Surely, there is no single route to increasing empathy and prosocial behaviors and decreasing aggressive behaviors in children and adolescents. This review suggests that considering a range of factors including children's development, process, and context can yield new insights into the ways in which we understand and address empathy in today's children.

REFERENCES

Anderson, C., & Keltner, D. (2002). The role of empathy in the formation and maintenance of human bonds. Commentary to Preston & deWaal, Empathy: Its ultimate and proximate basis. *Behavioral and Brain Science, 25*, 1–72.

Batson, C. D. (1991). *The altruism question: Toward a social-psychological answer*. Hillsdale, NJ: Erlbaum.

Batson, C. D., Fultz, J., & Schoenrade, P. (1987). Distress and empathy: Two qualitatively distinct vicarious emotions with different motivational consequences. *Journal of Personality, 55*, 19–39.

Battistich, V. (2003). Effects of a school-based program to enhance prosocial development on children's peer relations and social adjustment. *Journal of Research in Character Education, 1*, 1–17.

Battistich, V., Schaps, E., Watson, M., & Solomon, D. (1996). Prevention effects of the Child Development Project: Early findings from an ongoing multi-site demonstration trial. *Journal of Adolescent Research, 11*, 12–25.

Battistich, V., Schaps, E., & Wilson, N. (2004). Effects of an elementary school intervention on students' "connectedness" to school and social adjustment during middle school. *The Journal of Primary Prevention, 24*, 243–262.

Battistich, V., Solomon, D., Watson, M., & Schaps, E. (1997). Caring school communities. *Educational Psychologist, 32*, 137–151.

Battistich, V., Solomon, D., Watson, M., Solomon, J., & Schaps, E. (1989). Effects of an elementary school program to enhance pro-social behavior on children's cognitive social problem-solving skills and strategies. *Journal of Applied Developmental Psychology, 10*, 147–169.

Blair, R. J. R. (1999). Responsiveness to distress cues in the child with psychopathic tendencies. *Personality and Individual Differences, 27*, 135–145.

Blair, R. J. R. (1997). Moral reasoning and the child with psychopathic tendencies. *Personality and Individual Differences, 22*, 731–739.

Blair, R. J. R., Peschardt, K. S., Budhani, S., Mitchell, D. G. V., & Pine, D. S. (2006). The development of psychopathy. *Journal of Child Psychology and Psychiatry, 47*, 262–275.

Blair, R. J. R., Colledge, E., Murray, L., & Mitchell, D. G. V. (2001). A selective impairment in the processing of sad and fearful expressions in children with psychopathic tendencies. *Journal of Abnormal Child Psychology, 29*, 491–498.

Brown, J. L., Jones, S. M., LaRusso, M., & Aber, J. L. (2010). Improving classroom quality: Teacher influences and experimental impacts of the 4Rs Program. *Journal of Educational Psychology, 102,* 153–167.

Campos, J., Mumme, D., Kermoian, R., & Campos, R. (1994). A functionalist perspective on the nature of emotion. *Monographs of the Society for Research in Child Development, 59* (2–3), 284–303.

Caprara, G. V., Barbaranelli, C., & Pastorelli, C. (2001). Prosocial behavior and aggression in childhood and pre-adolescence. In A. C. Bohart & D. J. Stipek (Eds.), *Constructive and destructive behavior: Implications for family, school, and society* (pp. 187–203). Washington, DC: American Psychological Association.

Caprara, G. V., Barbanelli, C., Pastorelli, C., Bandura, A, & Zimbardo, P. G. (2000). Prosocial foundations of children's academic achievement. *Psychological Science, 11,* 302–306.

Carlo, G., Eisenberg, N., & Knight, G. P. (1992). An objective measure of adolescents' prosocial moral reasoning. *Journal of Research of Adolescence, 2,* 331–349.

Carter, D. S., Harris, J., & Porges, S. W. (2009). Neural and evolutionary perspectives on empathy. In J. Decety & W. J. Ickes (Eds.), *Social neuroscience of empathy* (pp. 169–182). Cambridge, MA: MIT Press.

Catherine, N. L. A., & Schonert-Reichl, K. A. (2011). Children's perceptions and comforting strategies to infant crying: Relations to age, sex, and empathy-related responding. *British Journal of Developmental Psychology*. Advance online publication.

Cohen, D., & Strayer, J. (1996). Empathy in conduct disordered and comparison youth. *Developmental Psychology, 32,* 988–998.

Collaborative for Academic, Social, and Emotional Learning [CASEL]. (2003). *Safe and sound: An educational leader's guide to evidence-based social and emotional learning programs.* Chicago: Author.

Conduct Problems Prevention Research Group (CPPRG). (1999). Initial impact of the Fast Track Prevention Trial for Conduct Problems II: Classroom effects. *Journal of Consulting and Clinical Psychology, 67,* 648–657.

Conduct Problems Prevention Research Group (CPPRG). (2010). The effects of a multiyear universal social-emotional learning program: The role of student and school characteristics. *Journal of Consulting and Clinical Psychology, 78,* 156–168.

Consortium on the School-Based Promotion of Social Competence. (1994). The school-based promotion of social competence: Theory, research, practice and policy. In R. J. Haggerty, L. R. Sherrod, N.

Garmezy, & M. Rutter (Eds.), *Stress, risk, and resilience in children and adolescents: Processes, mechanisms, and interventions* (pp. 268–316). Cambridge, MA: Cambridge University Press.

Dadds, M. R., Hawes, D. J., Frost, A. D. J., Vassallo, S., Bunn, P., Hunter, K., & Merz, S. (2009). Learning to 'talk the talk': The relationship of psychopathic traits to deficits in empathy across childhood. *Journal of Child Psychology and Psychiatry, 50,* 599–606.

Damon, W. (2004). What is positive youth development? *Annals of the American Academy of Political and Social Science, 591,* 13–24.

Davis, M. H. (1983). Measuring individual differences in empathy: Evidence for a multidimensional approach. *Journal of Personality and Social Psychology. 44,* 113–126.

Davis, H. (2002). Too early for a neuropsychology of empathy. Commentary to Preston & deWaal, Empathy: Its ultimate and proximate basis. *Behavioral and Brain Science, 25,* 1–72.

Decety J., & Lamm, C. (2006). Human empathy through the lens of social neuroscience. *The Scientific World Journal, 6,* 1146–1163.

Decety, J., & Jackson, P. L. (2004). The functional architecture of human empathy. *Behavioral and Cognitive Neuroscience Reviews, 3,* 71–100.

Denham, S. A., & Couchoud, E. A. (1991). Social-emotional predictors of preschoolers' response to adult negative emotion. *Journal of Child Psychology and Psychiatry, 32,* 595–608.

De Waal, F. B. M. (2008). Putting the altruism back into altruism: The evolution of empathy. *Annual Review of Psychology, 59,* 279–300.

Domitrovich, C. E., Cortes, R. C., & Greenberg, M. T. (2007). Improving young children's social and emotional competence: A Randomized Trial of the preschool "PATHS" curriculum. *Journal of Primary Prevention, 28,* 67–89.

Durlak, J. A., Weissberg, R. P., Dymnicki, A. B., Taylor, R. D., & Schellinger, K. B. (2011). Enhancing students' social and emotional development promotes success in school: Results of a meta-analysis. *Child Development, 82,* 474–501.

Eagly, A. H., & Crowley, M. (1986). Gender and helping behavior: A meta-analytic review of the social psychological literature. *Psychological Bulletin, 100,* 283–308.

Eisenberg, N. (1986). *Altruistic emotion, cognition and behavior.* Hillsdale, NJ: Erlbaum.

Eisenberg, N. (2002). Empathy-related emotional responses, altruism, and their socialization. In R. J. Davidson & A. Harrington (Eds.), *Visions of compassion: Western scientists and Tibetan Buddhists examine human nature.* New York: Oxford University Press.

Eisenberg, N., & Fabes, R. (1998). Prosocial development. In W. Damon (Editor-in-Chief) & N. Eisenberg (Vol. Ed.), *Handbook of child psychology: Vol. 3. Social, emotional, and personality development* (5th ed., pp. 701–778). New York: Wiley.

Eisenberg, N., & Fabes, R. A. (1990). Empathy: Conceptualization, assessment, and relation to prosocial behavior. *Motivation and Emotion, 14,* 131–149.

Eisenberg, N., Fabes, R. A., & Spinrad, T. (2006). Prosocial development. In N. Eisenber (Ed.), *Handbook of child psychology: Social, emotional, and personality development* (pp. 646–718). Hoboken, NJ: John Wiley & Sons.

Eisenberg, N., & Lennon, R. (1983). Gender differences in empathy and related capacities. *Psychological Bulletin, 94,* 100–131.

Eisenberg, N., & Miller, P. A. (1987). The relation of empathy to prosocial and relate behaviors. *Psychological Bulletin, 101,* 91–119.

Eisenberg, N., Spinrad, T. L., & Sadovsky, A. (2006). Empathy-related responding in children. In M. Killen & J. G. Smetana (Eds.), *Handbook of moral development.* (pp. 517–549). Mahwah, NJ: Erlbaum.

Eisenberg, N., Zhou, Q., & Koller, S. (2001). Brazilian adolescents' prosocial moral judgment and behavior: Relations to sympathy, perspective taking, gender-role orientation and demographic characteristics. *Child Development, 72,* 518–534.

Eisenberg, N., Martin, C. L., & Fabes, R. A. (1996). Gender development and gender differences. In D. C. Berliner & R. C. Calfee (Eds.), *The handbook of educational psychology* (pp. 358–396). New York: Macmillan.

Eisenberg, N., Murphy, B., & Shepard, S. (1997). The development of empathic accuracy. In W. Ickes (Ed.), *Empathic accuracy* (pp. 73–116). New York: Guilford Press.

Eisenberg, N., Shea, C. L., Carlo, G., & Knight, G. (1991). Empathy-related responding and cognition: A "chicken and the egg" dilemma. In W. Kurtines & J. Gewirtz (Eds.), *Handbook of moral behavior and development. Vol. 2. Research* (pp. 63–88). Hillsdale, NJ: Erlbaum.

Elias, M. J., Zins, J. E., Weissberg, K. S., Greenberg, M. T., Haynes, N. M., Kessler, R. et al. (1997). *Promoting social and emotional learning: Guidelines for educators.* Alexandria, VA: Association for Supervision and Curriculum Development.

Endresen, I. M., & Olweus, D. (2001). Self-reported empathy in Norwegian adolescents: Sex differences, age trends, and relationship to bullying. In A. C. Bohart & D. J. Stipek (Eds.), *Constructive and destructive behavior: implications for family, school, and society* (pp. 147–165). Washington, DC: American Psychological Association.

Espelage, D. L., Mebane, S. E., & Adams, R. S. (2004). Empathy, caring, and bullying: Toward an understanding of complex associations. In D. L. Espelage & S. M. Swearer (Eds.), *Bullying in American schools: A social-ecological perspective on prevention and intervention* (pp. 37–61). Mahwah, NJ: Erlbaum.

Fabes, R. A,, Martin, C. L., & Hanish, L. D. (2002, October). *The role of sex segregation in young children's prosocial behavior and disposition*. Paper presented at the Groningen Conference on Prosocial Dispositions and Solidarity, Groningen, The Netherlands.

Feshbach, N. D. (1975). Empathy in children: Some theoretical and empirical considerations. *Counseling Psychologist, 5,* 25–30.

Fogassi, L., Ferrari, P. F., Gesierich, B., Rozzi, S., Chersi, F., & Rizzolatti, G. (2005). Parietal lobe: From action organization to intention understanding. *Science, 302,* 662–667.

Fonagy, P., Twemlow, S. W., Vernberg, E. M., Sacco, F. C., & Little, T. D. (2005). Creating a peaceful school learning environment: The impact of an antibullying program on educational attainment in elementary schools. *Medical Science Monitor, 11,* CR317–325.

Frick, P. J., & Hare, R. D. (2000). *The psychopathy screening device.* Toronto: Multi-Health Systems.

Frick, P. J., O'Brien, B. S., Wooton, J. M., & McBurnett, K. (1994). Psychopathy and conduct problems in children. *Journal of Abnormal Psychology, 103,* 700–707.

Gallese, V., & Goldman, A. I. (1998). Mirror neurons and the simulation theory of mind-reading. *Trends in Cognitive Science, 2,* 493–501.

Garner, P. W., Jones, D. C., & Palmer, J. L. (1994). Social cognitive correlates of preschool children's sibling caregiving behavior. *Developmental Psychology, 30,* 905–911.

Gini, G., Albiero, P., Benelli, B., & Altoe, G. (2007). Does empathy predict adolescents bullying and defending behavior? *Aggressive Behavior, 33,* 467–476.

Goleman, D. (2006). *Social intelligence: The new science of human relationships.* New York: Bantam.

Gordon, M. (2005). *Roots of empathy: Changing the World child by child.* Toronto, ON: Thomas Allen.

Greenberg, M. T. (2010). School-based prevention: Current status and future challenges. *Effective Education, 2,* 27–52.

Greenberg, M. T., Kusche, C. A., Cook, E. T., & Quamma, J. P. (1995). Promoting emotional competence in school-aged deaf children: The effects of the PATHS curriculum. *Development and Psychopathology, 7,* 117–136.

Greenberg, M., Weissberg, R., O'Brien, M., Zins, J., Fredericks, L., Resnik, H., & Elias, M. (2003). Enhancing school-based prevention and youth development through coordinated social, emotional and academic learning. *American Psychologist, 58,* 466–474.

Hare, R. D. (1980). A research scale for the assessment of psychopathy in criminal populations. *Personality and Individual Differences, 1,* 111–119.

Hare, R. D. (1991). *The Hare psychopathy checklist-revised.* Toronto, ON: Multi-Health Services.

Hastings, P. D., Zahn-Waxler, C., & McShane, K. (2006). We are, by nature, moral creatures: Biological bases of concern for others. In M. Killen, & J. Smetana (Eds.), *Handbook of moral development* (pp. 483–516). Mahwah, NJ: Erlbaum.

Hastings, P. D., Zahn-Waxler, C., Robinson, J., Usher, B., & Bridges, D. (2000). The development of concern for others in children with behavior problems. *Developmental Psychology, 36,* 531–546.

Hoffman, M. L. (1981) Is altruism part of human nature? *Journal of Personality and Social Psychology, 40,* 121–137.

Hoffman, M. L. (1982). Development of prosocial motivation: Empathy and guilt. In N. Eisenberg (Ed.), *The development of prosocial behavior* (pp. 281–313). San Diego, CA: Academic Press.

Hoffman, M. L. (1984). Empathy, its limitation, and its role in a comprehensive moral theory. In W. M. Kurtines & J. L. Gewirtz (Eds.), *Morality, moral behavior, and moral development* (pp. 283–302). New York: John Wiley & Sons.

Hoffman, M. L. (2000). *Empathy and moral development. Implications for caring and social justice.* Cambridge, UK: Cambridge University Press.

Izard, C. (2002). Translating emotion theory and research into preventive interventions. *Psychological Bulletin, 128,* 796–824.

Izard, C. E., Trentacosta, C. J., King, K. A., & Mostow, A. J. (2004). An emotion-based prevention program for Head Start children. *Early Education and Development, 15,* 407–422.

Izard, C. E., Fine, S., Mostow, A., Trentacosta, C., & Campbell, J. (2002). Emotional processes in normal and abnormal development and preventive intervention. *Developmental and Psychopathology, 14,* 761–787.

Izard, C., King, K. A., Trentacosta, C. J., Morgan, J. K., Laurenceau, J. P., Krauthamer-Ewing, E. S., & Finlon, K. J. (2008). Accelerating the development of emotion competence in Head Start children: Effects on adaptive and maladaptive behaviors. *Development and Psychopathology, 20*, 369–397.

Joliffe, D., & Farrington, D. P. (2004). Empathy and offending: A systematic review and meta-analysis. *Aggression & Violent Behavior, 9*, 441–476.

Joliffe, D., & Farrington, D. P. (2006). Examining the relationship between low empathy and bullying. *Aggressive Behavior, 32*, 540–550.

Jones, S. M., Brown, J. L., & Aber, J. L. (2011). Two-year impacts of a universal school-based social-emotional and literacy intervention: An experiment in translational developmental research. *Child Development*, doi: 10.1111/j.1467-8624.2010.01560

Kaukiainen, A., Björkqvist, K., Lagerspetz, K., Österman, K., Salmivalli, C., Rothberg, S., & Ahlbom, A. (1999). The relationships between social intelligence, empathy, and three types of aggression. *Aggressive Behavior, 25*, 81–89.

Keltner, D. (2009). *Born to be good: The science of a meaningful life.* New York: W. W. Norton & Company.

Kiang, L., Moreno, A. J., & Robinson, J. L. (2004). Maternal preconceptions about parenting predict child temperament, maternal sensitivity, and children's empathy. *Developmental Psychology, 40*, 1081–1092.

Knafo, A., Israel, S., & Ebstein, R. P. (2011). Heritability of children's prosocial behavior and differential susceptibility to parenting by variation in the dopamine receptor D4 gene. *Development and Psychopathology, 23*, 53–67.

Knafo, A., Zahn-Waxler, C., Van Hulle, C., & Robinson, J., & Rhee, S. H. (2008). The developmental origins of a disposition toward empathy: Genetic and environmental contributions. *Emotion, 8*, 737–752.

Kohn, A. (1997) How not to teach values: A critical look at character education. *Phi Delta Kappan, 78*, 429–439.

Lamb, S., & Zakhireh, B. (1997). Toddlers' attention to the distress of peers in a day care setting. *Early Education and Development, 8*, 105–118.

Lennon, R., & Eisenberg, N. (1987). Gender and age differences in empathy and sympathy. In N. Eisenberg & J. Strayer (Eds.), *Empathy and its development* (pp.195–217). New York: Cambridge University Press.

Luntz, B. K., & Widom, C. S. (1994). Antisocial personality disorder in abused and neglected children grown up. *American Journal of Psychiatry 151*, 670–674.

Miller, P. A., & Eisenberg, N. (1988). The relationship of empathy to aggressive and externalizing/antisocial behavior. *Psychological Bulletin, 103,* 324–344.

Mostow, A. J., Izard, C. E., Fine, S., & Trentacosta, C. J. (2002). Modeling the emotional, cognitive, and behavioral predictors of peer acceptance. *Child Development, 73,* 1775–1787.

Mullins-Nelson, J. L., Salekin, R. T., & Leistico, A. R. (2006). Psychopathy, empathy, and perspective-taking ability in a community sample: Implications for the successful psychopathy concept. *International Journal of Forensic Mental Health, 5,* 133–149.

Nesdale, D., Milliner, E., Duffy, A., & Griffiths, J. A. (2009). Group membership, group norms, empathy, and young children's intentions to aggress. *Aggressive behavior, 35,* 244–258.

Oberle, E., Schonert-Reichl, K. A., & Thomson, K. (2010). Understanding the link between social and emotional well-being and peer relations in early adolescence: Gender-specific predictors of peer acceptance. *Journal of Youth and Adolescence, 39,* 1330–1342.

Patterson, G. R. (1995). Coercion as a basis for early age of onset for arrest. In J. McCord (Ed.), *Coercion and punishment in long-term perspectives* (pp. 81–105). New York: Cambridge University Press.

Patterson, G., DeBaryshe, B., & Ramsey, E. (1989). A developmental perspective on antisocial behavior. *American Psychologist, 44,* 329–335.

Patterson, G. R. (1982). *Coercive family process.* Eugene, OR: Castalia.

Pfeifer, J. H., Iacoboni, M., Mazziotta, J. C., &, Dapretto, M. (2008). Mirroring other's emotions relates to empathy and interpersonal competence in children. *NeuroImage, 39,* 2076–2085.

Preston, S. D., & deWaal, F. B. (2002). Empathy: Its ultimate and proximate bases. *Behavioural Brain Science, 25,* 1–20.

Robinson, J. L., Zahn-Waxler, C., & Emde, R. N. (2001). Relationship context as a moderator of sources of individual difference in empathic development. In R. N. Emde & J. K. Hewitt (Eds.), *Infancy to early childhood: Genetic and environmental influences on developmental change* (pp. 257–268). Oxford, England: Oxford University Press.

Saarni, C. (1999). *The development of emotional competence.* New York: Guilford Press.

Schonert-Reichl, K. A. (1999). Moral reasoning during early adolescence: Links with peer acceptance, friendship, and social behaviors. *Journal of Early Adolescence, 19,* 249–279.

Schonert-Reichl, K. A. (1993). Empathy and social relationships in adolescents with behavioral disorders. *Behavioral Disorders, 18,* 189–204.

Schonert-Reichl, K. A., & Oberle, E. (2011a). Teaching empathy to children: Theoretical and empirical considerations and implications for practice. In B. Weber & E. Marsal (Eds.), *"The politics of empathy": New interdisciplinary perspectives on an ancient phenomenon.* Berlin, Germany: Lit Verlag.

Schonert-Reichl, K. A., & Scott, F. (2009). Effectiveness of the "Roots of Empathy" program in promoting children's emotional and social competence: A summary of research findings. In M. Gordon (Ed.), *Roots of empathy: Changing the world child by child* (pp. 239–262). Toronto, Ontario: Thomas Allen Publishers.

Schonert-Reichl, K. A., & Stewart Lawlor, M. (2010). The effects of a mindfulness-based education program on pre- and early adolescents' well-being and social and emotional competence. *Mindfulness, 1,* 137–151.

Schonert-Reichl, K. A., Smith, V., Zaidman-Zait, A., & Hertzman, C. (2011a). *Promoting children's prosocial behaviors in school: Impact of the "Roots of Empathy" program on the social and emotional competence of school-aged children.* Manuscript submitted for publication.

Schonert-Reichl, K. A., Oberle, E., Lawlor, M. S., Abbott, D., Thomson, K., Oberlander, T. F., Diamond, A. (2011b). *Enhancing cognitive and social emotional development through a simple to administer school program.* Manuscript submitted for publication.

Schultz, L. H., Selman, R. L., & LaRusso, M. D. (2003). The assessment of psychosocial maturity in children and adolescents: Implications for the evaluation of school-based character education programs. *Journal of Research in Character Education, 1,* 67–87.

Selman, R. L. (1980). *The growth of interpersonal understanding.* New York: Academic Press.

Seligman, E. P., & Csikszentimihalyi, M. (2000). Positive psychology: An introduction. *American Psychologist, 55,* 5–14.

Shipman, K., Zeman, J., Penza, S., & Champion, K. (2000). Emotion management skills in sexually maltreated and non-maltreated girls: A developmental psychopathology perspective. *Development and Psychopathology, 12,* 47–62.

Shirtcliff, E. A., Vitaccio, M. J., Graf, A. R., Gostisha, A. J. Merz, J. L., & Zahn-Waxler, C. (2009). Neurobiology of empathy and callousness: Implications for the development of antisocial behavior. *Behavioral Sciences and the Law, 27,* 137–171.

Staub, E. (1979). *Positive social behavior and morality: Socialization and development* (Vol. 2). New York: Academic Press.

Staub, E. (1988). The evolution of caring and nonaggressive persons and societies. *Journal of Social Issues, 44,* 81–100.

Staub, E. (2003). Notes on cultures of violence, cultures of caring and peace, and the fulfillment of basic human needs. *Political Psychology, 24*, 1–21.

Sutton, J., Smith, P. K., & Swettenham, J. (1999). Bullying and "theory of mind": A critique of the social skills deficit view of anti-social behavior. *Social Development, 8*, 117–134.

Thompson, R. A. (in press). The emotionate child. Chapter to appear in D. Cicchetti & G. I. Roisman (Eds.), *The origins and organization of adaptation and maladaptation. Minnesota Symposium on Child Psychology*, Vol. 36. New York: Wiley.

Tregebov, R. (1993). *Sasha and the wiggly tooth*. Toronto, ON: Second Story Press.

Tremblay, R. E., Masse, L. C., Vitaro, F., & Dobkin, P. L. (1995). The impact of friends' deviant behavior on early onset of deliquency: Longitudinal data from 6 to 13 years of age. *Development and Psychopathology, 7*, 649–667.

Vaish, A., Carpenter, M., & Tomasello, M. (2010). Young children selectively avoid helping people with harmful intentions. *Child Development, 81*, 1661–1669.

van Baardewijk, Y., Stegge, H., Bushman, B. J., & Vermeiren, R. (2009). Psychopathic traits, victim distress and aggression in children. *Journal of Child Psychology and Psychiatry, 50*, 718–725.

Warden, D., Cheyne, B., Christie, D., Fitzpatrick, H., & Reid, K. (2003). Assessing children's perceptions of prosocial and antisocial behavior. *Educational Psychology, 23*, 547–567.

Warden, D., & Mackinnon, S. (2003). Prosocial bullies, bullies, and victims: An investigation of their sociometric status, empathy, and social problem-solving strategies. *British Journal of Developmental Psychology, 21*, 367–385.

Warneken, F., & Tomasello, M. (2006). Altruistic helping in human infants and young chimpanzees. *Science, 311*, 1301–1303.

Warneken, F., & Tomasello, M. (2007). Helping and cooperation at 14 months of age. *Infancy, 11*, 271–294.

Warneken, F., & Tomasello, M. (2008). Extrinsic rewards undermine altruistic tendencies in 20-month-olds. *Developmental Psychology, 44*, 1785–1788.

Warneken, F., & Tomasello, M. (2009). The roots of human altruism. *British Journal of Psychology. Target article with commentaries, 100*, 445–471.

Wentzel, K. R. (1993). Does being good make the grade? Social behavior and academic competence in middle school. *Journal of Educational Psychology, 85*, 357–364.

Wilson, S. J., Lipsey, M. W., & Derzon, J. H. (2003). The effects of school-based intervention programs on aggressive behavior: A meta-analysis. *Journal of Consulting and Clinical Psychology, 71,* 136–149.

Wispé, L. (1986) The distinction between sympathy and empathy: To call forth a concept, a word is needed. *Journal of Personality and Social Psychology, 50,* 314–21.

Zahn-Waxler, C., & Radke-Yarrow, M. (1990). The origins of empathic concern. *Motivation and Emotion, 14,* 107–130.

Zahn-Waxler, C., Robinson, J. L., & Emde, R. N. (1992). The development of empathy in twins. *Developmental Psychology, 28,* 1038–1047.

Zahn-Waxler, C., Radke-Yarrow, M., Wagner, E., & Chapman, M. (1992). Development of concern for others. *Developmental Psychology, 28,* 126–136.

Zahn-Waxler, C., Schiro, K., Robinson, J. L., Emde, R. N., & Schmitz, S. (2001). Empathy and prosocial patterns in young MZ and DZ twins: Development and genetic and environmental influences. In R. N. Emde & J. K. Hewitt (Eds.), *Infancy to early childhood* (pp. 141–162). New York: Oxford University Press.

Zhou, Q., Valiente, C., & Eisenberg, N. (2003). Empathy and its measurement. In S. J. Lopez & C. R. Snyder (Eds.), *Positive psychological assessment: A handbook of models and measures* (pp. 269–284). Washington, DC: American Psychological Association.

CHAPTER 8

Bullying Among Children and Adolescents
Social–Emotional Learning Approaches to Prevention

Dorothy L. Espelage and Sabina Low

INTRODUCTION: PREVALENCE, DEFINITIONS, AND CORRELATES

Bullying is recognized as one of the most significant public health concerns facing children in the United States today. Involvement in bullying among elementary and middle school students is quite prevalent with students assuming roles such as bully, victim, bully–victim, and various bystander roles (Espelage & Horne, 2008). Current estimates suggest that nearly 30% of American students are involved in bullying in one of these capacities (Nansel et al., 2001). Specifically, findings from this nationally representative sample indicated that among 6th to 10th graders, 13% had bullied others, 11% had been bullied, and 6% had both bullied others and been bullied. Bullying involvement has also been implicated as a predictor of school shootings. In the United States, an investigation was commissioned in 2000 by the Secret Service; family and friends of students involved in 37 incidents of targeted school shootings and school attacks between 1974 and 2000 were interviewed. Researchers discovered that 71% of the perpetrators had been victims of bullying (Vossekuil, Fein, Reddy, Borum, & Modzeleski, 2002).

Victims, bullies, and bully–victims often report adverse psychological effects and poor school adjustment as a result of their involvement in bullying that might also lead to subsequent victimization or perpetration and long-term effects (Juvoven, Nishina, & Graham, 2000; Nansel,

Haynie, & Simons-Morton, 2003). For example, targets of bullying evidence more loneliness and depression, greater school avoidance, more suicidal ideation, and less self-esteem than their nonbullied peers (Hawker & Boulton, 2000; Kaltiala-Heino, Rimpelae, & Rantanen, 2001; Kochenderfer & Ladd, 1996; Olweus, 1992; Rigby, 2001). Whereas victims tend to report more internalizing behaviors, bullies are more likely than their peers to engage in externalizing behaviors like anger, to experience conduct problems, and to be delinquent (Haynie, Nansel, & Eitel, 2001; Nansel et al., 2001). Furthermore, long-term outcomes for bullies can be serious; compared to their peers, bullies are more likely to be convicted of crimes in adulthood (Eron, Huesmann, Dubow, Romanoff, & Yarnel, 1987; Olweus, 1993). Bully–victims demonstrate more externalizing behaviors, are more hyperactive, and have a greater probability of being referred for psychiatric consultation than their peers (Kumpulainen et al., 1998; Nansel et al., 2003; Nansel et al., 2001).

Although bullying among schoolchildren is receiving increasingly more attention by policymakers and the media, it is not a new phenomenon. Professor Dan Olweus introduced the world to the problem of bullying among young boys through a nationwide Scandinavian campaign against bullying in the 1970s. This campaign was motivated by a suicide pact among three Norwegian children who were relentlessly bullied. This research set forth the following definition that still remains today, "A student is being bullied or victimized when he or she is exposed, repeatedly and over time, to negative actions on the part of one or more students" (Olweus, 1993). The preceding definition highlights the aggressive component of bullying, its associated inherent power imbalance, and repetitive nature. In recent years, scholars have recognized the wide range of behaviors consistent with bullying, including verbal, physical, and social manifestations. Smith and Sharp noted: "A student is being bullied or picked on when another student says nasty and unpleasant things to him or her. It is also bullying when a student is hit, kicked, threatened, locked inside a room, sent nasty notes, and when no one ever talks to him" (Sharp & Smith, 1991, pg.1).

A tremendous amount of research has been conducted on school-based bullying within the last few decades. Results consistently indicate a wide array of risk and protective factors linked to bullying perpetration and victimization that include individual, peer, familial, and community variables (see Espelage & Swearer, 2010 for a review). These significant factors have informed to varying degrees prevention and intervention planning. Risk factors for bullying perpetration include individual characteristics such as being male, sibling bullying history, less empathy, anger disposition, and positive attitudes toward bullying; in some cases, perpetration is also associated with other forms of delinquency. Risk factors for victimization have included physical characteristics, overprotective parents, and prior experiences of victimization. Protective factors for perpetration and victimization include the presence of positive social support and the ability to form strong attachments with peers, parents, and teachers. Peer group affiliation also plays an important role, as members appear to socialize one another to bully others through group norms that support bullying perpetration. Teacher and school characteristics were also noted as both risk and protective factors in perpetration and victimization.

META-ANALYTIC STUDIES OF BULLYING PREVENTION

Despite a burgeoning number of published studies on the topic of bullying, systematic evaluations of large-scale prevention programs are only now appearing in the literature. In 2008, a meta-analytic investigation of 16 studies published from 1980–2004 yielded disappointing results regarding the impact of antibullying programs (Merrell, Gueldner, Ross, & Isava, 2008). This meta-analysis included data from over 15,000 students (grades kindergarten to 12) in Europe, Canada, and the United States. Positive effect sizes were found for only one third of the study variables, which primarily reflected favorable changes in knowledge, attitudes, and perceptions of bullying. No changes were found for actual bullying behaviors. These authors indicated in a tentative fashion that school bullying interventions showed modest evidence of enhancing student social competence, self-esteem, and peer acceptance. In addition, it appears that programs shifted in a positive direction teacher's knowledge of effective practices and efficacy of intervening and responding to incidences at school.

Ttofi, Farrington, and Baldry (2008) expanded this meta-analysis to include many more studies. In a report for the Swedish National Council for Crime Prevention, they evaluated 44 bullying intervention studies. Results indicated that bullying and victimization were reduced by 17–23% in experimental schools compared to control schools. Ttofi et al. found that reductions in bullying were associated with classroom rules, classroom management, parent training, increased playground supervision, home–school communication, and the use of training videos. Further, there was a dosage effect; the more elements included in a program, the greater likelihood of reducing bullying.

Both meta-analyses indicated that anti-bullying programs were more efficacious in smaller-scale European studies and less effective in the United States, suggesting that U.S. scholars need to continue to explore different approaches to decrease bullying in schools or determine how existing programs need to be modified to produce positive results. Many of the programs included in both recent meta-analyses were based on the Olweus Bullying Prevention Program, which is largely focused on shifting the school environment to be less supportive of bullying (Olweus, 1991). However, this program focuses less attention on providing direct instruction in social–emotional learning or life skills development, which we argue here is an approach that is growing in school-based programming to prevent bullying and to prevent bullying involvement escalating into more severe aggression and violence in our society.

Indeed, bullying and peer victimization are phenomena that are the result of complicated exchanges between individuals and their broader social environment. All individuals influence and are influenced by their surroundings. In this chapter, we argue for the potential of incorporating a social emotional framework to bullying prevention. To accomplish this, we provide a brief historical perspective of the social emotional learning movement, describe social emotional learning components, and then review four bullying prevention programs that include, to varying degrees, social–emotional learning aspects.

SOCIAL–EMOTIONAL LEARNING AS A BULLY PREVENTION FRAMEWORK

According to the National Center for Education Statistics, during 2007–2008, 46% of public schools had at least one serious disciplinary action, and 31% of schools dealt with fighting or physical attacks. It is our contention that strong relationships among students, staff in classrooms, and schools can prevent many of the ills that schools suffer from. A social emotional learning approach has emerged as a way to prevent many of these school-based problems. Social–emotional learning as a framework emerged from influences across different movements that focused on resiliency and teaching social and emotional competencies to children and adolescents (Elias et al., 1997). In response, advocates for Social and Emotional Learning (SEL) use social skill instruction to address behavior, discipline, safety, and academics to help youth become self-aware, manage their emotions, build social skills (empathy, perspective-taking, respect for diversity), friendship skill building, and make positive decisions (Zins, Weissberg, Wang, & Walberg, 2004). Recently, a study of more than 213 programs found that if a school implements a quality SEL curriculum, they can expect better student behavior and an 11-point increase in test scores (Durlak, Weissberg, Dymnicki, Taylor, & Schellinger, 2010). The gains that schools see in achievement come from a variety of factors—students feel safer and more connected to school and academics, SEL programs build work habits in addition to social skills, and kids and teachers build strong relationships (Zins et al., 2004).

As we forge ahead in promoting an SEL approach to bullying prevention, it is important to understand the history of the SEL movement. Social–emotional learning is a framework that was introduced at a 1994 meeting hosted by the Fetzer Institute as a result of the concern of researchers, educators, and child advocates that prevention and health promotion efforts were producing null results (Elias et al., 1997). These individuals explored efforts to enhance positive youth development, to promote social competence and emotional intelligence, to develop effective drug education, violence prevention, health promotion, character education, service learning, civic education, school reform, and school–family–community partnerships. They believed that, unlike the many prevention programs that targeted one specific problem, SEL programming could address underlying causes of problem behavior while supporting academic achievement. Social emotional learning programs are based on many well-established theories including theories of emotional intelligence, social and emotional competence promotion, a social developmental model, social information processing, and self-management (e.g., Guerra & Bradshaw, 2008). In addition, behavior change and learning theories also informed the SEL framework, such as the health belief model, the theory of reasoned action, problem behavior theory, and social–cognitive theory (e.g., Greenberg et al., 2003; Hawkins, Smith, & Catalano, 2004).

A new organization, the Collaborative for Academic, Social, and Emotional Learning (CASEL), also emerged from this meeting with the goal of establishing high-quality, evidence-based SEL as an essential part of preschool through high school education (Collaborative for Academic, Social, & Emotional Learning, 2005). A social–emotional learning framework includes five interrelated skill areas: self-awareness, social awareness, self-management and organization, responsible problem-solving, and relationship management. Within each area, there are specific competencies supported by research and practice as essential for effective social-emotional functioning, including emotions recognition, stress-management, empathy, problem-solving, or decision-making skills (Elias et al., 1997). Further, the conceptualization of the skills is that they are important at all developmental levels; what changes is the level of cognitive-emotional complexity with which they are applied, as well as the situations in which they will be used.

Overall, school-based programs developed in the U.S. that are predicated on the belief that academic skills are intrinsically linked to children's social–emotional resources have yielded success (Durlak et al.,

2010). Self-regulated learning is both directly and indirectly targeted in these programs. As students are better able to control their feelings, thoughts, and actions, especially under emotional demands (i.e., cognitive complexity), academic learning is optimized. Self-regulated learning happens in a cyclical fashion, consisting of forethought, performance, and self-reflection stages. These types of bullying prevention programs have contributed to improvements in academic skills, engagement, and improved grades.

Steps to Respect: A Bullying Prevention Program

Steps to Respect: A Bullying Prevention Program is designed to help students build supportive relationships with one another (Committee for Children, 2001). The Steps to Respect program promotes a whole-school primary- and secondary-level approach to bullying prevention by addressing factors at four levels: school staff, peer group, individual child, and family. Intervening at multiple levels, the program developers believe, is the most effective way to reduce school bullying. Empirical support has shown reductions in playground bullying, acceptance of bullying behavior, and argumentative behavior. At the same time, it has demonstrated increases in agreeable interactions and perceived adult responsiveness in comparison with control schools (Frey et al., 2005). More recently, it has demonstrated reductions in observed aggression and destructive bystander behavior, and higher teacher ratings of peer social skills (Hirschstein & Frey, 2006; Hirschstein, Van Schoiack, Frey, Snell, & MacKenzie, 2007). Steps to Respect relies heavily on adults to deliver scripted training from a curriculum and to continually emphasize those lessons throughout the school year. The Steps to Respect prevention program is specifically respected for its well-established empirical support.

Primary bullying prevention strategies address risk factors from a systemic perspective that will influence the maximum number of students. Knowing that primary-level interventions have the potential to reach approximately 80% of students in a school encourages school officials and stakeholders to invest time and effort into these systemic efforts (Walker & Shinn, 2002). For example, the first component of the Steps to Respect program is staff training for *all* adults in the school building, emphasizing that the word "adults" includes janitors, bus drivers, mentors, receptionists, school nurses, volunteers, licensed staff, administrators, teachers, assistants, and other adults at school who are involved in the daily lives of students. Training meetings include a scripted training session that provides basic information on the Steps to Respect program, information on bullying, and training on how to receive bullying reports from students. Administrators, teachers, or counselors who will work directly with students who have been bullied or who are bullying others receive additional training.

Steps to Respect includes lessons to increase students' social–emotional competence and positive social values. Specifically, the program addresses three general skills: First, students learn skills of perspective-taking and empathy as well as how to manage their emotions. Second, academic skills are also encouraged by incorporating themes of friendship and bullying into literature unit activities such as oral expression, writing composition, and analytical reasoning. Third, the curriculum addresses students' social values by encouraging students' sense of fairness, and attempts to instill a desire for rewarding friendships. Also literature units for grades 3–6 are included that integrate previously learned components of Steps to Respect for activities such as writing activities, spelling lists, and reading books (Committee for Children, 2001).

The universal design of the Steps to Respect program makes it an easy fit for implementation in elementary schools. It relies mostly on teachers and adults, who assist students in modifying the school climate to encourage positive friendships and reduce bullying behaviors. As a universal intervention, it does not ignore the potential contribution of students who are not directly involved, either as bullies or as victims. These bystanders play a critical role in reducing and eliminating bullying from a school environment. As Frey and colleagues demonstrated (2005, 2009), reducing the acceptability of bullying behaviors and increasing perceived adult responsiveness are key components to building a positive school community. In this study, six elementary schools were randomly assigned to either receive the intervention or be a control group. Playground observations were collected in the fall and spring, along with surveys of student skills and attitudes identified as factors in bullying and victimization. Following staff training, intervention, schools created bullying policies and implemented the classroom curricula twice a week for approximately 12 weeks. Positive outcomes included a 25% reduction in playground bullying incidents, compared with a control group, and a decrease in bystanders to bullying episodes who encouraged it. Furthermore, the effects of the Steps to Respect program were most pronounced among students who were observed to do the most bullying before program implementation. A more recent study examined teacher implementation variables related to Steps to Respect (Hirschstein, Edstrom, Frey, Snell, & MacKenzie, 2007). Specifically, the study examined the effects of teachers "walking the talk"—that is, teachers who wove support for positive behaviors into daily interactions with students and coached those involved in bullying. After 1 year of the program, high levels of "walking the talk" were linked to less aggression and victimization among fifth- and sixth-grade students. The program also resulted in less observed victimization of all children who had previously been victimized and less destructive bystander behavior among all children who had previously been observed contributing to bullying as bystanders.

BULLY BUSTERS

Bully Busters is a program that can be implemented by schools with fewer resources and can be used at the primary, secondary, or tertiary levels. The program is designed as "a collaborative effort in which teachers, support staff (counselors, social workers, psychologists, and others), and administrators can become more aware of the bullying problem and develop the knowledge base and skills to deal with the problem confidently" (Newman et al., 2000, p. 1). The program is in two parts—Grades K–5 and 6–8—and contains seven learning modules on how to increase awareness, how to recognize the bully and victims, interventions for bullies and victims, classroom prevention, and coping skills, along with corresponding classroom activities for kids.

Teachers receiving Bully Busters training reported significantly higher levels of self-efficacy for managing bullying behavior, demonstrated greater knowledge of classroom behavior management, and had fewer classroom behavior problems and office referrals than comparison teachers (Newman-Carlson & Horne, 2004; Horne, Swearer, Givens, & Meints, 2010). The first of the seven modules is designed to increase teachers' and students' awareness of bullying. Teachers are encouraged to develop a definition of bullying by working collaboratively with students. Exercises facilitate a conversation among students about who is a bully, what bullying is, and where it takes place. Drawing upon social emotional learning standards of the importance of communication skills, students then participate in several activities to recognize how their words and actions can be hurtful, and they role-play more constructive ways of interacting. The second module includes a discussion with students about how bullying develops and the forms it can take. Activities in this module include viewing movies in which characters are victims or bullies. Students discuss both aggressive and passive forms of bullying. This second module ends with a focus on misconceptions about bullying.

In the third module, students discuss the effects of victimization and challenge myths about victims. Students are encouraged to recognize different types of victims, including individuals who are passive or provocative, and bystanders. The majority of students do not engage directly in bullying, but their reluctance to intervene when bullying occurs can promote this behavior in others. Thus, students are encouraged to break the "code of silence" and create a safer climate for all students. The fourth module includes specific strategies for teachers to create a bully-free classroom. Similar to the classroom-level interventions of the Olweus Bullying Prevention Program, teachers are given specific strategies (e.g., setting rules, acting quickly), but expand this repertoire to included SEL skills such as empathy skills training, social skills training, and anger management training.

The fifth module expands on these skills by providing specific strategies for working with victims. Several activities are used to help victims become aware of their strengths, view themselves in a positive manner, and build skills and confidence in joining groups. The sixth module includes a discussion of the role of prevention, and activities are designed to educate teachers about the need for prevention and to introduce prevention theory. Teachers are encouraged to identify how their attitudes and behaviors influence student behavior and how school-level factors relate to bullying. The final module focuses on teaching relaxation and coping skills to teachers because it is important that teachers manage their own stress to prevent aggression within their classrooms.

THE PEACEFUL SCHOOL PROJECT

The Peaceful Schools Project, developed in 2000 (Twemlow et al., 2001; Twemlow et al., 2010) (www.backoffbully.com), is a philosophy rather than a program (Twemlow, Fonagy, & Sacco, 2004). The goals are consistent with the SEL framework by the inclusion of developing healthy relationships between all stakeholders in the educational setting and altering the school climate in permanent and meaningful ways. The Project includes five main components. First, schools embark on a positive climate campaign that includes counselor-led discussions and the creation of posters that help alter the language and the thinking of everyone in the school (i.e., "Back off bullies!" or "Stop bullying now"). All stakeholders in the school are flooded with an awareness of the bullying dynamic, and bullying is described as a social relationship problem. Second, teachers are fully supported in classroom management techniques and are taught specific techniques to diffuse disruptive behavior from a relational perspective rather than from a punishment perspective. Third, peer and adult mentors are used to help everyone in the school resolve problems without blame. These adult mentors are particularly important during times when adult supervision is minimal (i.e., in hallways and on the playground). The fourth component is called the Gentle Warrior Physical Education Program." It uses a combination of role-playing, relaxation, and defensive martial arts techniques to help students develop strategies to protect themselves and others. These are essentially confidence-building skills that support positive coping. Fifth, reflection time is included in the school schedule each day. Teachers and students talk for at least 10 minutes at the end of the day about bully, victim, and bystander behaviors. By engaging in this dialogue, language and thinking about bullying behaviors can be subtly altered (Twemlow et al., 2005).

The Peaceful Schools Project is a holistic philosophy that attempts to alter negative social relationships in schools, which in turn, are hypothesized to reduce or eliminate bullying behaviors. In a recent study it was found that elementary students whose schools participated in the The Peaceful Schools Project had higher achievement scores than students from schools without the program; there were also significant reductions in suspensions for acting out behavior in the treatment schools, whereas the comparison schools had a slight increase in suspensions for problem behavior (Fonagy et al., 2009).

SUMMARY

Despite almost three decades of bullying research, as well as prevention and intervention efforts worldwide, progress has been slow in developing empirically-supported primary, secondary, and tertiary school-based prevention programs. What has been learned to date is that zero tolerance policies (policies that provide for punishment regardless of the basis of the problem behavior) are not effective in curbing aggressive behaviors (Casella, 2003), and expulsion appears to be equally ineffective (Morrison, Redding, Fisher, & Peterson, 2006). Despite this, Furlong, Morrison, and Grief (2003) noted that most formalized legislation addressing bullying and peer aggression in schools continue to emphasize taking action with bullies to the exclusion of addressing the needs of victims or addressing the larger school climate. Interventions that may be effective with other types of violence do not translate to effectiveness with bullying. These include conflict resolution, peer mediation, or group therapy, all of which target underlying social skills or personal resources. For example, many bullying interventions have tended to allocate more resources to identifying individual bullies and addressing their behavior than to developing universal programs that address the entire student body. Bullying, however, is not always a manifestation of social skill deficits (as with other forms of aggression); rather, it is rooted in and elaborated upon by social contingencies among one's peers, which are reinforced or ameliorated at the classroom- or school-wide level. Because bullying is maintained by social and tangible reinforcers, effective prevention must be predicated in peer- and school-level interventions that shift power dynamics and the value placed on contingencies (Whitted & Dupper, 2005). It is our contention, along with our fellow SEL colleagues, that the lack of connectedness in our schools is partially contributing to the many problems that children and adolescents encounter in our schools. We believe that in order to make schools safer, we need to equip kids and adults alike with the social–emotional learning skills to manage their own emotional states, their interactions with others, and to behave in civil ways toward others. It is only then that bullying involvement will not escalate into tragic events such as school shootings.

REFERENCES

Casella, R. (2003). Zero tolerance policy in schools: Rationale, consequences, and alternatives. *Teachers College Record, 105,* 872–892.

Collaborative for Academic, Social, and Emotional Learning [CASEL]. (2005). *Safe and sound: An educational leader's guide to evidence-based social and emotional learning programs—Illinois edition.* Chicago, IL: Author.

Committee for Children (2001). Steps to Respect: A Bully Prevention Program. Seattle, WA.

Durlak, J. A., Weissberg, R. P., Dymnicki, A. B., Taylor, R. D., & Schellinger, K. B. (2010). The impact of enhancing students' social and emotional learning: A meta-analysis of school-based universal interventions. *Child Development.*

Elias, M. J., Zins, J. E., Weissberg, R. P., Frey, K. S., Greenberg, M. T., Haynes, N. M., Kessler, R., Schwab-Stone, M. E., & Shriver, T. P. (1997). *Promoting social and emotional learning: Guidelines for educators.* Alexandria, VA: Association for Supervision and Curriculum Development.

Eron, L. D., Huesmann, L. R., Dubow, E., Romanoff, R., & Yarnel, P. W. (1987). Aggression and its correlates over 22 years. In D. H. Crowell & I. M. Evans (Eds.), *Childhood aggression and violence: Sources of influence, prevention, and control* (pp. 249–262). New York: Plenum Press.

Espelage, D., & Horne, A. (2008). School violence and bullying prevention: From research based explanations to empirically based solutions. In S. Brown & R. Lent (Eds.), *Handbook of counseling psychology* (4th edition, pp. 588–598). Hoboken, NJ: John Wiley & Sons.

Espelage, D. L., & Swearer, S. M. (Eds.) (2010). *Bullying in North American schools: A social-ecological perspective on prevention and intervention (2nd edition)*. New York: Routledge.

Fonagy, P., Twemlow, S. W., Vernberg, E. M., Nelson, J. M., Dill, E. J., Little, T. D. et al. (2009). A cluster randomized controlled trial of child-focused psychiatric consultation and a school systems-focused intervention to reduce aggression. *Journal of Child Psychology and Psychiatry*, 50(5), 607.

Frey, K. S., Hirschstein, M. K., Edstrom, L. V., & Snell, J. L. (2009). Observed reductions in school bullying, nonbullying aggression, and destructive bystander behavior: A longitudinal evaluation. *Journal of Educational Psychology*, 101(2), 466.

Frey, K. S., Hirschstein, M. K., Snell, J. L., Edstrom, L., Van Schoiack, MacKenzie, E. P., & Broderick, C. J. (2005). Reducing playground bullying and supporting beliefs: An experimental trial of the steps to respect program. *Developmental Psychology*, 41(3), 479–491.

Furlong, M. J., Morrison, G. M., & Grief, J. L. (2003). Reaching an American consensus: Reactions to the special issue on school bullying. *School Psychology Review*, 32, 456–470.

Greenberg, M. T., Weissberg, R. P., O'Brien, M. U., Zins, J. E., Fredericks, L., Resnik, H., & Elias, M. J. (2003). Enhancing school-based prevention and youth development through coordinated social, emotional, and academic learning. *American Psychologist*, 58, 466–474.

Guerra, N. G., & Bradshaw, C. P. (2008). Linking the prevention of problem behaviors and positive youth development: Core competencies for positive youth development and risk prevention. In N. G. Guerra & C. P. Bradshaw (Eds.), *Core competencies to prevent problem behaviors and promote positive youth development, 122*, 1–17.

Hawker, D. S. J., & Boulton, M. J. (2000). Twenty years' research on peer victimization and psychosocial maladjustment: A meta-analytic review of cross-sectional studies. *Journal of Child Psychology and Psychiatry and Allied Disciplines, 41*, 441–455.

Hawkins, J. D., Smith, B. H., & Catalano, R. F. (2004). Social development and social and emotional learning. In J. E. Zins, R. P. Weissberg, M. C. Wang, & H. J. Walberg (Eds.), *Building academic success on social and emotional learning: What does the research say?* (pp. 135–150). New York: Teachers College Press.

Haynie, D. L., Nansel, T., & Eitel, P. (2001). Bullies, victims, and bully/victims: Distinct groups of at-risk youth. *Journal of Early Adolescence, 21*, 29–49.

Hirschstein, M. K., Edstrom, L. V. S., Frey, K. S., Snell, J. L., & MacKenzie, E. P. (2007). Walking the talk in bullying prevention: Teacher implementation variables related to initial impact of the Steps to Respect program. *School Psychology Review, 36*, 3–21.

Hirschstein, M. K., & Frey, K. S. (2006). Promoting behavior and beliefs that reduce bullying: The Steps to Respect program. In S. Jimerson & M. Furlong (Eds.), *The handbook of school violence and school safety: From research to practice* (pp. 309–323). Mahwah, NJ: Erlbaum.

Hirschstein, M. K., Edstrom, L. V. S., Frey, K. S., Snell, J. L., & MacKenzie, E. P. (2007). Walking the talk in bullying prevention: Teacher implementation variables related to initial impact of the STEPS TO RESPECT program. *School Psychology Review, 36*(1), 3–21.

Horne, A. M., Swearer, S. M., Givens, J., & Meints, C. (2010). Bully Busters: Reducing bullying by changing teacher and student behavior. In Jimerson, S., Swearer, S., & Espelage, D. L. (Eds.), *The International Handbook of Bullying* (pp. 507–516). New York: Routledge.

Juvoven, J., Nishina, A., & Graham, S. (2000). Self-views versus peer perceptions of victim status among early adolescents. In J. Juvonen & S. Graham (Eds.), *Peer harassment in schools: The plight of the vulnerable and victimized* (pp. 105–124). New York: The Guilford Press.

Kaltiala-Heino, R., Rimpelae, M., & Rantanen, P. (2001). Bullying at school: An indicator for adolescents at risk for mental disorders. *Journal of Adolescence, 23*, 661–674.

Kochenderfer, B. J., & Ladd, G. W. (1996). Peer victimization: Cause or consequence of school maladjustment? *Child Development, 67*, 1305–1317.

Kumpulainen, K., Räsänen, E., & Henttonen, I. (1998). Children involved in bullying: Psychological disturbance and the persistence of the involvement. *Child Abuse & Neglect, 23*, 1253–1262.

Lochman, J. E. & Wells, K. C. (1996). A social-cognitive intervention with aggressive children: Prevention effects and contextual implementation issues. In R. Dev. Peters & R. J. McMahon (Eds.), *Prevention and early intervention: Childhood disorders, substance use, and delinquency* (111–143). Newbury Park, CA: Sage.

Lochman, J. E., & Wells, K. C. (2002). The Coping Power Program at the middle school transition: Universal and indicated prevention effects. *Psychology of Addictive Behaviors, 16*, S40–S54.

Merrell, K. W., Gueldner, B. A., Ross, S. W., & Isava, D. M. (2008). How effective are school bullying intervention programs? A meta-analysis of intervention research. *School Psychology Quarterly, 23*(1), 26.

Morrison, G. M., Redding, M., Fisher, E., & Peterson, R. (2006). Assessing school discipline. In S. R. Jimerson & M. Furlong (Eds.), *Handbook of school violence and school safety: From research to practice* (pp. 211–220). Mahwah, NJ: Erlbaum.

Nansel, T. R., Haynie, D. L., & Simons-Morton, B. G. (2003). The association of bullying and victimization with middle school adjustment. *Journal of Applied School Psychology, 19*, 45–61.

Nansel, T. R., Overpeck, M., Pilla, R. S., Ruan, W. J., Simons-Morton, B. G., & Scheidt, P. (2001). Bullying behaviors among US youth: Prevalence and association with psychosocial adjustment. *Journal of the American Medical Association, 285*, 2094–2100.

Newman, D. A., Horne, A. M., & Bartolomucci, C. L. (2000). *Bully busters: A teacher's manual for helping bullies, victims, and bystanders.* Champaign, IL: Research Press.

Newman-Carlson, D., & Horne, A. (2004). Bully-busters: A psychoeducational intervention for reducing bullying behavior in middle school students. *Journal of Counseling and Development, 82*, 259–267.

Olweus, D. (1991). Bully/victim problems among school children: Basic facts and effects of a school-based intervention program. In D. J. Pepler & K. H. Rubin (Eds.), *The development and treatment of childhood aggression* (pp. 408–444). Hillsdale, NJ: Erlbaum.

Olweus, D. (1992). Bullying among schoolchildren: Intervention and prevention. In R. D. Peters, R. J. McMahon, & V. L. Quinse (Eds.), *Aggression and violence throughout the life span* (pp. 100–125). London: Sage Publications.

Olweus, D. (1993). Bully/victim problems among schoolchildren: Long-term consequences and an effective intervention program. In S. Hodgins (Ed.), *Mental disorder and crime* (pp. 317–349). Thousand Oaks, CA: Sage Publications.

Rigby, K. (2001). Health consequences of bullying and its prevention in schools. In J. Juvonen & S. Graham (Eds.), *Peer harassment in school: The plight of the vulnerable and victimized* (pp. 310–331). New York: Guilford Press.

Sharp, S., & Smith, P. K. (1991). Bullying in UK schools: The DES Sheffield bullying project. *Early Child Development and Care, 77*, 47–55.

Smith, S. W., Lochman, J. E., & Daunic, A. P. (2005). Managing aggression using cognitive-behavioral interventions: State of practice and future decisions. *Behavioral Disorders, 30*, 227–240.

Ttofi, M. M., Farrington, D. P., & Baldry, A. C. (2008). *Effectiveness of programmes to reduce school bullying.* Stockholm: Swedish Council for Crime Prevention, Information, and Publications.

Twemlow, S. W., Fonagy, P., Sacco, F. C., Gies, M. L., Evans, R., & Ewbank, R. (2001). Creating a peaceful school learning environment: A controlled study of an elementary school intervention to reduce violence. *American Journal of Psychiatry, 158,* 808–810. doi: 10.1176/appi.ajp.158.5.808

Twemlow, S., Fonagy, P., & Sacco, F. (2004). The role of the bystander in the social architecture of bullying and violence in schools and communities. *Annals of New York Academy of Sciences, 1036,* 215–232.

Twemlow, S. W., Vernberg, E., Fonagy, P., Biggs, B. K., Nelson, J. M., Nelson, T. D., & Sacco, F. (2010). A school climate intervention that reduces bullying by a focus on the bystander audience rather than the bully and victim: The peaceful schools project of the Menninger clinic and Baylor college of medicine. In Jimerson, S., Swearer, S., & Espelage, D. L. (Eds.), *The International Handbook of Bullying* (pp. 365–377). New York: Routledge.

Vossekuil, B., Fein, R. A., Reddy, M., Borum, R., & Modzeleski, W. (2002). The final report and findings of the Safe School Initiative: Implications for the prevention of school attacks in the United States. Washington, DC: U.S. Secret Service and U.S. Department of Education.

Walker, H. M., & Shinn, M. R. (2002). Structuring school-based interventions to achieve integrated primary, secondary, and tertiary prevention goals for safe and effective schools. In M. R. Shinn, G. Stoner, & H. M. Walker (Eds.), *Interventions for academic and behavior problems: Preventive and remedial approaches.* Silver Spring, MD: National Association of School Psychologists.

Whitted, K. S., & Dupper, D. R. (2005). Best practices for preventing or reducing bullying in schools. *Children & Schools, 27*(3), 167–174.

Zins, J. E., Weissberg, R. P., Wang, M. C., & Walberg. H. J. (Eds.). (2004). *Building academic success on social and emotional learning: What does the research say?* New York: Teachers College Press.

CHAPTER 9

A Quick, Fun Method for Teaching Kids How to Stop Being Victims

Israel C. Kalman

The horrific school shooting at Columbine High School on April 20, 1999, brought awareness to the modern world of the terrible suffering of victims of teasing and bullying. In the website created by the gunmen Eric Harris and Dylan Klebald, they presented themselves as victims of loathing and abuse by other students and announced their plans to carry out an unspeakably ghastly act of revenge. Looking back at previous school shooters, social scientists noticed that almost all of them harbored similar victimization sentiments, though they may have not been as articulate about them as Harris and Klebald. This discovery ignited our determination to eliminate the scourge of bullying from schools.

Feeling victimized by peers, though, is not only a factor in school shootings but in youth suicide as well. Prof. Dan Olweus, the founder of bullying psychology, began research on bullying in the 1970s in response to a rash of student suicides (Olweus,1993). More recently, the term "bullycide" (a misnomer—linguistically, the word means "killing a bully") has been coined to refer to suicide by victims of bullying.

The dramatic cases of murder and suicide related to bullying are only the tip of the iceberg. There are one or two students in virtually every classroom that are relentlessly picked on by their peers, and they all feel miserable. Imagine what it's like to go to school and have your fellow students making fun of you, rejecting you, spreading rumors about you, threatening you, and pushing you around on a daily basis. Then you go home to find that they are continuing their nastiness over the cell phone and Internet. To top it off, nothing you are doing to make the bullying stop is working, and nothing the school is doing is working, either. There is even a good chance that your school has gone gung-ho on an antibullying campaign, and your school assured you that bullying will not be tolerated, yet the bullying continues unimpeded. If you followed the school's instructions to tell the staff when you are bullied, there is an excellent chance that it made your peers lose any remnant of respect they may have had for you. Maybe your parents went to the school for help or confronted the bullies' parents, and the only thing that changed was that your peers become even more convinced you're a total momma's boy/girl.

How do you think you would you feel if this happened to you? You'd feel like a complete loser, so pathetic that not even the adult authorities can help you. You'd be consumed with pain and rage and desire for revenge. Life becomes hell. If you go too long without relief, you begin considering the possibility of ending the pain by ending your life.

Schools throughout the modern world have made it a goal to eliminate bullying. Most state governments have passed laws requiring schools to make children safe from bullying. Hundreds, if not thousands, of research studies have been conducted on bullying. Unfortunately, these efforts to eliminate bullying are far from succeeding, as both the popular media and the research are finding. With increasing frequency, parents are suing schools for failing to stop their children from being bullied— and in most of these cases, the schools *do* have antibullying programs and policies in effect, but they fail to solve the problem. The December 2004 issue of the *School Psychology Review* published a research study of monumental importance (Smith et al., 2004). Canadian psychologist David Smith had conducted a metanalysis of the published research on whole-school antibullying programs—the approach developed by Prof. Dan Olweus and subsequently adopted by most of the world's antibullying programs and policies. He discovered that 86% of the studies showed the antibullying program had no benefit or made the problem even worse. Only 14% of the published studies showed that the antibullying program produced a minor reduction in bullying. Not one study showed that the program produced a major reduction in bullying. Since then, two more metaanalyses on antibullying programs have been published with similarly discouraging findings.

So how are we to help kids who are suffering from bullying when the programs developed by the leading experts are failing to solve the problem? How can we prevent tortured souls from harming themselves or their schools?

Fortunately, the solution to bullying is essentially effortless; the kids just need to be taught the effortless solution.

WHY ARE THE SOCIAL SCIENCES DOING SUCH A POOR JOB OF SOLVING THE PROBLEM OF BULLYING?

Despite years of intensive effort to get rid of bullying, the problem continues and is frequently called an epidemic. Other fields of science have had the most incredible accomplishments, yet the psychological sciences can't seem to figure out how to solve the problem of bullying. Why?

The reason is quite simple. The very conceptualization of the bullying problem as defined by Olweus and universally adopted by the academic educational and psychological establishments is not a scientific/psychological one but a law enforcement one. Bullying behavior is treated as a crime that is not to be tolerated (Olweus, 1993; Olweus & Limber, 1999). We declare that children have a right to go to school without being bullied by other kids. Bullies are seen as guilty perpetrators and victims as innocent targets that have no responsibility for the way they are treated. Educators and school mental health professionals are required to inform the student body about the myriad unacceptable behaviors that constitute bullying and the punishments ("consequences") that will be meted out to perpetrators. The staff is mandated to protect children from each other and to monitor all areas of the school (and cyberspace as well) so that the students can live in a completely safe environment. To help us perform these functions, we instruct kids to inform us when they are bullied so that we can apprehend and punish the bullies. Student bystanders are also conscripted in the effort to protect victims from bullies, and many schools punish bystanders who don't stand up for victims against bullies, as accessories to the crime.

The psychological research, though, shows that punitive, zero-tolerance approaches to child discipline don't work and cause more harm than good (Evenson et al., 2009; Skiba, 2008). Both the American Psychological Association and the National Association of School Psychologists have issued research-based opinion papers urging schools to shun this approach to discipline.

A logical examination of the law enforcement approach to bullying would make it clear why it isn't working. Let's say you and I are kids in school. You make fun of me and I get you sent to the principal's office for bullying me. Is that going to make you like me? No. You are going to hate me and want to beat me up after school, and/or you will look for an opportunity to inform the school that I bullied you so you can get *me* in trouble. So every time we get the school staff involved, the hostilities escalate and more serious incidents follow.

This same process is what causes so much fighting to go on among siblings in the home (Wolf, 2003; Faber and Mazlish, 1987). The children are telling the parents on each other. The parents get involved playing policeman, judge, and punisher. This makes the kids hate each other even more, and the losing side hates the parents, too, so the hostilities never end. The same approach that makes matters worse between kids at home is hardly likely to make matters better among kids in school.

Let's also examine what the antibullying education is teaching kids today. The following, in a nutshell, is the philosophy that is the foundation of antibullying programs, policies, and laws:

> You are entitled to a life in which no one is mean to you. If people are mean to you, please don't think it has anything to do with you, your behavior, or your attitudes. It is because they are bullies, but it has nothing to do with you. There is an imbalance of power, and you cannot handle the bullies on your own. Furthermore, since you are an innocent victim, it is not your responsibility to make people stop bullying you but that of society-at-large—student bystanders, staff, parents, and law enforcement officers. You must inform the school authorities about bullies so they can apprehend, punish, and/or rehabilitate them.

There is no serious school of psychology, philosophy, or religion in the world that promotes such an approach to life. Anyone living by this philosophy is bound to be miserable. They will be repeatedly disappointed to discover life is very different from their expectations. They will believe they are helpless to solve their problems on their own. They will think of anyone who upsets them as an evil person that preys on others' weaknesses and of themselves as virtuous saints. When they inform on others to the authorities, they will be despised and become pariahs in their communities.

To solve the problem, we need to take a scientific psychological approach to bullying. We don't simply decide that a phenomenon is unacceptable and needs to be eradicated. We expect the likelihood of unintended negative side effects to interventions. We recognize that life is replete with adversity and that we need to use our brains to understand and solve our problems; the idea that we can create a completely safe society by passing laws against all negative behavior is irrational. If it were possible to do so, governments throughout the world would have created Utopia ages ago. We understand that we are not passive passengers in the journey of life but that everything we do or don't do affects what happens to us, that the way we treat others influences how they treat us, and that our attitudes influence the way we feel.

If we are to assist children in becoming emotionally and socially successful, we need to present them with a realistic approach to the hardships of life rather than with the fantasy that we can guarantee them a completely safe environment.

THE DIFFERENCE BETWEEN CRIMINAL BEHAVIOR AND BULLYING

Before I continue, we need to consider what constitutes bullying. Because the academic definition of bullying comprises virtually all negative behavior, acts like rape, theft, murder, gang behavior, and arson are being called bullying. Even slavery, genocide, and terrorism are often called bullying. The cases of bullying highlighted by the media tend to be instances of extreme violence.

It is true that sometimes children are extremely violent. But such acts are true crimes and are relatively rare. Behaviors that cause objective harm to people's bodies or property are rightfully considered criminal. We deserve to be protected from these behaviors, and people who perpetrate them deserve to be punished. We need the law enforcement system to deal with true crime.

But most of the acts of bullying are not criminal. In fact, most are protected by the First Amendment. Acts like name-calling, rumors, social exclusion, gestures, and kids' hitting or pushing without injuring anyone are the normal problems of everyday life. We need to learn how to handle them on our own (Guldberg, 2009). Treating them like crimes in which the authorities need to be involved almost always make matters worse. Just imagine what life would be like if people called the police on you every time they felt you upset them!

HOW CAN WE HELP KIDS WHO ARE BULLIED?

Because awareness of bullying is growing, referrals of victims to professional counselors and therapists are growing as well. How can we help these tormented souls?

If you have worked with such clients, there is a good chance you have found yourself making little or no progress. Listening to their feelings and empathizing with them will make them feel better for a short while, but they return to school and continue to be bullied. You can discuss their family dynamics with them, but the bullying doesn't stop. You can do play therapy, art therapy, and dance therapy with them, but the bullying continues. You can inform them that no one has a right to abuse them in any way, but that will make them feel even more hurt and self-righteously angry the next time they are bullied. You can instruct them to tell the school authorities, but that will often fail to solve the problem and even intensify it. You can refer them to karate lessons, or teach them to stand up tall when facing their bullies, yet find that the bullying continues.

So what are we to do? First, we need to understand *why* kids get bullied. Please remember, we are not talking about isolated criminal or abusive acts, but routine and repetitive nastiness inflicted on the victim by the same kids.

WHY DO KIDS GET BULLIED?

There is only one reason that anyone gets bullied repeatedly by the same people. The reason is that they *get upset* by the bullying. Every victim of bullying is by definition upset by the way they are being treated. Otherwise it wouldn't be a problem. And no one who *doesn't* get upset by bullying is a victim of bullying. It is practically impossible to continue picking on someone if it doesn't bother them. When you use the approach I will be teaching you in this chapter, you will discover over time how true this is.

The solution, then, is to teach kids not to get upset by bullying. When they stop getting upset, the bullying stops within a matter of days. That, though, sounds easier said than done. Even we adults have a hard time not getting upset by abusive behavior. How do we teach kids to stop getting upset when people are mean to them?

THE GOLDEN RULE/FREEDOM OF SPEECH GAME

While I have been conducting this procedure in its current form for about two decades, I recently decided to call it The Golden Rule/Freedom of Speech Game. The reason should become apparent by the time you finish reading the description of the process.

There is nothing new in the principles kids learn through this game. Wise people have understood them for thousands of years. They are taught by all major schools of psychology, philosophy, and religion. Many counselors and therapists, as well as parents, give kids the right advice for dealing with bullying, but simply giving good advice is often not sufficient to get kids to actually follow the advice. It is far more convincing to convey the solution through role-playing. And this structured role-playing game makes it especially convincing. Once I play the game with kids, they are eager to try the solution on their bullies. It is effective with the average child of 7 years and older. I will also play it with kids as young as 5, but I will keep the dialogues simpler.

The single most important thing I can teach people is how to deal with verbal attacks. Most of the acts we call bullying are verbal, and even most physical fights begin with words. So if you know how to deal with verbal attacks, most of the bullying disappears.

My game is similar to the tactic of a pool hustler. If I am a pool hustler, I will go into a pool hall and play against you, betting five dollars. I will play mediocre, being sure I lose the game. I will play you again for five dollars, again making sure I lose. Then I will say, "You know what? I have a hundred dollars. Let's play for a hundred bucks." You rub your hands together in glee, eagerly anticipating making an easy hundred dollars.

Then we play again. But this time I do my best. I get all of the balls in their pockets and you don't stand a chance. I walk off with your hundred dollars and you're left standing there flabbergasted.

My game takes a similar tactic. I will be presenting the instructions with "you" being the client and "me" being the therapist.

Step One: I ask you to describe the problem to me.
I want to know **who** picks on you, how they do it, how often they do it, what **you've been doing** to try to get them to stop, and **why you think** they do it to you. This step takes perhaps 5 minutes.

Then I ask you if you want the kids to **stop** picking on you, and of course you say **yes.**

Step Two: I give you the instructions for the game.
Me: I'm going to play a game with you. This game will teach you the real reason the kids are picking on you and it will also teach you how to make them stop. In this game, your job is to insult me, and my job is to make you stop. But don't let me stop you, because then I win and you lose. Don't worry about really hurting my feelings. It's only a game, and I want you to do a good job.

Step Three: I get angry when you insult me.
It looks like I am trying hard to win the game, but I am really setting you up to believe that there is no way in the world I can win the game. It goes something like this:

You: Izzy, you're an idiot!
Me: No, I'm not!
You: Yes, you are! You have "idiot" written all over you!
Me: No, I don't! Stop calling me an idiot!
You: But you are! Everyone knows you're an idiot!
Me: I'm warning you, you had better stop calling me an idiot!
You: Yeah! Or what? What are you going to do to stop me?
Me: I know karate! I'll break every bone in your body!
You: Ha! You're going to stop me? Let me see you try!
Me: I will! Just do it one more time and I'll have no choice!

You: Idiot, idiot, idiot!
Me: Stop it already!

I keep this going for a while. Typically, the angrier I become, the more confident and insulting you become. If you are laughing, I know I am doing a good job. After a minute or two of being insulted, I sigh and say, "Okay, I give up."

   Step Four: I challenge you again.
In Step Three, you discovered how easy it is to insult me and are now convinced that I can't possibly make you stop. I ask you:

Me: So if you want to insult me, can I make you stop?
You: No.
Me: Good! We're going to play the game again. Your job is to insult me and my job is to make you stop. Remember, don't let me stop you or I win and you lose. I can't stop you, right?
You: Right.
Me: Okay. Insult me, and remember, don't let me stop you. I can't stop you, right?
You: Right.

   Step Five: I do nothing to stop you.
When you insult me this time, I stay completely calm and content. I let you know it is perfectly okay for you to insult me all you want. I will show appreciation for the things you say, and ask you if there is anything else wrong with me that you want to inform me about.

You: Izzy, you're an idiot!
Me: I do stupid things every day.
You: You do! So you know you're an idiot?
Me: Of course. I don't know about you, but I'm an idiot.
You: Boy, you're weird!
Me: I've always been weird.
You: I don't get you.
Me: A lot of people don't.
You: Okay, I give up.
Me: Are you sure? Because you don't have to. If you want to insult me some more I really don't mind.
You: Yes, I'm sure.

   Step Six: I question you about the experience.

Me: We just played the game two times. Which time was more fun for you, the first or the second?

You: The *first.*

Me: Who won the game the first time?

You: *I* won.

Me: Who won the second time?

You: *You* won.

Me: Who looked like an idiot the first time?

You: *You* did.

Me: Who looked like an idiot the second time?

You: *I* did.

Me: Which time could you respect me more, the first or the second?

You: The *second.*

Me: Which time did I work harder?

You: The *first.*

Me: The first time, was I treating you like a friend or an enemy?

You: Enemy.

Me: The second time, was I treating you like a friend or an enemy?

You: Friend.

Me: That's right. The first time I was treating you like an enemy and the second time like a friend. That is the real difference. Treating you like a friend was a lot easier than treating you like an enemy and it got me much better results.

Step Seven: I give you insight about the game.

I will help you understand what the game shows about your situation. First, I want to get you to understand *who* it is that has been making you angry all along.

Me: When you were insulting me and I was getting mad, who was making me mad?

You: *I* was.

Me: But that was really an illusion. Do you know who was *really* making me mad?

You: No.

Me: I was really making *myself* mad. I had you insult me two times. One time I got mad, and the other time I didn't. Do you have a remote control to my brain and are pressing the "Anger" button?

You: No.

Me: Of course not. If I don't want to get mad, you can't make me mad. And this is what's been happening with you and the kids in school. They have been making fun of you and you have been getting mad. Doesn't it feel like *they* make you mad?

You: Yes.

Me: But do they really have a remote control to your brain and are pressing the "Anger" button?

You: No.

Me: That's right. All this time you have been making *yourself* mad, but it feels like *they* do it *to* you.

Next, I will use the experience in the game to explain the real reason you have been getting picked on, as well as the way to make kids **stop** picking on you. Each time we played the game, there was an optical illusion. [If you are a young child or have limited vocabulary, I will say *magic trick* instead of *optical illusion.*] What you *saw* me doing was not *really* what I was doing. The first time, did you see me trying to *stop* you?

You: Yes.

Me: But that's not what I was *really* doing. Do you know what I was *really* doing the first time?

You: No.

Me: I was making you *continue.* I was making you *win.* I was making you have *fun.* I made myself look like a big *idiot.* Why should you stop? You were having such a good time! So it only *looked* like I was making you stop, but I was actually making you *continue* and I could have kept you going all day long. It's just that I got worn out and had to stop. And this is what's been happening with the kids who make fun of you. You have been getting mad and trying to make them *stop.* But you haven't been making them *stop.* You have been making them *continue*! Didn't you have a great time when *I* was getting upset?

You: Yes.

Me: Don't you think they have a great time when *you* get upset?

You: Yes.

Me: They don't call you fatso because you're overweight, or four-eyes because you have glasses, or idiot because you are in Special Education. They do it because you get *upset* when they call you fatso or four-eyes or idiot. The real reason they pick on you is *because* you're getting upset and trying to make them stop. You just couldn't see it. The second time we played the game, there was also an optical illusion. The second time, did you see me letting you insult me?

You: Yes.

Me: But that's not *really* what I was doing. You know what I was really doing the second time?

You: No.

Me: I was making you *stop.* Wasn't it harder to insult me the second time?

You: Yes.

Me: That's right. It was a lot harder the second time, you felt foolish and you stopped. You were *sure* I couldn't stop you, but I stopped you very quickly and you couldn't see what I was really doing.

Step Eight: I give you instructions.

Me: This is what I want you to do for the next week, and it only takes a week to see if it works. Until now you've been thinking, "Oh, no! They're making fun of me! I have to make them stop!" This is the wrong way to think. As long as you think you have to make them stop, they're *never* going to stop. Now, do you want to be the winner or the loser?

You: Winner.

Me: This is how you are going to win. For the next week, you are going to show kids they can insult you all they want and it's perfectly okay. If they insult you and you are calm and happy, who is going to look foolish?

You: They will.

Me: And who's going to feel foolish?

You: They will.

Me: Will you be *upset* if they look and feel foolish when they insult you?

You: No.

Me: In fact, you'll be *happy* if they look and feel foolish when they insult you. So from now on, you are going to be perfectly happy when they make fun of you because they are going to feel foolish and you are going to be the winner.

Now I will give you the following two warnings:

Me: I have to give you two warnings, or you may not succeed. The first warning is that they are not going to stop picking on you right away. In fact, they are going to do it even more in the beginning. They've been picking on you every day for a very long time, so when they see you are *not* getting upset, they are going to try even harder. So the first couple of days, if you see them treating you worse, don't think, *"Oh, no. This advice doesn't work! The problem's only getting worse!"* It does work. It is just that it gets worse before it gets better. The second warning is that you have to do it 100% of the time; 90% will probably not work. If they find that they can get you upset every once in a while, they will just try harder and more often until you do get upset. It's only when they see they can never upset you, then they'll stop trying to upset you.

Step Nine: I help you practice not getting upset.

Me: Now I'm going to help you practice. I'm going to insult *you* and I want you *not* to get upset no matter what I say. I'm warning you, I'm going to be really nasty. If you get upset, you lose. The truth is I don't *want* you to lose this one—I don't *want* you to get upset. I am just warning you that if you do, you lose.

Then I proceed to insult you. I do it for a full minute or two. As I am going on, you are likely to feel increasingly confident and happy, and I in turn become increasingly frustrated. In fact, there is a good chance you will even be laughing, especially if the insults are really good. My all-time favorite insult is, "You are so ugly, when you look in the mirror the reflection throws up!"

I have developed my own repertoire of insults, and I suggest you develop your own repertoire as well for working with kids. You can look up insult websites and choose your favorites. Don't be afraid of hurting the kids' feelings. They are not likely to get upset. Just gauge how much they can take. If it is going well, you should have the child smiling and laughing before long. If the child **does** look upset, stop and ask if it is upsetting them. If they say it is, explain it's only a game and you are try-ing to help them practice not getting upset. Then they will probably let you insult them and they won't get upset.

I insult you long enough for it to be clear that I can't upset you, and I am the big loser.

Me: I give up. You did a really good job. Who was winning?
You: *I* was.
Me: And who was looking like a jerk?
You: You were.
Me: Was it hard not to get upset?
You: No.
Me: Any effort at all?
You: No.
Me: That's right. Because once you realize that you *lose* when you get upset, and that you do it to *yourself*, you discover it's *effortless* not to get upset. You did a good job with me. Can you do a good job with the kids in school for the next week?
You: Yes.

Me: Good! I will see you in a week and you'll tell me how it went. Just remember—it's going to get worse before it gets better, and you have to do this all of the time. [I may also add:] If you're having a hard time during the week, come and see me and I'll help you some more.

And I'll see you in another week and you will probably inform me that it worked and the kids are stopping picking on you.

There are kids who have serious impulse control problems. They may do a good job not getting upset when I insult them in the last step of my game, but once they're back in the "real world" they give in to their impulses and get upset. If I discover the kid is having a hard time following my advice, I will try to touch base with them every day—only for a few minutes—and do some more role playing about whatever situation they are having difficulty handling. After a week or two, almost all kids "get it." They stop getting upset and the bullying stops soon thereafter.

OTHER TYPES OF BULLYING

Of course, there are other types of behaviors that are being called bullying, and I use a similar approach for teaching how to handle each one. A detailed presentation of them all is beyond the scope of this book chapter, and can be found in my publications and seminars, as well as in many of my free writings on my website, www.Bullies2Buddies.com, but I will explain them briefly here.

Whatever type of situation I am teaching how to handle, I have the child play the bully and I play the victim, and we do it two times. The first time we play the scenario I handle the bullying in the wrong way—that is, the way people *typically* respond—by getting angry, defensive, and/ or threatening. In other words, I treat the person like an enemy. Then we play the scenario a second time, and I treat the bully like a friend. This process enables the children to understand how their bullies feel when they (the children) get upset and to experience how the bullies would feel if they (the children) were to treat them like friends. Finally, I help the children practice the right approach. I play the bully, and instruct the children to treat me like a friend when I am mean to them.

PREJUDICIAL ATTACKS

Today, insults about people's race, religion, gender, or sexual orientation are considered much worse than other insults. They have become crimes that are not protected by Freedom of Speech. Many mental health professionals believe that we cannot possibly handle such insults on our own because they attack the "essence of our being." However, prejudicial insults can be handled just as easily and successfully as any other insults by applying Freedom of Speech.

Among kids in recent years, the most common insult is *gay*. They get mad and into fights when they're called gay. Some have even taken to committing murder or suicide because they couldn't tolerate being called gay.

I will provide several different situations of gay insults and how to handle them.

Scenario Number One: I am not gay, but you call me gay.

You: You are soooo gay!
Me: No, I'm not!
You: Yes, you are! Everyone knows you're gay!
Me: How can they know something that's not true?
You: Didn't you ever look in the mirror? You're *flaming* gay!
Me: No, I'm not! Stop calling me gay!
You: Why should I stop? I'm going to keep on calling you gay until you admit it's true!
Me: But it's not true! Shut your mouth already or I'll shut it for you!
You: A little fairy like you! Hah! How are *you* going to shut my mouth?
Me: I will! You call me gay one more time and I'll have to do it!
You: Gay, gay, gay, gay, gay! Go ahead! Try and stop me!

This, of course, will lead to nowhere but a fight. Now we'll do it differently. I will give you Freedom of Speech and treat you like a friend.

You: You are soooo gay!
Me: How come you think I'm gay?
You: Just look in the mirror and you'll see.
Me: I do look in the mirror. What about me do you think makes me look gay?
You: The way you dress. Those pants are so tight. Only gays would wear pants like that.
Me: They are 50s style. Marlon Brando and James Dean used to wear pants like that.
You: Well, they must have been gay.
Me: I don't think so. I think they were really hot with the women.
You: They were?
Me: Yeah! You should watch some of their movies. They're real classics.

You: Only gays like old movies.
Me: Oh, you'd be surprised. You should watch *On the Waterfront* and *Rebel Without a Cause*. You'd love them.
You: Well, maybe I'll watch them sometime.
Me: You won't regret it!
You: Thanks.

Much better, isn't it? And it was so easy. I just treated you like a friend and told myself you have the right to say whatever you want.

> *Scenario Number Two:* I am gay and have "come out," and you hate gays with a passion. Let's say we are in high school because by that age we are likely to be aware of our true sexual orientation.

You: You know, you are going to burn in hell!
Me: No, I'm not!
You: Yes, you will! The Bible says all gays are going to burn in hell!
Me: The Bible is nonsense! It was written by homophobic men!
You: No, it wasn't! God wrote the Bible and it says you are going to suffer eternal damnation!
Me: No, I won't! You're the one who's going to burn in hell because God hates bigots!
You: God loves me! He hates you! That's why he sent AIDS to kill you off!
Me: How dare you talk to me like that? You are violating my civil rights!
You: Oh, yeah? What are you going to do? Call the police?
Me: Maybe I should!
You: Yeah, go ahead, you gay sissy! Guess what? The police hate gays, too! They're not going to help you!
Me: Yes, they will! It's the law!
You: Hah, hah! No law can help you! Gays are beyond help!
Me: Shut your mouth already!

Again, this results in endless hostility. This time I'll give you Freedom of Speech and treat you like a friend. (I don't expect kids to respond in as sophisticated a manner as I will be demonstrating here. It is simply how I do it to get the message across, and to teach kids to take a friendly attitude when they are insulted.)

You: You know, you are going to burn in hell!
Me: Why do you say that?
You: Because you are gay!
Me: And you think gays are going to hell?

You: Yes! The Bible says so!

Me: Well, I sure hope it's not true.

You: It is!

Me: How do you know?

You: I told you already. The Bible says so. And that's what my priest says, too!

Me: Yes, a lot of priests say that. You know, there were a lot of stories in the news about priests molesting young boys. Does that mean they are gay, too?

You: I guess so.

Me: Will they go to hell, too?

You: Sure.

Me: Boy, I'm sure glad there will be some priests to confess to in hell!

You: Stop kidding around. I mean it. You are going to go to hell if you stay gay.

Me: Why do they think it is so terrible to be gay?

You: Because the Bible says "Adam and *Eve*," not, "Adam and *Steve*."

Me: If God didn't want there to be gays, why did he make me gay?

You: He didn't make you gay. You *chose* to be gay!

Me: You think I *chose* to be gay?

You: Of course. Everyone knows it's a choice.

Me: Are you *straight*?

You: Of course!

Me: Do you remember *choosing* to be straight?

You: I didn't have to choose. I was *born* straight.

Me: That's right. You didn't choose to be straight. You never had to ask yourself, "Should I be straight, or should I be gay? Hmmm … I think I'll be straight!" Well, I never chose, either. If it were a choice, do you think I would have chosen to be gay?

You: Well, you obviously did!

Me: Believe me, if it were a choice, I would have chosen to be straight. You know how tough it is to be gay?

You: No.

Me: Oh, it's a bummer! People hate you just for what you are. They treat you like a freak and tell you you're going to hell. When I first realized I was gay, I thought, "Oh, no. What am I going to do? People are going to hate me. How am I going to live a normal life? And how am I going to tell my parents?" Believe me, if it were a choice, I would have picked straight.

You: Well, it's not too late! You can still choose to become straight.

Me: Believe me, I tried. I went out with girls. I figured if I go out with enough girls, I'd learn to be attracted to them. But it didn't work. I mean, I love their company. We have so much in common. But I was never *attracted* to them.

You: Maybe you didn't go out with the *right* girl.

Me: Dude, it's nice that you care so much about me, but believe me, I went out with the "right" girls. But it didn't help. I just had to become cool with the fact that I'm gay, and then I became happier.

You: I think you should still try anyway. In my church, they run this program that turns gay people straight.

Me: I went to a program like that for a whole year. All it did was make me feel guilty. It didn't make me straight.

You: Well, maybe the program in my church is better. You should try it.

Me: Thanks again for wanting to help me. I really appreciate it. But I'm gay, and I'm okay with it now.

You: Well, if that's what makes you happy ...

Me: Yes, it does. Thanks for the concern.

You: You're welcome.

It obviously worked out much better this time. If we go to school together, are in the same classes, and I always treat you this way, you may even become my friend despite your antigay prejudice. And you may even end up thinking, "well, maybe gays aren't so bad after all." So why do I need the government's help with this? I can turn you into a less prejudiced person all by myself if I give you Freedom of Speech and treat you like a friend.

INSULTS AGAINST HANDICAPPED PEOPLE

It is in particularly bad taste to insult people's handicaps. Nevertheless, it often happens among kids because they are less restrained than adults.

If a child is handicapped but has intact intelligence, there is no reason they can't handle verbal aggression on their own. There is a very simple and effective way to defeat the aggressors in a way that makes them feel like real jerks.

Let's say I am a paraplegic, and you are going to call me a cripple. (The word *cripple* has become unacceptable).

You: Hey, you're a cripple!

Me: No I'm not! Don't call me a cripple!

You: But you are! Look! You can't get out of that wheelchair!

Me: It's because I'm disabled! Don't call me a cripple!

You: Cripple, cripple, cripple! Ha, ha, ha ha, ha!

Me: Stop it!

Now we'll do it again and I'll respond differently.

You: Hey, you're a cripple.
Me: You're so lucky you can walk and run.

This shuts you up right away while making you feel sympathy for me. And you're not likely to ever put me down again.

PHYSICAL ATTACKS

There is a great deal of confusion about physical attacks. On the one hand, mental health professionals inform us that verbal attacks can be even more destructive than physical attacks. On the other hand, they almost universally treat physical attacks much more seriously than verbal attacks. They don't instruct people to call the police when their spouse was verbally insulting, but they do tell them to call the police when their partner has hit them.

The reason for this confusion is that words can, indeed, cause terrible harm to people. People's lives have been destroyed because of insults. However, verbal attacks are fundamentally different in nature from physical attacks. That is why our Bill of Rights guarantees us Freedom of Speech, not Freedom to Hit. Freedom of Speech is actually the Constitutional version of the slogan, "Sticks and stones may break my bones but words can never harm me." This slogan has been routinely called "a lie" in recent years (Bolton and Hawker, 1997; Conoley, 2008; Garbarino and De Lara, 2002; Merkwan, 2009). However, this slogan was never meant as a statement of fact. It is meant to be a *solution*—a solution to verbal bullying. If I get upset by insults, you are going to love insulting me and you will do it relentlessly. If I don't get upset by insults, it is no fun to pick on me, and you will leave me alone.

The "sticks and stones" slogan expresses the fundamental difference between verbal aggression and physical aggression. If you hit me with sticks and stones, my attitude toward the sticks and stones has no bearing on how much pain and damage I will experience; *you* are the one who's hurting me and injuring me. On the other hand, if you insult me, my attitude toward your words will determine if they hurt me. It is not up to *you* if the words hurt me. So if you insult me and I get upset, I really upset *myself*. Once I realize that it is my choice to get upset by insults, then I can stop getting upset, and you will stop insulting me.

Before you read my explanation of how I teach kids to deal with physical attacks, it is important to realize a couple of things. First, kids are far more physical than adults are, and the younger they are, the more physical they are. We cannot treat hitting among kids the same way we treat hitting among adults. We don't call the police when our children at home hit each other, but we very well may call the police when our spouse or neighbor hits us.

Secondly, when kids hit each other, rarely is there injury or even much pain. If you're a kid in school and another student purposely injures or causes you significant pain, they *should* be disciplined by the authorities. But most often the routine hitting and pushing, while unpleasant and humiliating, is not painful or injurious. So how should you handle it? I do the following demonstration.

I ask you to push me hard.

Me: (Pushing back) Hey! Get your hands off of me!
You: (Push me back even harder).
Me: (Pushing you again) I said get your hands off of me!

This of course leads to escalating fighting. Then I have you push me again.

Me: Oh, are you mad at me?
You: No.
Me: Oh, good!

And that usually puts a stop to it.

Situations tend to escalate, and very often there is little conscious thinking behind the hitting and pushing that kids do. They simply do it for the fun of it without any premeditation. If I hit you back, you immediately want to retaliate. So I bring it down from the physical level to the verbal level by asking you, "Are you mad at me?" If you're not, you realize you have no good reason to be mad at me and you leave me alone.

But perhaps you *are* mad at me. Let's say we're in high school and you saw me talking to your girlfriend. So I have you push me.

Me: Oh, are you mad at me?
You: You bet I am! You were talking to my girlfriend!
Me: I was? Who's your girlfriend?
You: Susie!

Me: Susie's your girlfriend? Wow, you're so lucky! I think she's the cutest
    girl in the whole school.
You: That's right! So you better stop talking to her!
Me: Do you think I'm trying to steal her away from you?
You: Yeah!
Me: Do you really think Susie would leave you for someone like me?
You: Of course not!
Me: That's right! I'm a nerd, and you're tough and cool. Susie would
    never go for someone like me.
You: That's right!
Me: That's right!

So if you do have a legitimate reason for being mad at me, my asking
you, "Are you mad at me?" still turns the situation from a physical into
a verbal one. Of course you have no right to injure me just because you're
mad at me, and if you do, you *should* get in trouble. But I will always try
to work out the situation with you on my own before I get the authorities involved.

RUMORS

A very common way that kids upset each other is through rumors. So I
ask you to bring me a rumor about me.

You: Izzy, I heard that you wet your bed at night!
Me: No, I don't!
You: Yes you do! Johnny slept over your house and said he saw your
    mother hanging out the wet sheets!
Me: No she didn't! We have a dryer! We don't hang out laundry!
You: Everyone knows you wet the bed, and everyone in class is talking
    about it!
Me: It's a big fat lie! I don't wet the bed!
You: Yes, you do!
Me: No, I don't! Shut your mouth already!

Then we do it again, and I respond as follows.

You: Izzy, I heard that you wet your bed at night!
Me: You did?
You: Yes!
Me: Do you believe it?
You: Yes!

Me: You can believe it if you want.
You: I do!
Me: I can't stop you.
You: That's right! You can't!
Me: No, I can't.

And it fizzles out.

You would like to see me defending myself from the rumor. But it's a trap. I lose by defending myself because the defensive position is the weaker position, and since you are biologically programmed to try to win, you will keep on attacking me with the rumor. So the second time, I turn the tables on you. I make you defend *yourself* by asking you, "Do you believe it?" Now you have to decide if you want to believe a nasty rumor about me. We can't stop people from believing what they want. So if you say you believe it, I say you can believe it if you want, and I win. And in case you say you *don't* believe it, I also win.

Sometimes rumors are incredibly humiliating and they happen to be true, and everyone *knows* that they're true. What do you do then? Imagine being the child of a celebrity or a politician and your parent had an affair or committed a crime, and it's being reported all over the news. You have to go to school and face the ridicule of your peers. Or let's say you are a girl in high school, and you got drunk at a party and had sex with the entire football team. Kids took pictures of you with their cell phones or digital cameras and are spreading the pictures around. (I will not deal here with the legitimate issue of the possibility of rape having been committed, only with how to handle ridiculing peers.) There are kids who have committed suicide because they didn't know how to handle such situations. So I demonstrate, with me playing the girl.

You: Izzy, you're a slut!
Me: No I'm not!
You: Yes you are! You slept with the football team!
Me: No I didn't!
You: Yes you did! I saw the pictures!
Me: That wasn't me! The pictures were PhotoShopped!
You: No they weren't! The pictures are you! And everyone saw you, anyway!
Me: Shut your mouth! It wasn't me!

This is obviously not going to get you to stop calling me a slut. Now we'll do it again and I'll treat you like a friend.

You: Izzy, you're a slut!

Me: What do you mean?

You: You slept with the football team!

Me [Sounding melancholy]: I know. It was the biggest mistake of my life.

You: And now everyone is talking about you!

Me: I know. I completely destroyed my reputation. I can't believe I actually did it.

You: And everyone's spreading the pictures around.

Me: I know. We were all at the party, and I was so happy that our football team won. Before I knew it I was drunk, and I felt so cool celebrating with the players, I didn't even realize what I was doing. I don't know what I'm going to do when my parents find out.

You: Maybe they won't.

Me: They probably will. I don't know what I'm going to tell them. I wish I were never born.

You: Don't talk like that. You parents will get over it.

Me: I don't think so. And neither will I. Life will never be the same again.

You: Don't say that. Maybe you should go to talk to the counselor. I think she can help you.

This time, not only are you no longer calling me a slut, you are trying to comfort me. So if the rumor is true and everyone knows it, or it's easily verifiable, it is much better for me to acknowledge it than to try to deny it.

SOCIAL EXCLUSION

The final situation I will deal with in this chapter is a very common one—kids being excluded from cliques. To teach you how to respond, I will ask you play the head of our clique and you will inform me that I'm excluded.

You: Izzy, the group had a meeting and decided you're out.

Me: What do you mean, "I'm out?"

You: You heard me. We kicked you out. You can't hang with us anymore.

Me: You can't kick me out!

You: Yes we can! And we did!

Me: I wasn't there for the meeting! You can't kick me out if I'm not there to vote!

You: Oh, yes we can!

Me: You can't kick me out! Even the teacher said you can't leave anyone out of a group!

You: Oh, what a cry-baby! Go ahead! Go tell the teacher!

This approach is going to *guarantee* that I will be out of the group. Now we'll do it again and I'll respond differently.

You: Izzy, the group had a meeting and decided you're out.
Me: So I'll be out.
You: You mean you don't care?
Me: If you don't want to be my friends, you don't have to.
You: Okay ... so you're cool with it?
Me: I'm cool.
You: Okay. See you around.

I come out looking much better this way. Of course there's no guarantee the group will have me back if I respond the second way. But the first way it is guaranteed that I'll be out.

If I make it important to be part of the group, I am giving you power over me. The way for you to experience that power is by excluding me. So the more I insist that I must be in the group, the more you want to leave me out. The second way, I don't care, so you have no power over me and I can't be the loser.

You can't force anyone to be your friend, and neither can the school. The truly popular kids do not go around begging other kids to be their friends. If you want to have more friends, tell yourself that it's perfectly okay if no one wants to be your friend. Then no one has power over you and you can't be a loser. Kids will respect you more and will be more likely to want to be your friend.

CONCLUSION

I have had tremendous success using this approach with both kids and adults, and the professionals who have learned it are also getting great results. It is fun for both the clients and the professionals, and is much more effective than simply explaining. If you are not accustomed to using role-playing on the job, you should find that with time you become increasingly comfortable doing it, and you will be able to come up with a role play to teach the solution to just about any interpersonal problem a client brings to you.

I wish you great success!

REFERENCES

Bolton, M., & Hawker, D. (1997) Verbal bullying—the myth of "sticks and stones." In D. Tattus & G. Gerbert (Eds.), *Bullying: Home, school and community* (pp. 53–63). London: David Fulton Publishers.

Conoley, J. (2008) Sticks and stones can break my bones and words can really hurt me. *School Psychology Review, 37*(2), 217–220.

Evenson, A., Justinger, B., Pelischek, E., & Schulz, S. (2009) Zero tolerance policies and the public schools: When suspension is no longer effective. *NASP Communiqué, 37*(5), 1, 6–7.

Faber, A., & Mazlish, E. (1987). *Siblings without rivalry: How to help your children live together so you can live too.* New York: Norton.

Garbarino, J., & De Lara, E. (2002). *And words can hurt forever: How to protect adolescents from bullying, harassment, and emotional violence.* New York: Free Press.

Guldberg, H. (2009). *Reclaiming childhood: Freedom and play in an age of fear.* Abingdon, Oxon: Routledge.

Merkwan, C. (2009, April 30). Sticks and stones may break my bones, but words can kill. Retrieved June 30, 2009, from Twin Cities Daily Planet website: http://www.tcdailyplanet.net/article/2009/04/28/sticks-and-stones-may-break-my-bones-words-can-kill.html.

Merrell, K. W., & Isava, D. M. (2008). How effective are school bullying intervention programs? A meta-analysis of intervention research. *School Psychology Quarterly, 23*(1), 26–42.

Olweus, D. (1993). *Bullying at school: What we know and what we can do (understanding children's worlds).* Malden, MA: Blackwell.

Olweus, D.; Limber, S. (1999). Bullying prevention program. Boulder, CO: Center for the Study and Prevention of Violence. Document Type: Book Citation.

Skiba, R. (2008). Are zero tolerance policies effective in the schools?: An evidentiary review and recommendations. *American Psychologist, 63*(9), 852–862.

Smith, J. D. et al. (2004). The effectiveness of whole-school antibullying programs: A synthesis of evaluation research. *School Psychology Review, 33*(4), 547–560.

Vreeman, R., & Carroll, A. (2007). A systematic review of school-based interventions to prevent bullying. *Archives of Pediatric Adolescent Medicine, 161*(1), 78–88.

Wolf, A. (2003). *"Mom, Jason's breathing on me!": The solution to sibling bickering.* New York: Ballantine Books.

CHAPTER 10

Early Interventions
Preventing Aggression and Enhancing Connection Among Youth and Adults

Kathleen Nader and William S. Pollack

INTRODUCTION

Years after a shooting at an elementary school, exposed student survivors described, to the authors and their colleagues, a number of lingering effects from the trauma.* For example, Chandra's good friend died in the shooting. Chandra had undergone successful therapy, following the shooting, and described functioning well but never having forgotten the experience. Occasionally, a reminder of the shooting or a new life experience (e.g., a college course, having a child) made it necessary to reprocess what had happened and to reevaluate choices (e.g., life goals, parenting). Mat and Kyra spoke of being very aware of the violence and other dangers in the world and described continued difficulty feeling safe. Daniel expected harm or hostility from others, had trouble trusting, and overreacted with anger and/or aggression in stressful situations. Lana spoke of how she had never gotten over feeling like she had left her dead friend behind when she ran for safety. Even though she thought her friend was right behind her, she felt like she had somehow betrayed her. The experience influenced her relationships and feelings about herself as a friend. Sean, who was shot twice, had periods of depression and of anxiety, had self-esteem problems, was overly cautious, felt like he attracted bad

---

* Names have been changed to protect anonymity and, in some cases, represent composite cases of the authors.

things, and felt damaged by the experience (emotionally and physically). Sometimes, he stabbed at his wounds with a pencil .... Surviving parents felt lucky that their children were alive, or they mourned the loss of dead children. Some had difficulty functioning in their marriages or as parents after a death. Some functioned well but described, "an ongoing pain in the heart that has never left." Some became overprotective of their children and frequently worried .... Years later, teachers in the youth's high school described them as sometimes "dark" or "moody"—"They'd been to hell and back and you could tell." Teachers said that the youth were often allowed to do things that other students were not allowed to do, such as walk in the halls without a hall pass. Teachers felt unequipped to handle these youth and complained that no one prepared them to do so. Some of them felt unsupported and were angry with their superiors.

Student-perpetrated homicides are rare in U.S. schools (Borum, Cornell, Modzeleski, & Jimerson, 2010; Cornell, 2006). When they do occur, they may severely impact surviving individuals, their senses of safety, expectations, mental and emotional well-being, and much more. In addition, they have an important effect on schools, their climates and functioning. As can be seen in the examples given ("years later ... in the youth's high school ...") such events also may affect schools where the shooting did not occur as well as the school and community where they occurred. Our most powerful tools are those employed in creating changes before tragedies occur. Effective preventive interventions must be both wide ranging and focused in multiple directions (e.g., toward children, home, school, community) and be sensitive to multiple risk factors within each domain. For example, interventions in schools and/or homes for affect regulation (Chapter 5; CD/workbook) and attachment (Chapter 6) have been used to treat youth with conduct disturbances (Keiley, 2002).

As the chapters of this book have demonstrated, among important interventions are those that enhance positive connection among and between adults and youth and include respect, vigilance, and enhancing important resilience-based skills (e.g., coping, social, self-regulation). The preceding chapters have demonstrated the importance of creating environments that help youth to feel safe and respected, as well as assisting them with personal, social, and coping skills. The success of programs that emphasize respectful and supportive communication between and among adults and youth as well as low tolerance for victimization help to demonstrate the importance of creating, at school and at home, an atmosphere in which youth feel safe and respected. *Targeted* school shootings—a significant differential concept distinguishing it from general gun violence—youth depression, and suicides demonstrate that disconnection is not conducive to positive outcomes (See Fein, Vossekuil, Pollack et al., 2002 on the Safe School Initiative investigation and findings). The disconnection that occurs when children are not treated empathically and sensitively—demonstrating that they are valued—has been shown in studies of attachment, examinations of targeted school shootings, and the observations of those who work with youth. In contrast, feeling valued, having opportunities to develop and display personal areas of competence, and having a safe atmosphere in which to function enhances the likelihood that youth will thrive. Increasing youth–adult connection is at the heart of antiviolence and antibullying methods, and is important to the creation of emotional stability in youth, their health resilience and academic achievement in the classroom (Cohen, 2001; Pollack, 2004a, b; Pollack, Modzeleski, & Rooney 2008; see also Cornell and groundbreaking work of Resnick, Bearman, Blum et al., 1997).

The Need for Early Interventions

The National Research Council and Institute of Medicine (2009) has concluded that developmentally appropriate, early youth interventions offer the greatest promise for preventing mental, emotional, and behavioral disorders. Given the high prevalence and costs of youth disorders such as aggression or depression, prevention efforts are clearly warranted (Gladstone, Beardslee, & O'Connor, 2011). Violence and suicides are among the most distressing outcomes that affect school communities. Additionally, exposure to these outcomes is a risk factor for other negative outcomes such as behavioral, cognitive, emotional, physical, and social problems (Griffin, McEwen, Samuels, Suggs, Redd, & McClelland, 2011). Aggressive victimization has multiple deleterious effects (Nader, 2008), including symptoms that perpetuate the cycle of aggression. As noted in Chapter 2, youth with early onset aggression tend to commit more crimes and more serious crimes than youth with late-onset aggression and may continue to do so into adulthood (Douglas & Bell, 2011; McBurnett et al., 2003; Nader, 2008). Early-onset depression also tends to recur in adulthood, is difficult to treat, and, the longer the duration of a depressive episode, the less likely it is to respond even to proven treatments (Gladstone et al., 2011). Disorders may combine with or contribute to other disorders. For example, substance abuse and suicide are among possible outcomes of depression. Symptoms (e.g., depression or anxiety) of disorders (e.g., depression or PTSD after bullying) without a diagnosable disorder may precede fully erupted disorders in youth and may warrant early intervention. Moreover, individuals who have experienced repeated or multiple types of trauma, such as repeated forms of bullying and/or abuse combined with other distressing experiences, may develop more complicated forms of traumatic reaction without exhibiting classically diagnosable PTSD (Habib & Labruna, 2011). Complicated traumatic reactions manifest themselves as a wide continuum of difficulties with emotional and behavioral regulation (e.g., aggression; see Table 10.1).

The Multiple Targets of Interventions

Among variables associated with negative outcomes (e.g., aggression, depression, suicide) for youth are (a) *family environments*: faulty attachments, parenting style (e.g., failure of monitoring, lack of warmth; harsh parenting), low SES, low levels of support (from family, school, and/or peers; Chapters 1, 4, 6; Cassidy & Shaver, 1999; Kilpatrick et al., 2007; Klein & Cornell, 2010); (b) *community environments*: community violence, low structure and support, regular exposure to violent media (Chapter 4; Chung & Steinberg, 2006; Huesmann, 2007, 2010; Klein & Cornell, 2010); (c) *child traits and history*: lack of empathy and self-awareness, temperament, unacknowledged or unresolved shame, poor coping, inadequate self-regulation skills, inadequate social skills, victimizations (Chapters 2, 5, 6, 7; Buckner, Mezzacappa, & Beardslee, 2009; Fletcher, in press; Posner & Rothbart, 2007); (d) *school environments*: school cultures/climates lacking respect, open communication (between and among students and adults), and/or value for individuality or individual learning needs; ineffective methods of identifying risk and inability for taking appropriate and swift action to ensure safety (Chapter 3; Borum et al., 2010; Cornell, Sheras, Gregory, & Fan, 2009; Cornell et al., 2009; Fein et al., 2002; Gregory, Cornell, Fan, Sheras, Shih, & Huang, 2010; Pollack et al., 2008); and (e) *peer relationships*: deviant peer associations, peer rejection or bullying (Chapters 1, 8; Graham, 2010; Klomek et al., 2010; Laird, Jordan, Dodge, Pettit, & Bates, 2001; see also Pollack et al., 2008). For example, insecure disorganized attachments are consistently demonstrated to be quite stable in the absence of intervention and to be a significant and ongoing risk factor for psychopathology, including aggression (Lyons-Ruth & Jacobvitz, 2008; Moss, Cyr, Bureau, Tarabulsy, & Dubois-Comtois, 2005; Chapter 6). This chapter discusses some of these issues and their relationship to the importance of enhancing connections among individuals.

The Multidimensionality of Target Variables

The emergence and maintenance of aggression and other youth disturbances is multidimensional (Keiley, 2002; Nader, 2008). Combinations of

TABLE 10.1 Youth Problems and Interventions

Variables	Risk Factors	Needs
Family environments	Harsh parenting or abuse Failure of monitoring Low socioeconomic status (SES) Low levels of support Parental mental disorders or substance abuse	Repair of faulty attachment relationship and styles Positive parenting (e.g., monitoring, warmth, sensitivity; firm, appropriate discipline) Mutual support
Community environments	Traumatic exposure (e.g., violence) Exposure to violent media or media that perpetuates ill will among sexually, ethnically, or otherwise differing members of the youth population Few resources Easy access to weapons	Safety and protection Structure/cohesiveness Positive role models Support and monitoring
Child traits and history	Lack of empathy and self-awareness Aggressive or negative temperaments or genetic predispositions Unacknowledged or unresolved shame Poor coping Inadequate self-regulation (e.g., poor ability to delay response or gratification; dysregulated, impulsive, hostile, and/or aggressive reactivity) Cognitive biases (e.g., expectations of hostility or harm; belief in rewards for aggressive behavior)	To be valued and respected; sensitive care Early interventions for problem behaviors and symptoms, risk factors, and/or traumatic exposures Training in coping, social, and self-regulation skills Ethical/moral training Supportive home and school environments Respect for individual emotional and academic needs

Continued

TABLE 10.1 (*Continued*) Youth Problems and Interventions

Variables	Risk Factors	Needs
School environments	Poor school climates (e.g., lack of respect and open communication between and among students and adults) Failure of school culture (e.g., in providing positive values, concrete displays of positive values) Failure to promote school connection Failure of monitoring (e.g., lack of vigilance for threat; ineffective methods of identifying risk or separating real threats from transient situations that can be easily assisted)	Providing a safe and peaceful climate (e.g., protection from all forms of aggression, including bullying) with open communication between youth and adults, respect and support for individual differences, respect among youth Providing a school climate and culture in which there is concrete evidence that adults respect each other and youth, are attentive to youth and their needs (supportive), are attentive to threat, and individuality is valued Teaching youth skills such as social skills (e.g., empathy, rapport building—e.g., listening, communicating), self-regulation (e.g., delay of gratification or reaction), coping skills (e.g., tension reduction, mental soothing, displacement of attention, information gathering), and skills to defuse bullying
Peer relationships	Relational bullying (e.g., cyber-bullying, rejection/exclusion, defamation/gossip) or overtly aggressive bullying (e.g., hitting, pushing, spilling on, throwing things at a person) Deviant peer associations	Bullying prevention Training in dealing with bullies Empathy and problem solving training Monitoring

risk and vulnerability factors along with particular experiences (e.g., victimization, loss) and conditions or contexts (e.g., school climate, parenting, and attachment) increase the possibility of school aggression and suicides and of other internalizing and externalizing problems. Problem behaviors are sometimes linked to specific combinations of variables. For example, preliminary evidence suggests that higher levels of risk-taking may be more likely for youth with both a propensity for risk taking and low but not high distress tolerance (MacPherson, Reynolds, Daughter, Wang, Cassidy, Mayes et al., 2010). Whether in specific or nonspecific combinations, a number of risk factors have been repeatedly associated with negative outcomes. It is important that those variables that can be influenced by intervention be addressed in and outside of schools before they escalate (Table 10.1). Training and interventions for very young and elementary school age children (adjusted/adapted for age and cognitive levels) are a part of the preventive process. Elementary schools are one important locus for *primary* prevention (Fonagy, Twemlow, Vernberg, Sacco, & Little, 2005), because early interventions may prevent or reduce the severity of later problem behaviors (Chapter 7).

SCHOOL-FOCUSED INTERVENTIONS

The creation of a caring community in which students feel safe and secure is the foundation for a safe school (Cornell, 2006). Among conditions for a safe school are an orderly and predictable environment characterized by consistent and reliable supervision and discipline, and a school climate that is characterized by school connectedness and an atmosphere of open communication, support, and respect (Cohen et al., 2009; Cornell, 2006; Daniels, Volungis, Pshenishy, Gandhi, Winkler, Cramer et al., 2010; Pollack, 2004a,b; Chapter 3). School values are evidenced in posters and communications that include safety and respect (e.g., no tolerance of bullying; value of diversity; Chapter 3; in Chapter 8, *Peaceful Schools Project*). It is also essential to have a team in place to assess conflict and problems before they escalate into aggression (Cornell, 2006; Daniels et al., 2010). Such a school environment would put emphasis upon achieving an emotional climate of interpersonal civility, empathy for others, and a clear sense of safety as modeled by adult behaviors and processes, and manifest by student–teacher and student–administrator connections (with serious attention paid to repairing any disconnections which may ensue). Such a climate would also emphasize a general ethos of trust and meaningful positive interpersonal relationships within the academic milieu where such adult–student connections not only forestall harm or alert the community to threat so it may be removed before harm ensues, but form the "emotional glue" that is the latticework at the heart of sustaining the educational endeavor within the school and, by extension, form a model for the other stakeholders involved in such positive school climates: parents, student caretakers, and the surrounding community of responsible adults (see Cohen et al., 2009; Cornell, 2006; Pollack, 2004a,b)

School Climate

> The more students feel connected, understood, and treated fairly at school, the less likely they are to become suicidal, abuse drugs and alcohol, become addicted to nicotine, or engage in impulsive sexual activities. Youth do best when they feel cared for and understood by their teachers and when they sense that teachers have high hopes for them academically. ... The potency of loving adult–child relationships is much stronger than even the best (and potentially useful) antiviolence program, certainly greater than any simple-minded, required, zero-tolerance curriculum, and more productive and less traumatic than any magnetometer or gun-sniffing dog. (Pollack, 2004a, p. 24)

Positive school climates serve as protection against negative outcomes (Loukas, Suzuki, & Horton, 2006; Chapter 3). Negative school climates are linked to student aggressive behavior (Holtappels & Meier, 2000; Chapter 3). Youth thrive in schools where there is a pervasive sense that they are genuinely liked and welcomed (Pollack, 2004a; Pollack et al., 2008). Research has demonstrated that a sustainable, positive school climate and school connection is associated with healthy youth development and academic achievement, as well as with the skills, knowledge, and dispositions necessary for students to be responsible and productive individuals (National School Climate Council [NSCC], 2007; Pollack, 2004a; Resnick et al., 1997). Reduced dropouts are also linked to positive school climate. Such a climate is characterized by values and norms that promote safety, engagement, involvement in the physical environment, satisfaction in learning, and respect, as well as the joint efforts of youth, parents, educators, and other community-based stakeholders. The framework for maintaining a positive school climate includes, among other guidelines, policies that specifically promote and sustain the development of social, emotional, ethical, civic, and intellectual skills, knowledge, dispositions, and engagement in an environment where all members are welcomed, supported, and genuinely feel safe (physically, emotionally, socially, and intellectually) (NSCC, 2007).

Threat Assessment

Even though school homicides are rare, threat of homicide or other violence cannot be ignored (Cornell, 2006). Individuals who make threats do not always pose a danger. Substantive threats must be distinguished from transient ones that may be easily resolved. School attacks are usually planned in advance (Fein et al., 2002; Randazzo & Plummer, 2009). Most school shooters have caused serious concern among peers, family members, and/or teachers before carrying out attacks. Many school shooters were suicidal prior to their attacks (Vossekuil et al., 2002; Randazzo & Plummer, 2009). They may have tried to commit suicide earlier but failed and/or may be at a point of desperation in which they wish to die or do not care what happens to them. Threat assessment methods include vigilance. These methods usually employ a threat assessment team, promote a school climate in which youth are likely to report suspected threats, promote school connectedness and conditions that deter aggression (including prevention of bullying), have established liaison with law enforcement and mental health professionals, and have a crisis plan (Cornell, 2006; Daniels et al., 2010; see Table 1.2). Methods such as the Virginia threat assessment method have shown to resolve threats without violence and to reduce bullying and long-term suspensions (Cornell, Allen, & Fan, under review; Cornell et al., 2009).

School Interventions

Preventive interventions for elementary-school-age children for a number of negative youth outcomes, including aggression and suicide, have employed training (e.g., parent, student, and/or teacher training), counseling efforts (e.g., mental health interventions), school-wide programs (e.g., threat assessment; enhancing school climate), and even dietary methods (e.g., providing omega 3 fatty acids). Although traumatic reactions may require mental health interventions in order to prevent ongoing externalizing and internalizing problems (Nader, 2008), preventive interventions such as building coping and social skills can assist youth to confront future adverse experiences (Griffin et al., 2011). Beyond any antidotal effects (e.g., on traumatic risk factors), instilling such protective factors is relevant to children's overall well-being and academic achievement, including youth who never become traumatized. Such protective factors can help a child recover from developmental disruptions, as well as help to prevent disruption of normal development. Strong relationships between and among students and teachers are also protective (Pollack, 2004a,b; Pollack et al., 2008; see Chapter 8).

Among the important areas of children's social-emotional development that can be addressed in schools are (a) emotional self-regulation (e.g., identification and management of strong emotions such as anger, excitement, and frustration; the ability to delay gratification or emotional reactions); (b) social competence (e.g., prosocial problem solving, sharing, helping, cooperation, positive peer interactions; social emotional learning); (c) coping effectiveness that may enhance or be a part of both emotional self-regulation and social competence; (d) emotional identification (e.g., self-awareness skills; empathy), and (e) school cooperation and willingness/desire to follow rules and internalize values (Ayduk et al., 2002; Webster-Stratton & Reid, 2010; Chapters 5–9). Programs described in this book are linked to improved behavior (i.e., reduced behavior problems and bullying; increased prosocial behaviors and social skills), increased academic performance (e.g., improved test scores, better work habits, a more positive orientation toward learning), and increased school connectedness and positive school climate (e.g., improved teacher-responsiveness and appropriately open teacher–student relationships; see Chapter 8). Some of the programs presented in this book for a variety of target areas accomplish multiple goals. For example, the *Caring School Community* (CSC) program is linked to increased prosocial (e.g., reflecting norms and values such as caring, justice, responsibility, and learning) and fewer aggressive behaviors as well as a range of positive outcomes—improved school connectedness, participation, and climate; higher academic scores/grades; and fewer problem behaviors; Chapter 7). Similarly, use of the 4Rs (Reading, Writing, Respect, and Resolution) demonstrated reductions in self-reported hostile attributional bias, aggressive interpersonal negotiation strategies, and depression as well as teacher-reported improvements in attention skills, academic performance, aggression, and socially competent behavior (Chapter 7). Some programs can be integrated into a standard curriculum; others are designed as separate school-based interventions. Research on the *Incredible Years* programs has demonstrated the importance of providing training for parents, teachers, and youth (Webster-Stratton & Reid, 2010; Chapter 5)

PARENT-FOCUSED INTERVENTIONS

From birth, parents influence neurocognitive brain development, self-esteem, adaptive coping, self- and other-awareness with a bedrock of early empathy, and other aspects of resilience and well-being. For example, sensitive and multiple interactions with an infant promote healthy brain growth and development. In adolescence (beginning as early as age 10), when the prefrontal cortex and its neural connections are in a state of pro-liferation and pruning, parents may increase protective factors by deter-ring alcohol use, attending to dietary needs (e.g., omega 3s), and assisting the child to practice desirable behaviors. In addition to caregiver–infant attachment bonds, positive parenting methods may increase children's resilience, deter their tolerance of bullying, and reduce vulnerability to aggression, depression, and other youth problems (see Nader, in press). Effective parental monitoring may influence the reduction of youth behav-iors associated with aggression, such as youth's exposure to violent media or time spent with antisocial peers. Parents may create an atmosphere of respect and support. In general, research demonstrates the importance of environments that make youth (and adults) feel safe, valued, and valuable. Additionally, school training programs (e.g., to enhance social and coping skills) that include long-term coordinated efforts involving parents as well as children and schools are more effective than short-term isolated efforts (Cohen, 2006; Conoley & Goldstein, 2004; Resnick et al., 1997; Zins, Weissberg, Wang, Walberg, 2004; Chapter 5).

Family

> Targeted school violence represents the "tip of an iceberg"; that is, it is the most extreme example of disconnection-turned-to-violence, existing on a continuum all the way down to emotional teasing and psychologically induced blows to self-esteem. It is the family that can make all the difference in this society as to whether our youth grow into happy, well-adjusted adults or whether they become depressed, dysfunctional, or even violent and hateful. By protecting them from the harm of emotional disconnection, we in turn are protected from being harmed by violence as their desperate last attempt at connection. (Pollack, 2001, p. 4)

Pollack (2001) suggests that in order to survive the tribulations of adolescence, what youth need most is to know that they have meaning-ful connections with their parents and other family members, as well as with their peers. Such positive connections are needed throughout child-hood. Years of research on attachment have clearly demonstrated the importance of improving parent–child relationships (Chapter 6).

Attachment

Decades of research have demonstrated that the parent–child attach-ment relationship is associated with later socio-emotional competence, emotion regulation skills, more positive self-esteem and view of others, and other positive outcomes (DeKlyen & Greenberg, 2008; Chapter 6). Attachment insecurity, and disorganization in particular, is linked to the development of later difficulties, for example, in cognitive abilities, self-regulation, interrelating, and academic achievement (Jacobsen, Edelstein, & Hoffmann, 1994; Moss & St-Laurent, 2001; Chapter 6). Secure attachments are associated with resilience (Nader, 2008). Resilience is the ability to function well, despite adversity. Resilience suggests low vulnerability associated with higher levels of self-esteem, sense of personal control, trust, and coping skills (Ingram & Price, 2001; Nader, 2008; Price & Lento, 2001). Evidence supports the early promotion of secure attachment patterns in order to increase resilience and to interrupt risk trajectories for children with socio-emotional difficulties, including a propensity to aggression.

Parent Interventions for Attachment

A parent directly influences development of an infant's stress response system through sensitively, interactively regulating the child's positive and negative states from birth onward (Nader, 2008; Schore, 2003; Siegel, 2003). When a caregiver recognizes the child's individual style and rhythmically synchronizes to the infant's affect, communications, gestures, and play, modifying his/her own behavior to fit the child's rhythms, the caregiver facilitates the infant's unique information-processing capacities (Schore, 2003). Infants learn to self-soothe and to self-reflect (i.e., to monitor their own cognitive processes; to become self-aware) through these reciprocal interactions. As noted in Chapter 1, awareness of one's own thoughts and emotions is central to developing and utilizing the capacity for empathy.

Most successful attachment interventions focus on improving caregiver–infant attachment (Svanberg, Mennet, & Spieker, 2010). Meta-analysis suggests that such interventions are most successful in improving infant attachment patterns when they improve maternal sensitive responding to child cues (Bakermans-Kranenburg, Van IJzendoorn, Pijlman, Mesman, & Juffer, 2008). Assisting parent's mental representations, as well as targeting maternal sensitivity, has also proven beneficial (Cicchetti, Rogosch, & Toth, 2006). Paternal behaviors are also linked to outcomes (e.g., deliberate self-harm, externalizing, perceptions of family as a secure base; Gratz & Chapman, 2007; Williams & Kelly, 2005; Woodhouse, Dykas, & Cassidy, 2009; see Chapter 4). Additional methods are available for preschoolers and/or early school age children and caregivers (Chapter 6). *Parental child interaction therapy*, a long-term mother–child intervention program, has proven effective for children (ages 4 to 12) with aggressive behavior problems (Chaffin, Silousky, Funderbunk, Valle, Brestan, Balachova et al., 2004; Chapter 6). Presented in Chapter 5 and the CD that accompanies this book, Moss et al. provide methods for teachers to use in order to assist the attachment styles of school children. New methods are available to improve attachments for traumatized children ages 8 and older (e.g., maltreated children; Kagan, Douglas, Hornik, & Kratz, 2008). The latter employs individualized interventions with youth (e.g., to teach coping and self-monitoring and awareness skills) and utilizes a workbook for adult and youth joint participation to enhance attachment. With a little rewording, the workbook can be used with nontraumatized youth.

PEER-FOCUSED INTERVENTIONS

Chronic peer rejection predicts negative self-confidence, depression, anxiety, and delinquency (Ladd and Troop-Gordon, 2003; Chapter 4). Situations that result in humiliation, helplessness, hopelessness, or rage—such as victimization or failure—may translate into aggression, depression, and/or suicidal ideation and behaviors. Victimizers and victimized may be among popular and unpopular students. On the one hand, even a good-natured, friendly star football player has been the object of resentful aggression. On the other hand, athletes or other successful competitors may be among bullies (Thunfors & Cornell, 2008). Healthy competition can be used to build skills such as teamwork, team spirit, and healthy sportsmanship; or, in its more negative forms, may add to stress and leave youth feeling diminished. Pushing children to outdo others has resulted in stress, ill will, and sometimes humiliation or rage. Without instilling an atmosphere in schools in which talents are valued and all youth are respected, resentments may grow. Additionally, school failures may result in the emotional states associated with later aggression. In a field test of the Virginia threat assessment guidelines, Strong and Cornell (2008) found students in special education classes and those who had failed at least 1 year were well represented among individuals who threatened violence in Memphis City Schools.

CONCLUSIONS

Experiences that permit youth successes, the feeling of connection and of being valued, and an ongoing sense of safety are essential to safe schools, academic achievement, and positive youth development. As Pollack (2004a) points out, youth do best when they feel cared for and understood by their teachers and other adults, as well as when they sense that adults have high hopes for them academically.

Section I of this book demonstrated that experiences, which result in feelings of rejection or separation, exclusion, humiliation or shame, being disrespected or of little worth, might engender rage or a sense of powerlessness. Such experiences may translate into specific retaliation, multidirected aggression, or self-destructive acts. Conversely, experiences that enhance a sense of connection between youth and their parents, other adults, peers, and schools in an atmosphere of open communication, respect, and vigilance reduce the likelihood of bullying and other aggression, as well as reduce rates of school dropouts. Such atmospheres and experiences increase the probability that youth will report threats to school safety as well.

Youth are more likely to thrive when they feel respected and valued. Home and family environments, school climates and cultures, and peer relationships that provide safety, support, mutual respect, and an ongoing sense of positive emotional connection among individuals—particularly the positive caring/trusting relationships between adults in positions of school responsibility and their students—reduce the likelihood of school violence, suicides, and other undesirable outcomes. As described in the chapters of this book, a number of school training programs, threat assessment programs, and parent-training programs can enhance youth well-being and with it increase the likelihood of safer, emotionally supportive, academically excellent, and systemically genuine self-esteem-enhancing schools. Such schools can serve as models for a more equitable, civil, and democratic society, which schools are meant to reflect, create, and protect for the children vouchsafed to our care.

REFERENCES

Ayduk, O., Mischel, W., & Downey, G. (2002). Attentional mechanisms linking rejection to hostile-reactivity: The role of "hot" versus "cool" focus. *Psychological Science, 13*(5), 443–448.

Bakermans-Kranenburg, M., Van IJzendoorn, M., Pijlman, F., Mesman, J., & Juffer, F. (2008). Experimental evidence for differential susceptibility: Dopamine D4 receptor polymorphism (DRD4 VNTR) moderates intervention effects on toddlers' externalizing behavior in a randomized controlled trial. *Developmental Psychology, 44,* 293–300.

Borum, R., Cornell, D., Modzeleski, W., & Jimerson, S. (2010). What can be done about school shootings? A review of the evidence. *Educational Researcher, 39*(1), 27–37.

Buckner, J., Mezzacappa, E., & Beardslee, W. (2009). Self-regulation and its relations to adaptive functioning in low income youths. *American Journal of Orthopsychiatry, 79*(1), 19–30.

Cassidy, J., & Shaver, P. R. (Eds.). (1999), *Handbook of attachment: Theory, research, and clinical applications.* New York: Guilford Press.

Chaffin, M., Silovsky, J., Funderbunk, B., Valle, L., Brestan, E., Balachova, T. et al. (2004). Parent-child interaction therapy with physically abusive parents. Efficacy for reducing future abuse reports. *Journal of Consulting and Clinical Psychology, 72,* 500–510.

Chung, H., & Steinberg, L. (2006). Relations between neighborhood factors, parenting behaviors, peer deviance, and delinquency among serious juvenile offenders. *Developmental Psychology, 42*(2), 319–331.

Cicchetti, D., Rogosch, F., & Toth, S. (2006). Fostering secure attachment in infants in maltreating families through preventive interventions. *Development and Psychopathology, 18,* 623–649.

Cohen, J. (Ed.). (2001). *Caring classrooms/intelligent schools: The social emotional education of young children.* New York: Teachers College Press.

Cohen, J. (2006). Social, emotional, ethical and academic education: Creating a climate for learning, participation in democracy and well-being. *Harvard Educational Review, 76*(2), 201–237 (www. hepg.org/her/abstract/8).

Cohen, J., McCabe, E., Michelli, N., & Pickeral, T. (2009). School climate: Research, policy, practice, and teacher education. *Teachers College Record, 111*(1), 180–213.

Conoley, J., & Goldstein, A. (Eds.) (2004). *School violence intervention: A practical handbook* (2nd edition). New York: Guildford Press.

Cornell, D. (2006). The Virginia model for student threat assessment: From the Public Entity Risk Institute (PERI). Downloaded 4/19/11 from www.policeone.com.

Cornell, D., Sheras, P., Gregory, A., & Fan, X. (2009). A retrospective study of school safety conditions in high schools using the Virginia threat assessment guidelines versus alternative approaches. *School Psychology Quarterly, 24,* 119–129.

Daniels, J., Volungis, A., Pshenishy, E. Gandhi, P., Winkler, A., Cramer, D., & Bradley, M. (2010). A qualitative investigation of averted school shooting rampages. *The Counseling Psychologist, 38*(1), 69–95.

DeKlyen, M., & Greenberg, M. (2008). Attachment and psychopathology in childhood. In J. Cassidy & P. Shaver (Eds.), *Handbook of attachment: Theory, research, and clinical applications* (pp. 637–665). New York: Guilford Press.

Douglas, K., & Bell, C. (2011). Youth homicide prevention. *Psychiatry Clinics of North America, 34,* 205–216.

Fein, R., Vossekuil, B., Pollack, W., Borum, R., Modzeleski, W., & Reddy, M. (2002). *Threat assessment in schools: A guide to managing threatening situations and to creating safe school climates.* Washington, DC: U.S. Secret Service and Department of Education.

Fletcher, K. (in press). Understanding and assessing guilt, shame, and anger among children, adolescents, and young adults. *Journal of Child and Adolescent Trauma.*

Fonagy, P., Twemlow, S., Vernberg, E., Sacco, F., & Little, T. (2005). Creating a peaceful school learning environment: The impact of an antibullying program on educational attainment in elementary schools. *Medical Science Monitor, 11,* CR317–325.

Gladstone, T., & Beardslee, W. (2009). The prevention of depression in children and adolescents: A review. *Canadian Journal of Psychiatry, 54*(4), 212–221.

Gladstone, T., Beardslee, W., & O'Connor, E. (2011). The prevention of adolescent depression. *Psychiatric Clinics of North America, 34,* 35–52.

Graham, S. (2010). What educators need to know about bullying behaviors. *Kappan, 92*(1), 66–69.

Gratz, K., & Chapman, A. (2007). The role of emotional responding and childhood maltreatment in the development and maintenance of deliberate self-harm among male undergraduates. *Psychology of Men & Masculinity, 8*(1), 1–14.

Gregory, A., Cornell, D., Fan, X., Sheras, P., Shih, T., & Huang, F. (2010). Authoritative school discipline: High school practices associated with lower student bullying and victimization. *Journal of Educational Psychology, 102,* 483–496.

Griffin, G., McEwen, E., Samuels, B., Suggs, H., Redd, J., & McClelland, G. (2011). Infusing protective factors for children in foster care. *Psychiatry Clinics of North America, 34,* 185–203

Habib, M., & Labruna, V. (2011). Clinical considerations in assessing trauma and PTSD in adolescents. *Journal of Child and Adolescent Trauma, 4*(3), 198–216.

Holtappels, H., & Meier, U. (2000). Violence in schools. *European Education, 32*(1), 66–79.

Huesmann, R. (2007). The impact of electronic media violence: Scientific theory and research. *Journal of Adolescent Health 41,* S6–S13.

Huesmann, R. (2010). Nailing the coffin shut on doubts that violent video games stimulate aggression: Comment on Anderson et al. (2010). *Psychological Bulletin, 136*(2), 179–181.

Ingram, R., & Price, J. (2001). The role of vulnerability in understanding psychopathology. In R. E. Ingram & J. M. Price (Eds.), *Vulnerability to psychopathology: Risk across the lifespan* (pp. 3–19). New York: Guilford Press.

Jacobsen, T., Edelstein, W., & Hoffmann, V. (1994). A longitudinal study of the relation between representations of attachment in childhood and cognitive functioning in childhood and adolescence. *Developmental Psychology, 30,* 112–124.

Kagan, R., Douglas, A., Hornik, J., & Kratz, S. (2008). Traumatic stress in children: Real life heroes pilot study: evaluation of a treatment model for children with traumatic stress. *Journal of Child & Adolescent Trauma, 1,* 5–22.

Keiley, M. (2002). The development and implementation of an affect regulation and attachment intervention for incarcerated adolescents and their parents. *The Family Journal, 10,* 177–189.

Kilpatrick, D., Koenen, K., Ruggiero, K., Acierno, R., Galea, S., Resnick, H. et al. (2007). Serotonin transporter genotype and social support and moderation of posttraumatic stress disorder and depression in hurricane-exposed adults. *American Journal of Psychiatry, 164*(11), 1–7.

Klein, J., & Cornell, D. (2010). Is the link between large high schools and student victimization an illusion? *Journal of Educational Psychology, 102,* 933–946.

Klomek, A., Sourander, A., & Gould, M. (2010). The association of suicide and bullying in childhood to young adulthood: A review of cross-sectional and longitudinal research findings. *Canadian Journal of Psychiatry, 55*(5), 282–288.

Ladd, G., & Troop-Gordon, W. (2003). The role of chronic peer difficulties in the development of children's psychological adjustment problems. *Child Development, 74,* 1344–67.

Laird, R., Jordan, K., Dodge, K., Pettit, G., & Bates, J. (2001). Peer rejection in childhood, involvement with antisocial peers in early adolescence, and the development of externalizing behavior problems. *Development and Psychopathology, 13,* 337–354.

Loukas, A., Suzuki, R., & Horton, K. (2006). Examining school connectedness as a mediator of school climate effects. *Journal of Research on Adolescence, 16*(3), 491–502.

Lyons-Ruth, K., & Jacobvitz, D. (2008). Attachment disorganization: Genetic factors, parenting contexts, and developmental transformation from infancy to adulthood. In J. Cassidy & P. R. Shaver (Eds.), *Handbook of attachment, second edition: Theory, research, and clinical applications* (pp. 666–697). New York: Guilford Press.

MacPherson, L., Reynolds, E., Daughter, S., Wang, F., Cassidy, J., Mayes, L., & Lejuez, C. (2010). Positive and negative reinforcement underlying risk behavior in early adolescents. *Prevention Science, 11,* 331–342.

McBurnett, K., King, J., & Scarpa, A. (2003). The hypothalamic-pituitary-adrenal system (HPA) and the development of aggressive, antisocial, and substance abuse disorders. In D. Cicchetti & E. Walker (Eds.), *Neurodevelopmental mechanisms in psychopathology* (pp. 324–344). Cambridge, UK: Cambridge University Press.

Moss, E., Cyr, C., Bureau, J-F., Tarabulsy, G., & Dubois-Comtois, K. (2005). Stability of attachment between preschool and early school-age and factors contributing to continuity/discontinuity. *Developmental Psychology, 41,* 773–783.

Moss, E., & St-Laurent, D. (2001). Attachment at school age and academic performance. *Developmental Psychology, 37,* 863–874.

Nader, K. (2008). *Understanding and assessing trauma in children and adolescents: Measures, methods, and youth in context.* New York: Routledge.

Nader, K. (in press). Assessing trauma in children and adolescents. In P. Clements & S. Seedat (Eds.). *Mental health issues of child maltreatment.* St Louis, MO: STM Learning, Inc.

National Research Council, Institute of Medicine (2009). In O'Connell, M. E., Boat, T., & Warner, K. E. (Eds.), *Preventing mental, emotional, and behavioral disorders among young people: Progress and possibilities.* Washington, DC: The National Academies Press. Available at: http://www.iom.edu/CMS/12552/45572/64120. aspx

National School Climate Council (2007). The school climate challenge: Narrowing the gap between school climate research and school climate policy, practice guidelines and teacher education policy. Available online at: http://nscc.csee.net/ or http://www.ecs.org/school-climate

Pollack, W. (2001). The importance of family: Preventing violence through family connection. *The Brown University Child and Adolescent Behavior Letter, 17*(12), 1, 3–4.

Pollack, W. S. (2004a). Parent–child connections: The essential component for positive youth development and mental health, safe communities, and academic achievement. *New Directions for Youth Development, 103,* 17–30.

Pollack, W. S. (2004b). "Real" boys, "real" girls, "real" parents: Preventing violence through family connection. In R. Rozensky, N. Johnson, C. Goodheart, & W. Hammond (Eds.), *Psychology builds a healthy world* (pp. 35–47). Washington: American Psychological Association.

Pollack, W. S., Modzeleski, W., & Rooney, G. (2008). Prior knowledge of potential school based violence: Information students learn may prevent a targeted attack. Washington: United States Department of Education and United States Secret Service.

Posner, M., & Rothbart, M. (2007). *Educating the human brain.* Washington, DC: American Psychological Association.

Price, J., & Lento, J. (2001). The nature of child and adolescent vulnerability. In R. E. Ingram & J. Price (Eds.), *Vulnerability to psychopathology: Risk across the lifespan* (pp. 20–38). New York: Guilford Press.

Resnick, M. D., Bearman, P. S., Blum, R. W., Bauman, K. E., Harris, K. M., Jones, L. H. et al. (1997). Protecting adolescents from harm: Findings from the National Longitudinal Study on Adolescent Health. *Journal of the American Medical Association, 278,* 823–832.

Randazzo, M., & Plummer, E. (2009). Implementing behavioral threat assessment on campus: A Virginia Tech demonstration project. Blackburg, VA: Virginia Polytechnic Institute and State University.

Schore, A. (2003). Early relational trauma, disorganized attachment, and the development of a predisposition to violence. In M. Soloman & D. Siegel (Eds.), *Healing trauma* (pp. 107–167). New York: W. W. Norton.

Siegel, D. (2003). An interpersonal neurobiology of psychotherapy: The developing mind and the resolution of trauma. In M. Soloman & D. Siegel (Eds.), *Healing trauma* (pp. 1–56). New York: W. W. Norton.

Strong, K., & Cornell, D. (2008). Student threat assessment in Memphis City Schools: A descriptive report. *Behavioral Disorders, 34,* 42–54.

Svanberg, P., Mennet, L., & Spieker, S. (2010). Promoting a secure attachment: A primary prevention practice model. *Clinical Child Psychology and Psychiatry, 15*(3) 363–378.

Thunfors, P., & Cornell, D. (2008). The popularity of middle school bullies. *Journal of School Violence, 7,* 65–82.

Vossekuil, B., Fein, R. A., Reddy, M., Borum, R., & Modzeleski, W. (2002). The final report and findings of the Safe School Initiative: Implications for the prevention of school attacks in the United States. Washington, DC: U.S. Secret Service and U.S. Department of Education.

Webster-Stratton, C., & Reid, J. (2010). A school-family partnership: Addressing multiple risk factors to improve school readiness and prevent conduct problems in young children. In S. L. Christenson & A. L. Reschly (Eds.), *Handbook on school-family partnerships* (pp. 204–227). New York: Routledge/Taylor & Francis.

Williams, S., & Kelly, D. (2005). Relationships among involvement, attachment, and behavioral problems in adolescence: Examining father's influence. *The Journal of Early Adolescence, 25,* 168–196.

Woodhouse, S., Dykas, M., & Cassidy, J. (2009). Perceptions of secure base provision within the family. *Attachment & Human Development, 11*(1), 47–67.

Zins, J., Weissberg, R., Wang, M., & Walberg, H. (Eds.). (2004). *Building academic success on social and emotional learning: What does the research say?* New York: Teacher's College Press.

Author Index

Subject Index

CASEL (Collaborative for Academic, Social and Emotional Learning; see also Author Index), 115, 177, 190, 209, CD34, CD36
Childhood, CD63
 adaptation (see also Adaptive abilities/adaptation), 67
 age group
  infant/infancy
   attachment, 21, 51–52, 53, 56, 88, 104, 128–130, 131, 135, 136, 137, 139–140, 142, 145, 255, 256
   development, 84, 104, 254
   empathy, 164, 171, 180, 182–184
   high-risk, 136, 137, 140–141
   loss/death, 35
   references, 29, 30, 32, 61, 63, 70, 99, 150, 151, 153–157, 194, 200, 202, 203, 259, 261
  toddler
   attachment, 131, 140
   empathy, 165, 169, 170, 171
   normal behavior, 131, 165
   references, 29, 30, 150, 151, 155, 199, 258
   risk, 140–141
  early childhood/preschool
   attachment, 130–132, 133, 135–136, 149
   competencies, 111
   empathy, 170–171, 178, 179, 209
   high-risk children, 137–141
   interventions, 23, 110, 112–113, 115–116, 116–117, 136, 141–145, 209, 256
   problems/disorders, 135
   references, 61, 99, 119, 121, 122, 123, 125, 152–157, 195, 197, 200, 203, 218, 262
   victimization, 50

 middle childhood (7–10)
  aggressiveness, 23
  attachment, 134, 135, 142
  competencies, 89, 106, 130
  problems, 133
  references, 60, 61, 65, 67, 150, 151, 152, 154, 155
 adolescent/adolescence (see Adolescent/adolescence)
 aggression (see also Aggression), 62, 69, 88, 89
 attachment (see also Attachment), 52, 56, 61, 67
 competencies/skills (see also Self-regulation; Skills), 89
 coping, 106
 development, 60, 100
 humiliation/shame (see also Aggression-shame/humiliation; Humiliation; Shame), 41
 psychopathology, 21, 27, 103
 rejection (see Aggression-rejection; Parental abandonment/rejection; Peer rejection; Rejection; Rejection sensitivity), 28
 self-perception (see also Adolescent-self-perception; Self-perception), 52
 social difficulties, 52
 traits/personality, 31
 trauma (see also Abuse), 21, 24, 26, 29, 60, 62, 63, 64, 65, 66, 67, 70, 96, 97, 98, CD19, CD29, CD71
Climate (see School climate)
Cognitive Behavior Therapy (CBT), 186, 218, CD19
Cognitive development (see also Skills), 85, 169
Cognitive/metacognitive functioning (see also Information processing; Skills-cognitive; Functioning), 135, 136, 140, 152, 261
cognitive bias (see Bias)